Findings

Vatican Rehearsal, 1973

Findings

LEONARD BERNSTEIN

ANCHOR BOOKS
DOUBLEDAY
New York London Toronto Sydney Auckland

AN ANCHOR BOOK
PUBLISHED BY DOUBLEDAY
a division of Bantam Doubleday Dell Publishing Group, Inc.
1540 Broadway, New York, New York 10036

ANCHOR BOOKS, DOUBLEDAY, and the portrayal of an anchor
are trademarks of Doubleday, a division of Bantam Doubleday Dell
Publishing Group, Inc.

Findings was originally published in hardcover by
Simon & Schuster in 1982. The Anchor Books edition is
published by arrangement with the Estate of the Author.

Library of Congress Cataloging-in-Publication Data

Bernstein, Leonard, 1918–1990
Findings/Leonard Bernstein.—1st Anchor Books ed.
p. cm.
Originally published: New York: Simon and Schuster, © 1982.
Includes bibliographical references.
1. Bernstein, Leonard, 1918–1990. 2. Musicians—United States—
Biography. 3. Music—History and criticism. I. Title.
ML410.B566A3 1993
780—dc20 93-15553
CIP MN

ISBN 0-385-42437-x

Contents

PART FOUR·*The Last Decade till Now*·*1969–1980*

Preface

Today is my sixty-fourth birthday, and the occasion presents itself to round out, with this latest entry, a half century of written observations. Assuming (from its solemnly earnest tone) that the first piece in this collection must have been written around the age of fourteen, it pleases me to think that these words today come a good round fifty years later. I like round figures; they give one an oddly comfortable sense of arrival, even of achievement.

In reviewing this compilation for the last time before it goes to press, I find myself with mixed feelings. First off, needless to say, I wish I had been (and were now) a better writer. I have always loved words fully as much as musical notes; I find the same joys of ambiguity, structural surprise, anagrammatic play and grace of phrasing in both. Would that I had the skill with which to bring these into being—the art of a Nabokov, a Merrill, an Auden—but facts are facts: I am not a writer by profession; I have simply written words all my life, for the love of it. I accept this fact, and I hope, Gentle Reader, that you do as well. In which case this preface can remain a preface, not an apologia.

My mixed feelings involve a certain pride in some of the college writings, particularly the Cara Verson review and the honors thesis. I take pleasure in rereading my sabbatical poem, and particularly the Commencement Address at Johns Hopkins. I am touched by the reverence in the several writings on my father, and on my musical fathers Copland and Koussevitzky (and my musical forefathers Beethoven and Mahler). Other pieces may move me less, but seem worthy of being offered to a general reading public that delights in the sharing of ideas. The Harvard thesis, in particular, seems to me as valid today as it was some four decades ago, in spite of the volcanic changes in our musical universe since then (and in spite of a certain gratuitous tone of collegiate smart-assery. If time had permitted, I should have presented this thesis with highly critical marginal notes from today's perspective. But Time's winged chariot . . .).

These *Findings* are in no way to be construed as memoirs; they are indeed *findings* of past feelings and ideas ranging through an adolescent and increasingly adult lifetime. The Memoirs are yet to be written, slowly, carefully, in depth and at length, telling all—at least all I can call to consciousness; and they will take some time, all the time my declining years, with God's grace, will permit me.

Perhaps the most stunning surprise I have had in this last swift rereading is the gaping hiatus that occurs between my university graduation (1939) and the end of World War II (1945). There is literally nothing there; and this surprises me so strongly because it was not only a period of war, but especially of the Holocaust—perhaps the most traumatic and cruel period in my life, or in that of any contemporary adult for that matter. Besides, I note with equal surprise that almost as much material in this volume stems from my feelings of Jewishness as stems from the musical universe I inhabit. All the more curious, then, that I seemed to have no impulse to document my emotions of the *Hitlerzeit*. Perhaps I did and the words were lost; after all, I had no secretary or files in those days, and was constantly moving from city to city. Or perhaps I was traumatized, as were so many others, including *real* writers, repressing the pain, averting the inner eye from the implications of a Holocaust after which the world could never again be the same.

There are other *lucunae* as well: Hiroshima, another world trauma; the Boulez-Stockhausen phenomenon; the infamous McCarthy era. I am reminded of a marvelously pithy preface by Israel Zangwill: "I am sorry this book is not some other kind of book, but the next one shall be." Indeed it shall; but on the whole, mixed feelings and all, I like this book (I hadn't expected to); I like the sum of its parts, and I am grateful to all those who caused it to exist: my friend-manager Harry Kraut, who found the idea in the first place; my loyal secretary Helen Coates, who found the files and the photographs; my assistant-plus Craig Richard Nelson, who found the form; and to my splendid editor Michael Korda, who found the title. Good findings.

But I am most grateful to my mother, the gallant Jennie Bernstein, a lady of perspicacity and charm, without whom . . . and to whom the ensuing pages are most lovingly dedicated.

25 August 1982

Leonard Bernstein

Part One
JUVENILIA
1935–1939

With Samuel J., Shirley and Jennie Bernstein, ca. 1935

FATHER'S BOOKS

My father is a very complicated human being. A man of irregular temperament and unusual convictions, he is a rare combination of the shrewd businessman and the ardent religionist. It is rare that one finds such a combination. In my father's case, I attribute whatever degree of material success he has attained to this very suboccupation, religious activity.

His books follow very closely along the line of religious teaching and religious thought. His life's textbook is the Talmud. The Talmud is his guide to business ethics and economic construction. It has been so from his earliest childhood, and he has known no other teacher. He finds an analogy in the Talmud for every problem that arises in his business. If you should open his desk drawer nearest his right hand, you would find therein a small edition of the Bible and a well-thumbed copy of the Talmud.

The Talmud is his guide to moral and social ethics. If he is called upon to speak, his discourse invariably begins with a quotation from the Talmud. Nor does he omit it from casual conversation. It is his unfailing source of reference. He lives according to its principles, and it hurts him to see that others do not.

The Talmud is his reading matter. He can derive more pleasure from one of the many stories offered by it to illustrate a Biblical technicality than he could ever get from a novel. He is unacquainted with the English classics because he has no desire to be acquainted with them. He does not know English poetry because the music of Talmudic prose is sufficient diversion for him.

Why are all these things true? Why can the Talmud supplant all other literature for him? Because, first of all, his mind is adapted to the study of the Talmud; his studious nature is sated by nothing less erudite than the Talmud. Because, secondly, the Talmud is sufficiently diversified to offer every type of literary material. Because, lastly, the Talmud has been his food since he could first read; he has become part of it, and it of him. And, because of his diligent study, his work has flourished materially, and he is a leader in his field—living proof that the wise man combines the spiritual and material in order to ensure a sound life.   □

Written for English Composition Class
Harvard University
20 March 1938

THE FEEB

I

Never in my eight long years of life had I been so frightened. The woman was running as only a madwoman can run. She was ten yards or so from the main entrance of the State Hospital when I first saw her, her dirty gray hair weirdly concealing her face, her arms clutching forward in a desperate attempt at escape, her right hand shut tightly around the handle of a soup ladle. Her white smock had come undone, and her huge breasts, slapping cruelly against her as she ran, were plainly visible to the astounded crowd that had collected on the street corner. Behind her lumbered two buxom nurses, panting in their frantic attempt to catch her. Behind them, a tall, bony man came running at an incredible pace.

"Charlie!" I screamed within myself.

In a flash Charlie had passed the nurses and was at the heels of the nearly spent woman. He caught her firmly as she stumbled in her exhaustion and fell to the ground bleeding violently from the nose. Charlie released his hold and bent over, speaking very calmly to her.

"You shouldn't run away, Bessie. You belong there. Me, I ain't no feeb. But you're a feeb. You gotta stay there or

Ca. 1922

you'll get hurt. That's why you're hurt now, 'cause you ran away. It'd be different if you wasn't a feeb. Then they'd let you out too, the way they let me. Only you wouldn't come back, Bessie, see? That's why they don't let you out. Now me, I ain't no feeb. . . ."

The nurses arrived puffing and crimson, immediately followed by an ambulance. Together they lifted the unconscious woman into the compartment and seated themselves beside her. Charlie followed them with his eyes, still talking in his low, rational tone. "I told you a hundred times not to grab off," he said. As the ambulance started back for the building, one of the nurses leaned out and smiled gratefully at him. Charlie's face was a fan opening out into a broad smile. He took from his pocket a packet of Bull Durham, and with a proud beam at his curious audience deftly rolled a cigarette.

II

Charlie had been part of my existence as far back as I could remember. He was of uncertain old age, very thin, very strong. Through him I first learned to feel the word "wiry." None of us knew anything about the previous life of this strange man with the sparse threads of long white hair, except that he had for years been an inmate of the State Hospital, which was situated on the hill above our house. He was a member of the small privileged group that was permitted to cross Asylum boundaries during the afternoon. He would spend his time every day doing odd jobs for residents of the neighborhood in order to make spending money. Every Saturday afternoon he could be found in our kitchen, vigorously rubbing the water pipes behind the stove. This was his favorite job at our house; the pipes had a strange fascination for him. He would sit much longer than necessary on the warm floor beside the stove and rub away at the metal until it seemed to perspire with gleaming. His Bull Durham wagged up and down between his lips as he talked. For Charlie always talked—to himself.

I do not remember the first time I dared to hide behind the door and listen to his monologue. I did not think it funny; I listened with earnest respect to every word. I discovered that Charlie's favorite topic of autoconversation was inviting himself to parties that he was planning. The man's imagination, as I look back upon it, was nothing short of admirable. My mouth would become full when he would begin to describe his long lists of choice delicacies. His talent for decorating tables would put to shame our model hostess. Then he would tell himself very carefully who was coming to the party ("so's I'll be sure to remember," he said). Every week there was a new party. Charlie always saved this subject for last; and when he had exhausted all the details he would sigh happily, and yet regretfully, since now he had to leave the pipes.

One day when he had just finished one subject and was about to proceed to the next, I stepped out of my hiding place into the room.

"Hello," said Charlie in a very friendly way.

"Hello," I said, delighted at my boldness. "You're Charlie, aren't you?"

"Sure," he answered. "But I'm no feeb."

I was very much impressed with that, having not the slightest idea of the meaning of "feeb."

"Those pipes look very bright," I said, hoping that he would invite me to his party.

"That's 'cause they *are* bright," he said very seriously. "I could look at bright pipes forever. Could you?"

"Yes," I answered doubtfully. "You work very hard on them."

"That's so's they won't get dark and dirty when I go away." I have never forgotten that statement. I was profoundly touched for some reason. Now I can understand why. I think of Turgenev's little remark about the leaves on the tree, and I understand why that inspired, uneducated, brilliant, sick mind always insisted on proclaiming itself different from its fellow minds. I understand the yearning of that simple but prodigiously creative soul for an ivory tower of its own. "Me, I ain't no feeb" was his Hello and his Goodbye, the pitiful motto on which his existence was based.

During one of the many conversations that we held regularly after that, I asked him what he did with the money he earned.

"Oh, I gotta lotta money," said Charlie. "*They* give me my tobacco there. So I don't have to spend it. I'm saving up for a typewriter."

I looked at him admiringly. "That must be wonderful to have."

Charlie suddenly jumped to his feet. "I'll give it to you if you want it," he said, his eyes lighting up. "Only you must let me use it sometime."

"Why?" I asked, showing the natural lack of gratitude of a child of eight.

"So's I can remember . . ." He checked himself. Then, cautiously, "Did I ever tell you about my parties?"

"No," I lied.

"Well, I give parties," he answered.

I was stubborn.

"But why do you want the typewriter?"

"So's I can remember who's coming," he answered, his eyelids stretched out into fierce circles.

"Where do you give the parties?" I asked.

"In my room up there. They let me. They trust me up there. 'Cause I ain't a feeb."

III

On a Saturday afternoon several weeks later my mother and I went to see a moving picture. Mother had become very fond of Charlie and had no qualms about leaving him alone in the house.

"See if Charlie is still at work in the kitchen," she said as we were entering the house.

When I came into the kitchen, I was struck dumb. Charlie was standing looking miserable by the stove, surrounded by rushing water.

I was far too puzzled by this picture to be frightened. When I did speak, my voice shrieked.

"What happened?"

Charlie was mute. His arms hung limp by his sides; his shoulders sagged forward; his head drooped. He was holding something in his right hand. I looked, and realized what had happened. Charlie, in his naive curiosity, had unscrewed the pipe joint with his abnormally powerful hands. The water streamed out of the pipe, swirling about the poor man's feet. He was wet up to the shins.

Within five minutes the thing was over. I had screamed for Mother, there had been the expected reaction, and the water had been turned off in the cellar. There was no sound but that of Mother's footsteps slowly ascending the cellar staircase. Charlie could not speak; I would not. Mother stood at the doorway.

"Why did this happen?" she asked *sotto voce*, her face pale with disappointment rather than anger.

Charlie stood painfully silent. We waited for a word. Charlie was silent.

"I am afraid you must not come back here again," said Mother.

Charlie's eyes closed. For the first time I realized how old he was. He placed the pipe joint carefully on the stove and swished through the flooded room to the back door. Then he suddenly clapped his hands to his ears, and was gone.

IV

The next time I saw Charlie, he was a hero. He had just caught an escaping madwoman. He had just received a look of gratitude from the nurse. He was rolling a cigarette. He looked very old and very tired. He gasped for breath and his cheeks purpled. The run had been too much for him. He suddenly saw me, and beamed with a proud, triumphant joy. He stood gasping and grinning alternately like some fantastic automaton. Then he struck a match to light his cigarette, but the wind blew it out.   □

Written in 1938
while a student at
Harvard University
Published in
Modern Music

NEW MUSIC IN BOSTON

Boston has just recovered from a second attack of Prokofiev. That incredible man, winding up his brilliant American tour in this city, conducted the Boston Symphony Orchestra in an all-Prokofiev concert which compared rather favorably with the Prokofiev works conducted in January by Koussevitzky and reviewed in a previous issue of this magazine. The concert opened brilliantly with a suite from his ballet *Chout*, which strains the word "cleverness" to a snapping point. It is a very well written work, with geniality to spare. One is very thankful these days for a concert piece that has a finale one can whistle while leaving the hall. The *First Piano Concerto*, played by the composer, showed up wretchedly in the light of its predecessor. Truthfully, it is not a good piece. It is full of difficult and brilliant piano passages which can really be heard because of the unpretentious size of the orchestra; but its one real tune is worked to death (especially, it seemed, since it was always in D-flat), it lacks continuity, and it sounded like the student work that it is. When it was over, you asked, "Why?"

But then he redeemed himself. His "Orchestral Fairy Tale" *Peter and the Wolf* is a masterpiece of its kind. It purports to teach the instruments of the orchestra to little Russian children by having each animal in the story (and animals abound in this story) represented by a particular instrument which follows the duck or bird or wolf through its complicated wanderings. There is a narrator who serves to forward the plot; he is at least a better device than the operatic *recitativo*. He at least makes a clean breast of it. The piece itself falls into "bits" which hang together quite unreasonably and beautifully. The best possible description of the work can be had from the little tune that is assigned to Peter, the little-boy hero.

The concert closed with the Second Suite from his ballet *Romeo and Juliet.* This is a more serious work, inclined to be too long for a suite. Some of it has a very strange kind of beauty, which results naturally from the paradox of a composer who cannot write profoundly tragic music trying to picture in tones the grief of Romeo at Juliet's grave. It was more gentle sadness than grief; more poignancy than *Weltschmerz*; and if you could forget that there was a program to it, it could have been very beautiful indeed to hear. The whole work, however, fell just short of success because of the discrepancy between its great length and extension and its musical material.

A very important premiere was the *First Symphony* of Walter Piston, a composer who can always be depended upon for the best in workmanship. Adverse criticisms were profuse and diverse: some thought the Largo unduly long and uninteresting; others thought that the work lacked emotional appeal. Whatever the case (for opinions at a time as transitional as this must be conceded as personal), no one could deny the expert handling of the orchestra, the innovations in instrumental tone color, the never-failing good taste, the masterly proportioning of the structure, and the fine lyric sense which Mr. Piston has not often betrayed in the past.

Other modern works have not been many, and the credit for most of them goes to Dr. Koussevitzky. He gave us Ravel's *Shéhérazade*, a rarely heard and very charming song-triptych for soprano and orchestra. Madame Olga Averino sang with amazing understanding and beauty of tone. Recently Dr. Koussevitzky gave a stirring performance of Florent Schmitt's *Forty-ninth Psalm* for orchestra, organ, chorus, and solo voice. We were feted with Pizzetti's interesting and pleasant *Concerto dell'Estate*, and Malipiero's *Second Symphony*, the "Elegiaca," soon to be played in New York.

Bad music found its way in also. We recently had the misfortune to hear a cello concerto by one Thomas de Hartmann, another Gallicized Russian. It was nothing short of meaningless rubbish; but the cellist, Paul Tortelier of the orchestra, a perfect wonder of a cellist (one of those rare artists who have "everything"), did so expert a job that many were deceived about the value of the piece. Because of duty, and unwillingly, I mention Alessandresco's *Actaeon*, a symphonic poem of no importance played by Mr. Enesco while guest conductor here. □

Written in 1938 while a student
at Harvard University
Published in Harvard Advocate

TRUE STORY WITH A MORAL

"CARA VERSON TO GIVE ALL MODERN PROGRAM," said *The Boston Sunday Herald*. I was incredulous; but joyfully incredulous. After all, perhaps she is a martyr to the cause of diffusing art at any cost. But all modern music! That a woman—especially a woman—should be courageous enough to seat herself before a hired grand piano in hired Jordan Hall and play a program that would draw a liberal maximum of a hundred people seemed strange to me. Either the woman is extremely wealthy, I argued, and enjoys appearing before an audience; or she is a martyr; or she is a bad pianist who hopes to hide behind a program that nobody knows, and be hailed as a martyr however badly she plays; or she is an idiot.

Boston, you must remember, is not a city to be trifled with. If it chooses to sleep, it can be very nasty when forcefully awakened. Its temper is like its weather, which is conducive to sleep; and with all these naps, Boston is unusually strongly armed during its waking hours. Its resistance to change and artistic progress is phenomenal.

Therefore I shouted with joy when I read that Cara Verson was about to attempt an awakening of the sleeping cat. Never in my memory had an all-modern piano recital been given in Boston. I saw at last a chance for the poor old Hub of the Universe to hear some good modern music. I also squealed in anticipation of the countenances in the fifth row.

It was not, moreover, just the principle of the thing. Miss Verson, whoever she was, had put together a program of startling proportions. It was difficult, long, and varied; it included American music (which was really startling); and almost all of it was representative modern music, viz:

Malipiero: *Maschere Che Passano*
Kodaly: *Epitaph*

Castelnuovo-Tedesco: *Sonata*
Rudhyar: *The Call Sontata*
             Venus Born of the Foam (!)
Verrall: *Four Pieces*
Copland: *Piano Variations*
Szymanowski: *Scheherazade*
Hindemith: *Pantomime*

Of course, the most welcome sight on that list was the Copland *Variations*.

I spoke of the forthcoming event to everybody with whom I talked. It persisted in cropping up in every conversation until the name Cara Verson seemed to be perpetually perched on my vocal cords, waiting for a breath to urge it out. I was truly excited. I even bought a ticket.

Some fifty curiously assorted people sat in the hall, looking like varicolored location pins on a map. I recognized some aspiring composers, some budding piano talents, two critics (another one came in very nonchalantly half an hour later), three dilettantes, several avant-gardists. There was a strange, strained silence, and everybody looked either supercilious or guiltily ashamed. There was none of the secure mass feeling of watching unwatched that we are accustomed to experience at concerts. Everybody was watching everybody else. One felt the emptiness of the place as one feels a chilly draft. One felt precariously poised, as on the top limb of a tree, with only the air on all sides.

I discovered then that it is possible to mutter darkly. As I had expected, Boston had neither the interest nor the courage to come and find out what it was all about. I also muttered darkly because my dream of the countenances in the fifth row was unfulfilled. There was nobody in the fifth row.

The lights dimmed and the programs rustled madly. Every customary concert sound that is usually lost in the homogeneity of similar sounds was whip-clear that night. The ushers shut the doors with a Symphony Hall gesture, and quiet apprehension reigned. Then from the magically opened door at the rear of the stage there entered a long

1945

train of blue gauze of some sort, dragged on the ground by a middle-aged-looking, very ordinary woman with short, artificially waved hair and one exotic earring depending from her left ear. She was neither nervous nor unduly used-to-it-all; she moved meatily, with method. She bowed to applause that reminded me of twigs snapping under-foot, and sat down. There was a prolonged overture, dur-ing which she put her handkerchief down on the piano and arranged countless redundant bits of blue gauze over her neck and shoulders and throat. Then suddenly, in the midst of one of these maneuvers, she began to play.

Now, I admit that I don't know the *Maschere Che Passano* very well, but I am sure that Malipiero did not ask to have the pedal put down at the beginning and kept there until the end. It sounded like a Chopin Scherzo played by some-body's niece. Furthermore, the poor woman was un-equipped to make a piano sound. The Steinway she used had a thunderous bass, and no amount of punching by her right hand could possibly balance it. We might therefore say that it sounded like a Chopin Scherzo played by some-body's niece with the right hand omitted. Or at best, only vaguely suggested.

I began to see a gleam of hope in the Kodaly *Epitaph*; it was slow, and hence somewhat clear. But the gleam van-ished with Merlinesque rapidity when Miss Verson began the *Sonata* of Castelnuovo-Tedesco. The old faults coupled with new ones popped up. Lapses of memory; a lack of subtlety of shading that stuffed one's ear full of one point on the dynamic continuum. And the agonizing thing about it was that she possessed some facility on the keyboard, and was therefore more easily able to dupe her audience. The listeners themselves were in a peculiar situation: they were obviously restless, but afraid even to shift position for fear of betraying an insensibility to contemporary culture. Poor souls, I said, poor silly souls: they're waiting to be fed.* Another weird interlude followed, in which Rudhyar and Verrall received their respective punishments at the hands of this astonishing woman.

* Lewis Carroll suddenly seemed the finest artist on the program so far. —L.B., 1982.

Then Miss Verson calmly and deliberately pulled the rope to the confirming bell of my suspicions, and there issued forth the first clanging notes of the Copland *Variations*. Oh, God, I said, *la commedia è finita*. I was wrong. It was only the beginning.

I know I shall never be believed, but I must try nonetheless to tell what happened. Miss Verson began at the beginning (which is now hard for *me* to believe). She played half the theme or so, leaving out half the notes in the measures she did play. Then a fleeting suggestion of the first three variations. Then a quick shift to page 12. A few measures, and back to the end of Variation VII. Then Variation IX, as though she were handcuffed; a sprinkle of XVI through XIX; a mad rush to the end; and it was over. And all this without the slightest conception of the rhythms or tempi. All this with a butcher's lack of sensitivity, with the tone of a Woolworth xylophone, the halfheartedness of a professor in his twenty-fourth year of reading the same lectures. I felt, after a minute of it, that I must leave or scream. But therein lay the unpleasantness of being followed out by such muttered epithets as "arty," "temperamental," "aesthetical." So I stayed, and screamed silently until I was wet. I wanted to shout, "Don't you know what she is doing?" But more than that, I wanted simply to shout.

I was out of the hall with the last chord, which was misplayed.

There is no need to moralize. Let us supplant the moral with a prayer: God speed the Bureau of Fine Arts! ☐

Written for English Composition Course
Harvard University
24 February 1938

THE OCCULT

I

The room was filled with Greek people when Carl entered. It was a full minute before he was free of the bewilderment

Harvard University, 1949

which always attended his first glance at a crowded room. He could see that the people were dividing themselves into two rectangular phalanxes facing the front of the room, leaving a wide aisle between. Spartans, thought Carl, vaguely amused. He looked furiously about for the guest of honor, Eros Mavro, but could see only a flutist and pianist preparing to play, and the crowd staring intently at them. Overintently, Carl thought. Suddenly he sensed that he was standing right in the aisle and blocking someone's vision. Without turning, he knew that Eros Mavro was sitting at the head of the aisle, watching his back.

As he slipped into the mass on his left, he looked furtively back at the great Greek conductor for whom this reception was being given. He saw the massive head—a great dome of a hairless head which reflected the brilliant California sun like a halo. Only the head and the half-closed eyes did Carl see, and he quickly turned, embarrassed, to the soloists at the front of the room. Chaminade's *Flute Concertino* had never seemed so long and dull. Once again Carl turned cautiously in the direction of Mavro. The conductor was obviously suffering greatly from ennui.

The piece did end finally, and Mavro was suddenly surrounded by innumerable people, some offering him tea and ices, others eager only to speak the meaningless formulae of greeting to him. It was fifteen minutes before Carl convinced himself that he too should follow this procedure. As he advanced, Mavro suddenly rose and came toward him. The backs of Carl's thighs went rigid, and he stopped, paralyzed.

"You are a student here?" He saw the wide, full mouth barely move, accompanied by the subtlest movements about the strong nose, and a disarming gentleness in the small blue eyes that seemed to recede into the core of that phenomenal head.

"Yes," answered Carl. "That is—yes, sir."

"What do you study?"

People all around stared at him mercilessly.

"I study music."

"Music? Mmmm. *Bene. Molto bene.*" He caressed the boy's head. "What is your name?"

"Carl Fevrier." Suddenly Carl remembered a line he had read that morning: "Plato makes Eros the center of all emotions."

"Do you play?" Mavro illustrated with his long, bony fingers.

"Yes." Carl had just begun to notice Mavro's strange cosmopolitan speech, identifiable with no country he could think of.

At Harvard University, 1973

"Will you perhaps play something for me?"

"If you want it," answered Carl, unable to control the dazing hammer blows of his blood.

Mavro sat down just next to the piano, as Carl tried to steady his fingers. He struggled through a Chopin Nocturne, his damp fingers slipping all over the keys. It was a fantastically passionate interpretation. "Eros is the center of all emotions," he thought in his semi-coma. He played for half an hour, including, at Mavro's request, some compositions of his own. The afternoon became more and more confused, a mad mélange of more flute music, tea, and cakes; and culminating in the climactic moment when Eros invited him to all rehearsals that week.

"If they will not allow you in, ask for to see me," he said in parting, taking Carl's outstretched hand in both his own.

II

Carl flung himself hysterically on the bed. The thing lacked reason, this greatest of all his experiences. Surely there was something occult in it. I am a boy, he tried to rationalize, eighteen years old, studying at this university. I want to be a musician. He is the greatest conductor I have ever heard; he is wildly acclaimed by every audience. Why, then, should he have singled me out, and spoken to me? Why should he have left so abruptly the people talking to him? He certainly didn't know I was a musician. He knew nothing about me. He talked to me; he asked me to play.

But the whole affair, from its minutest beginnings, has an unnatural flavor. There I was, two days ago after dinner, debating whether or not to go into the common room and play the piano. Friends were urging me; yet I knew that I had work to do. Something drew me in. Number one. In the room was Peter reading a magazine. Now, I don't know Peter well; I could count the words I have spoken to him. But he invited me to that party. I thought I might go—it was barely possible, I told him, that I would drop in if I had the chance. I forgot about it.

And I went. Why I don't know. Number two. I was at that ridiculous party, with many people trying to believe they were in the highest spirits. And there was Pan, a Greek boy I had not seen for years. He asked me to a reception that his society was giving on Sunday for Eros Mavro, who was guest conductor for two weeks in San Francisco. Very casually, of course. "You might like to shake hands with him" was all he said. I forgot about that too.

But I went. That's number three. Again I don't know why. I was practicing the piano when I thought of it. It was late; the reception was over, I was sure. I was there before I had realized that I had left my room. I didn't shake his hand. I played for him. It is no use to reason. Everything is enveloped in a supernatural atmosphere. It is good that I am falling asleep.

III

The week that followed was the most memorable in Carl's life, and the most confused. It was the week before examinations. Carl forgot about that. Monday morning he was at the rehearsal ten minutes before schedule. He was sitting in the last row of the auditorium, awaiting with the orchestra the arrival of Eros Mavro. When he came upon the stage, on the dot of ten o'clock, there was much applause from the members of the orchestra. He saw Carl and motioned him down to the front row. He gave him the score to follow, for the music was all in Mavro's incredible head. The music was glorious. Mavro, in his never-ceasing excitement, broke two chairs by dropping down on them with all the force of his wiry body, in order to signify a sudden *diminuendo* to the orchestra. The first time, he went right through the cane seat. The concertmaster rushed to the rescue. The second time, the orchestra tittered. Mavro pulled himself up still conducting, too full of the music to stop even for an instant. Carl began to feel a great and awful love for the man.

After the rehearsal, Carl left in haste, afraid even to speak to his wonderful idol. It was not until after the Wednesday rehearsal that he resolved to ask Mavro if he might show him a trio he had just written. He jumped onto the stage and followed Mavro out the exit. Mavro turned, and

bumped into him. "I was just coming back to look for you," he said. "Will you take lunch with me?" Carl winced. It was cruel. He said yes with many thank-yous.

At lunch Eros revealed himself as a truly great man, with the sort of greatness that embodies liberalism, complete tolerance, unbounded enthusiasm for and devotion to his art. Carl nearly fainted when Eros offered him an oyster on his fork.

On Thursday there was lunch again. They had been joined by two associates of Mavro's. The conductor was sitting silently at the table. There was no word spoken. Suddenly Eros looked up, and began to traverse Carl's face with his now dilated eyes. Carl was uneasy.

"Do you know," he said slowly and with difficulty, "the moment I set eyes on this boy, I felt a—something"—he struggled for expression—"a feeling of the presence of—of greatness; of something—genius." Carl's eyes closed involuntarily. He was limp with realization. The man had spoken it; the man had clarified the whole problem.

There was no rehearsal on Friday, and Carl remained at home all day in torment. Saturday night would be the final concert; after that Eros would be gone, he had learned; back to Greece or to Monte Carlo or somewhere else beyond reach. Friday was a day of writhing, and of doing things jerkily; of wondering how to make the time go swiftly, of complete inability to work. Carl had to blurt out the whole story to his sweet but unresponsive little French mother, in order that he should not go mad. He had to hear her answer with such remarks as "How you have grown thin this week!" He had to eat and dress and undress. He had to wait. He waited for two days.

The night of the concert arrived, and Carl's sensitivity, aggravated and deepened by the confused emotions of the week, reacted to the music in greatly magnified wells of feeling. Sitting with his friends, he felt at once utter humbleness before the master, and a sense of propriety as he watched the audience thrill to the dynamic conducting. He heard Eros play Ravel's *Spanish Rhapsody*, and the whole poignancy and fire of the Spanish temperament became apparent to him. He felt that he would burst with a terrifying mixture of pride and despondency as he listened to the tender slow movement of Schumann's *Second Symphony*. He did not leave his seat during intermission.

After the concert, Eros was recalled thirteen times. The audience, which filled the hall to overflowing, stamped and rattled the seats. Everybody seemed to be shouting. Women threw their corsages onto the stage. The orchestra cheered and beat upon their instruments. Mavro beamed, bowed with humility again and again, picked up all the flowers one by one and kissed them gallantly to the audience.

The dressing room was packed with friends, admirers, and autograph seekers. As soon as Carl entered, Eros stopped talking to somebody and beckoned to him. Carl, now feeling only a bright pride, wormed through the mass to him. Eros took him into the bathroom for privacy. He closed the door gently and put his hands on Carl's shoulders.

"You must make me very proud of you one day," he began. "It is plain to me that you have every talent for a composer. You are sensitive in an ideal way—I know, do not say a word. You must work, work very hard. You must devote all your time to your art. You must keep yourself pure. Do not let friends spoil you with flattery. You have everything to make you great; it is up to you only to fulfill your mission." He took something from his pocket and gave it to Carl. "This is for you," he said. "Do not fail me."

He left the room. Carl was staggering. Slowly he opened the envelope Eros had handed him. It was an informal picture of Mavro, the head more noble than ever, the lips set in a firmly gentle position—the subtlest of smiles. The photograph had been inscribed to Carl *"Very sympathetically."* Carl thought madly of the beautiful connotations of the word *simpatico* which the English word lacks. He began to laugh out loud. Sweating profusely, flushed beyond description, he leaned against the cold bathroom wall holding the picture before him, and laughed until exhaustion quieted him.

IV

A year went by. Carl was working furiously on a ballet which showed great promise. He had made astonishing progress, developed in every way. He was writing music which caused considerable favorable comment. He was a recognized pianist in his city.

Tired from hours of writing, Carl put down his pencil and looked long at Mavro's framed photograph in front of him. He noticed with a start that this was the anniversary of his meeting with the great man. The year had been full of Eros Mavro; time had magnified his personality for Carl out of all proportion. Carl had flushed at every mention of his name. He recalled sadly that Mavro had promised to write him, and even to send him some of his own compositions. Yet he had had no word from him. He had made sufficient excuses for this to himself, but he could not help feeling that perhaps his relationship with Eros had been only the result of the great man's need to give his love to every human. He had told the story many times throughout the year, each time at great length, dwelling lovingly on every detail. Most people had reacted by venturing that there was something of the occult involved. Carl himself could still not rid his mind of this thought.

News came one day soon that Mavro was conducting a season in a Midwestern city. Carl's first thought was that now he should hear from him. No letter came, and after waiting two weeks Carl decided with an effort that he would write Mavro. "I have no right, after all, to expect a man with so little time . . ." he argued just a little regretfully. But when he began to write, the whole experience was magnificently re-created in him, and his letter proved to be, after the fourth draft, a series of declarations of faith. From beginning to end it was an alternation of confessions of admiration and longing. *"Please let me hear from you,"* he wrote, *"and fill the void which nothing else has been able to fill since you left."* At the end he wrote, *"Very sympathetically."*

Then he waited. It would take three days, he calculated, for the message to reach Mavro; three days for his answer to return. Six days Carl waited.

On the sixth day he rushed home from classes as fast as he could. His mother greeted him at the door.

"There's a letter for you from your friend whatever-his-name-is," she said. Carl tore the envelope from her hands and ran up to his room. He read the letter through several times; then he put it into a drawer and came slowly down the stairs. He sat at the table staring out in front of him. His mother was making the table ready for lunch.

"Plato makes Eros the center of all emotions," Carl kept thinking over and over. "Eros the center of all emotions." The dactyls made a maddening refrain in his head. His mouth was drawn down in bitterness. He began to murmur to himself dazedly.

"*I want you—I dared not believe it before. Come to me . . .*"

"Was it a nice letter?" broke in his mother. "You know, it has always seemed to me that there was something occult in all your affair with this man."

Carl stiffened with anguish. His face was a deadly white. "There certainly was," he whispered.   □

Harvard University
1938

SONNET: ON ACQUIRING KNOWLEDGE

I still remember, in the beginning, thinking
That Ivory Soap contained something to keep it from sinking.
But now that I'm grown I have learned—although never by rote—
That its being lighter than water's what keeps it afloat.

Learning is hare versus hounds, and teaching is worse.
One can be clear but lengthy, murky but terse.
People communicate badly, mumble and grope,
Exception: in art. But art will not analyze soap.

Learning is probably one's most private affair,
More intimate far than a bath, or saving one's hair.
For example, I once knew some physics, through ardent endeavor;
But I know what I know about Ivory Soap forever.

Another example: with all the research in cancer
No one has yet come up with a suitable answer.

At Harvard University, 1973

HARVARD BACHELOR'S THESIS

THE ABSORPTION OF RACE ELEMENTS INTO AMERICAN MUSIC

BY

Leonard Bernstein, '39

Submitted in partial fulfillment of the requirement for the degree with honors of Bachelor of Arts
HARVARD UNIVERSITY
10 April 1939

CONTENTS

PREFATORY NOTE

I propose a new and vital American nationalism; it is my task to define it. A certain lack of balance must necessarily result, since the movement is so recent that most of the paper will treat only of most recent years. The core of this dissertation will be found in Chapter Two of the Second

Part, the chapter dealing with Negro rhythms. This occasions a consequent additional lopsidedness, which is, however, inevitable, and in some ways even advantageous. It is hoped that the reader will retain, throughout this paper, the conception of the broader outlines of the thesis, however elliptical they may be.

I should like to express my gratitude to Professors A. T. Merritt and D. W. Prall for invaluable assistance, and to Mr. I. B. Cohen for stylistic suggestions. *Rem tene, verba sequuntur.*

PART ONE

1: The Problem of Nationalism in American Music

Nationalism is not an element arbitrarily inflicted upon music; it must be organic. To be organic, it must grow, a process implying the formation of roots and a consequential development. This development is manifested in two general stages, which we shall call "material" and "spiritual," respectively. These terms must be redefined for our purposes; they are used most literally.

The first stage (we are assuming that the roots are already existent, in the form of an indigenous folk music) is called "material" because it is in this phase of growth that we find the actual folk material brought into music which is in no other way nationalistic. Thus, the earlier Russian nationalists, Glinka for one, are often found using folk songs and dances in the midst of a piece otherwise in the German symphonic style. Glazounov, of course, is *Exhibit A* for this kind of thing.

The folk materials resolve themselves into a cogent and authentic art; the metamorphosis from "material" to "spirit" begins; and we arrive at the second stage, where folk material is not necessarily used *qua* folk material, but begins to permeate the whole of a composition, so that the entire piece sounds typical of the country. The "spirit" of the material, then, becomes the basis for composition, rather than the material itself. Thus we hear many passages in Tchaikovsky or Moussorgsky which are free from any identifiable Russian folk music, and which are, notwithstanding, immediately felt as Russian. This is the permanent, mature phase of the nationalistic process.

The word "spiritual" is, of course, inadequate, but most useful. It is, in fact, much more than *spirit* that characterizes this music; with arduous work one can usually reduce this "feeling" to musical elements expressible in musical terminology. But in general it is this feeling about which the musician so often finds himself making absurd motions with his fingers, or puffing out his cheeks, or mysteriously rolling his eyes—all for lack of words to express the German or French or pseudo-French "spirit."

In the developmental process, influences are constantly exchanged among countries. Italianisms are readily found in Mozart and Bach, Russianisms in Debussy, Gallicisms in Stravinsky, Germanisms in Elgar. Yet Mozart, Debussy, Stravinsky, and Elgar remain essentially German, French, Russian, and English. There is no one, for example, more German than Schütz, who was the transplanter of the late-sixteenth-century Italian style in Germany. A dogmatic or puristic attitude toward nationalism is therefore inexcusable, even if the priority of roots cannot be denied. That is, we must avoid the procedure of those who stretch the nationalistic element to its limit by making a fetish of it, and deliberately confuse it with political or social nationalism. We must return to our first statement, that *nationalism is not an element arbitrarily inflicted upon music, nor even cultivated within music; it must be organic. To be organic it must grow, a process implying the formation of roots and a consequential development. This development is manifested in two general stages, which we shall call "material" and "spiritual," respectively.*

This analysis can be applied with reasonable success to a nationalistic epoch in the music of almost any country but America. Here we are faced with a dilemma indeed. There are three factors contributing to the problem, none of which can be controlled by the musician. First, there is no aboriginal race at present active or important in American life: the Indians, of course, are socially almost negligible. Second, the country is based primarily on heterogeneity, with the result that no one race can claim to be more American than another, except in point of length of residence.

Third, the country is still so young that with the stoppage of wholesale immigration only in recent years, assimilation and the movement toward homogeneity are still in their primary stages. We are therefore left with a country boasting no fundamental racial unit, and composed of numerous unrelated racial units which have not yet had time to melt together.

For every race in America there is a characteristic art, primitive or advanced; and the musical situation consequently becomes similar to the social. Now, if it is true that a composer functions for the sake of society (which we certainly hope is true), the American composer is presumably confronted by a blank wall. If he seeks to develop any one folk art, he is not characteristically American. He is faced with a situation in which there is no *common* American musical material.

Imagine an American composer trying to be materially nationalistic under the following conditions: of the total white population in this country (108,864,207), 13,366,407 * (or almost 13 percent) are actually foreign-born, and among the 95,497,800 native-born, 25,361,186 (about 26 percent) are of foreign or mixed parentage. In fact, 16,890,221 of those native-born are of strictly foreign parentage. And when we consider that of all the 13,366,407 foreign-born whites only 2,627,187 are from England, Scotland, Wales, Northern Ireland, or the Irish Free State, we can gain some idea of the extraordinarily wide distribution of nationalities in America. In these figures, moreover, we have not even mentioned the great number of nonwhites—Negroes, Mexicans, Chinese, and so on.

Such is the problem, then, confronting the American composer. Where, in all this maze of racial codes, is the opportunity for the material-to-spiritual development of an indigenous American music? Granted that we have the roots, they are too variegated to produce a flower that will symbolize all of America. The cultivation of a single racial root can never satisfy Americans as a people; at best it will be only exotic.

* Census of 1930, Vol. I, Part 1.

The solution lies in the possibility that one or more of these racial musical elements can attain to universality—that they can infiltrate every part of the country to establish a constant factor common from coast to coast. Only upon such a universally representative basis can the process of nationalistic growth be realized.

Now—in the twentieth century—the possibility has become a fact. Two of these elements have achieved such a universality, independently of each other, and in totally different ways. The first is the music of the New England colonists, which includes the hymn, or Protestant chorale, with its American modifications, and the wealth of English, Irish, and Scottish folk music. The spread of this element is only to be expected, for these greater-British races form the racial and social backbone of the country; they are the most definitely established races, numerically the largest, and geographically the most common. Their music, then, spread as they themselves did, carried westward in the great emigrations of the last century, becoming as much the ballads, hymns, and dances of California, Minnesota, and Kentucky as of Massachusetts and Georgia.

But the second element—and this is even more important—relies for its spread not on emigration but on a phenomenon of the twentieth century known as jazz. Through the incredible popularity of this art, Negro music has finally shown itself to be the really universal basis of American composition.

Hence the American composer makes use of either or both of these elements, depending upon his ancestry. The jazz influence is common to *all* Americans; the New England influence only to those for whom it is a heritage and, being so universal, can be anybody's heritage. Add to these the tempering influence of each individual composer's own heritage, and the result is a personal, yet American, musical style, with jazz as the ultimate common denominator.

It may indeed seem bold to advance so mannered an idiom as jazz as a common denominator, but it must be remembered that in the two-stage development of which we have been speaking, the material itself is gradually lost in the generality of its "feeling." We are now at the incipience of this second, mature stage. We are constantly coming upon signs that point the way to an *American* music—American because the "feeling" is American. There may be a rebuttal to this, but I doubt it; travelers to this country speak of an American feeling, or tempo, or rhythm. *"L'esprit américain"* has become a French idiom. But we cannot be satisfied in this paper to indulge in generalities; and we certainly cannot move our hands or puff out our cheeks in the search for an expression of the American "feeling." We shall devote most of the paper, in fact, to the translation of this feeling into tangible musical terminology.

2: The Periods of Pre-Nationalism

We now have enough perspective to realize four separate periods in the growth of American music. The first, embracing the extent of time from the earliest Puritan days up to the nineteenth century, is important rather because it was so nonmusical than for any other reason. As to the second, we have already spoken of the two kinds of music that constituted the musical life of this period. With the shackles of Puritanism gradually worn away, and with "America" coming to denote more than a mere strip along the Atlantic Seaboard, a new musical consciousness begins to set in. Composers appear in various places; orchestras and choral societies are founded. But the character of the musical composition itself throughout this second period was based almost without exception on current European musical styles. Even the infrequent originality that can be discovered in this music is European in conception and technique.

The third period began, to all intents and purposes, at the turn of the century, when a new movement toward nationalism was felt among composers. It was a kind of taking oneself by the hand and saying, "This imitation cannot go on." Composers became aware of the great and varied store of material in America: Negro, Indian, and so on. Thus began the artificial induction of "American" material into the basically European music. This is apparently the first stage of the nationalistic process.

The next great punctuation came with the World War, by which time three phenomena had occurred: a more solid assimilation of races, producing a greater *Americanness* among the basic peoples of the country; a tremendous influx of immigrants from all over the world, adding a new color to the prevailing picture; and the advent of jazz. The fourth period depends on two of these three factors. A social universality had been achieved through the solidification of Anglo-Saxon races in America, and through the building of the West; and a musical universality had appeared in the form of jazz. The third factor—the sudden large-scale immigration—was to become the great tempering and personalizing force in American composition.

Let us first briefly consider the two initial periods, the era of pre-Nationalism. We have already pointed out the two musical currents of Puritan times—English, Irish, and Scottish folk music, and the Protestant chorale. The latter is certainly not particularly English; it is German in origin and quality. The exchange of influences among countries is again evident; the chorale had traveled a long way from sixteenth-century Germany to the Ozark Mountains. It is surely unnecessary here to point out the great extramusical force—religion—which so often controls this sort of absorption.

The hymns, characterized by the rude qualities that were inevitable in a pioneer society, were almost the only music heard in America for two centuries. As to the folk music, there is still much controversy relating to its prominence in Puritan society.

With the recent vigorous interest in the Puritans and their living habits, much material has been unearthed to show that they were not such disagreeable people after all. This has created two schools of thought—one older and more harshly critical, the other newer and more generous. But at best the state of music in Puritan times is confusing. We find such opposing views as these: Rupert Hughes quotes a bit of opposition to the revolutionary measure introduced in the early eighteenth century of adopting "regular singing," or hymn singing by note, rather than rote:

First, it is a new way, an unknown tongue; 2nd, it is not so melodious as the old way; 3rd, there are so many tunes that nobody can learn them; 4th, the new way makes a disturbance in churches, grieves good men, exasperates them, and causes them to behave disorderly; 5th, it is popish; 6th, it will introduce instruments; 7th, the names of the notes are blasphemous; 8th, it is needless, the old way being good enough; 9th, it requires too much time to learn it; 10th, it makes the young disorderly.*

On the other hand, Cotton Mather, in an article called "The Accomplished Singer" dated 1721, encourages "regular singing":

The skill of regular singing is among the gifts of God unto the children of men. . . . For the congregations wherein 'tis wanting, to recover a regular singing would be really a Reformation. . . . We ought certainly to serve God with our best, and regular singing must needs be better than the confused noise of a Wilderness.†

We do know, however, that the chorale, "regularly" sung or not, was virtually the only music the Puritans permitted themselves. The folk music was allowed in very restricted degrees: the songs—especially the sentimental ones and ballads—were, of course, sung. But the danced music, always so important in a people's music, was banned by very stringent laws along with dancing itself, or what they called "promiscuous dancing."

But the research of the newer Puritan scholars suggests that perhaps there were a few who broke the laws. Besides, it is reasonable to assume that if there had been no jig dancing there would have been no laws passed against it. Whatever the truth is, we know that all this music has persisted through the centuries, so that we find it now— hymn, jig, and ballad—constituting a major influence upon the music of all America.

But it took a long time. Mr. Hughes, writing in 1900, points out that

. . . the throttling hands of Puritanism are only now fully loos-

* Rupert Hughes, *Contemporary American Composers* (Boston: L. C. Page & Co., 1900), p. 15.
† Miller and Johnson, *The Puritans* (New York: American Book Co., 1938), p. 452.

ened. Some of our composers recall the parental opposition that met their first inclinations to a musical career, opposition based upon the disgracefulness, the heathenishness, of music as a profession.*

This "loosening" process filled the nineteenth century, constituting what I have called the second period of American musical history. It was only natural that these new composers, created suddenly without a tradition, should grasp at the nearest and most familiar salvation—imitation of European styles. As a result, there is almost no American music of the early or middle nineteenth century that is interesting, or ever heard today. And there is little enough in the later part of the century. It does seem an added disadvantage, furthermore, that American music "began" in the nineteenth century. Our composers entered directly into the general Romantic looseness of structure and freedom of idea that Europeans had had to approach so slowly. In other words, America has never had a classical music.

Out of this strange beginning sprang composers presumably fully armed, Minerva-like: Harvey Worthington Loomis, Edgar Stillman Kelley, Ethelbert Nevin, Henry Holden Nuss, and Edward MacDowell. Some of these composers are still alive, others only recently dead. Yet almost all of them based their aesthetic on imitation; and since they were all imitating the same model, they sound more or less similar. I assume that examples are not necessary.

When the music happened to be programmatic in its function, exotic subject matter was often the escape mechanism. Thus the flood of little salon pieces about Japanese gardens and Neapolitan nights; and the formidable array of Oriental operas. In other words, America was for these composers the last place in the world to look to for either musical or extramusical material.

This situation became intolerable for certain composers, and steps were accordingly taken in the direction of "material" nationalism.

3: Nationalism: First Stage
Dr. Dvořak caused a great furor in American musical circles

* Hughes, op. cit., p. 16.

Dvořák

by constantly pointing out that America had a great treasure of material that had never been used. He was particularly impressed by the music of the Southern Negroes, who
had taken advantage of their emancipation by spreading
themselves throughout the whole country. These, said Dr.
Dvořak, were America's musical forebears. He even went
so far as to write a symphony based on Negro themes,
although it must be admitted that most of the themes
sound more Slavic than anything else.

Immediately composers took up the idea, and, shortly,
Negro fantasies were everywhere to be heard. I do not
mean to indicate that Dvořak alone was responsible for
this; the idea of "American" material had to come sooner
or later. But the precedent of a *New World Symphony* by so
eminent a European carried much weight at that time, and
exerted a great influence.

This, then, was the material stage of the nationalistic
process, beginning, for our purposes, about 1900. It was
simply a case of artificial respiration; the new indigenous
materials were merely imposed upon an otherwise neutral
kind of musical scheme, in order to give that scheme a new
life and meaning. But unfortunately, it usually worked the
other way. The "American" material, instead, lost its own
luster and appeal, unhappily surrounded as it was by much
Brahmsian or Wagnerian matter. The whole work was then
an anomaly, partly one thing and partly the other, with
both parts suffering in the juxtaposition. There was Negro
material, but no Negro style. Perhaps the composers were
to blame—being, in a sense, pioneers, and not satisfacto-
rily equipped; but this is too severe an interpretation. Most
of these musicians had been extensively trained, usually in
Germany, so that we are at liberty to put all the blame upon
the natural circumstances concomitant with the initial
stages of the nationalistic development.

Perhaps the most noteworthy composer to emerge from
those who used Negro material at all extensively was
Henry F. Gilbert. Despite faults of one sort or another,
Gilbert was basically a sensitive and sound musician. He
had a profound feeling for the Negro folk art, and never
hesitated to build his most pretentious works around it.

One or two of these works, notably *The Dance in the Place Congo*, are enjoyable and exciting; the *Dance* might very possibly develop a great popularity if it were more often heard.

But even in this piece, the faults attendant on the artificial introduction of Negro material are apparent. Gilbert states, in a prefatory note to his score:

> It has been for a long time an ideal of mine to write some music which should be in its inspiration truly native to America. The efforts of my compatriots, though frequently very fine technically, failed to satisfy me. To my mind they leaned far too heavily upon the tradition of Europe. . . . I was therefore moved to strike out boldly on a different course. . . .

Writing in 1920, he was already able to see the defects in the "material" approach to nationalism. Yet there was still no universal basis upon which he himself could rely, in attempting to use "the very genuine touches of inspiration which exist in *our* history, *our* temperament, and *our* national life." It is therefore surprising to observe how homogeneous and convincing a piece the *Dance* is. But this is achieved mainly by the continuous use of a basic rhythm peculiar to the Creole Negroes:

This figure, along with an allegedly Negro theme, forms the core of the piece. Whenever Gilbert deserts that core and becomes more lyrical, he inevitably becomes more European, although his individuality is strong enough to remain prominent. Between passages of rhythmic, Negroid writing, there appear sections full of overlush Wagnerian harmonies, with harp chords in abundance. Then there are triumphant reiterations of thematic material, "much after the manner of Grieg or Tschaikovsky," as Gilbert himself writes. Nevertheless, the piece as a whole is surprisingly coherent and direct. This is unfortunately the exception among composers of the period.

In Gilbert's *Comedy Overture on Negro Themes*, the opening is direct, forceful, characteristic. But then we come suddenly upon passages that might easily be Franck or Bruckner. The same is true of the *Humoresque on Negro Minstrel Tunes*, where the slower passages are not particularly in the manner of Franck, but not particularly American either. The methods of development, again, are the old ones: *strettos* progressing over pedal points, making the round of keys, etc. In other words, there is no consequential development emerging inevitably from the thematic ideas themselves; there is no basic American "feeling."

Of course, it is ridiculous to expect any better results from this experiment; Gilbert was, in fact, one of the very best results. The purely musical difficulties inherent in the system were augmented by the fact that the composer was not writing *American* music. At best—and this only infrequently—he was writing a kind of artificial Negro music, which must in all events remain strange and exotic to all Americans but the Negroes [and on second thought, even to the Negroes themselves]. Obviously, the plan failed because of its artificiality—because it was, after all, a plan, with no natural, universal basis.

Another camp of American nationalists opposed the Dvořák theory and deplored the use of Negro material as the fundamental American folk music. For them the solution was embodied in the music of the American Indian. MacDowell, the most prominent of these, was "not sympathetic with negro music . . . if we are to found a national school based on some local manner, we should find the Indian more congenial than the lazy, sensual slave."[*] MacDowell always preferred the Northern type of music, and Huneker points out in MacDowell a great similarity to Grieg—a similarity depending not on Norwegian music, but on Scottish, since Grieg's grandparents were Scottish Greggs. The theory of Nordic music has been carried to an extreme; relationships among the musical lores of various Teutonic peoples and the American Indians have been pointed out again and again. The pentatonic scale, for instance, is common to both Scottish and Indian music. This

* Hughes, *op. cit.*, p. 48.

may account in some way for the attraction of Indian music for MacDowell; but we must bear in mind that the pentatonic scale is also to be found in the music of China, Japan, Siam, and Hungary.

At any rate, there was a prolonged and ecstatic vogue of music based on Indian themes. MacDowell's *Indian Suite* was followed by an innumerable host of Indian cantatas, operas, operettas, songs, mandolin solos, and the like, most of which are still to be found stacked pile by dusty pile in remote corners of almost any secondhand-music store. Again, the Hiawatha-opera plan failed because it was only a plan; because it was not an organic fruition; because Americans could never be content to call Indian music *their* music. Moreover, the same inevitable fault is here to be found that weakened the corresponding Negro attempts: the material is too characteristic to stand shoulder to shoulder with the more prosaic European imitation without suffering pollution.

Still other composers claimed that the really fundamental music of America was the personal racial heritage of each individual musician. In this theory lie the seeds of the later nationalistic development—the application of particular racial idioms to a generally American foundation by the respective composers. This development was not presumably in their minds. To them it was a question of greatest self-expression via the ancestral medium. This too was a plan and suffers the same fault of restricted appeal as the other two plans discussed above.

Mr. Hughes's book, from which we have been quoting so freely, is really a valuable piece of work, despite the sometimes indiscriminate praise meted out to his contemporaries. Ample excuse is afforded, of course, by Mr. Hughes's obvious desire to encourage American composition as a whole. But aside from his particular evaluations, the introduction contains remarks astonishingly prophetic and clear, written as they were in the rather unsettled year of 1900. We find the case neatly summed up:

The vital objection, however, to the general adoption of Negro music as a base for an American school of composition is that it is in no sense a national expression. . . . The music of the

American Indian . . . would be as reasonably chosen as that of these imported Africs. . . . But the true hope for a national spirit in American music surely lies, not in the arbitrary seizure of some musical dialect, but in the development of just such a quality as gives us an individuality among the nations of the world in respect to our character as a people; and that is a Cosmopolitanism made up of elements from all the world, and yet in its unified qualities, unlike any one element.*

But the result has been even greater than Hughes hoped for. The cosmopolitanism has come; the individuality is assured; but the great universal basis that we now have was beyond his horizon. He could not foresee the incredible phenomenon of jazz.

PART TWO

1: Nationalism, Second Stage, and the Negroes

The greatest single racial influence upon American music as a whole has been that of the Negroes. But Negro music itself has affected our music not purely as the original African systems, but as an agglomeration of many influences in its own history. It is not our concern here to trace it from its many African sources, in all its ritual ramifications, through to its present state in America. It need only be remarked that this music, since the beginnings of slave trade with the Western Hemisphere, has undergone influences, and entered into combinations with such other music as Spanish and Latin American (this mostly in Cuba and Florida) or French (the Creole potpourri in New Orleans) or Protestant hymn singing (throughout the South and North) or the mountain music of Tennessee. At this point the problem becomes too diverse for our purposes; it would require a careful investigation of all these mergers, from the point of view not only of Negro music, but of all the others as well. It is enough to point out that the

* Hughes, *op. cit.*, pp. 22–23.

effect of Negro music upon American music has been more international than is commonly supposed.

We have seen how the composers of the nineteenth century drew upon the great amount of Negro material in the country. We have seen how artificial this was, because at best the composers had to regard their material as exotic. The manifestations of this material were, after all, highly localized. Before the emancipation, there was only the plantation singing to look to; after the emancipation there was the dancing and blues singing of Charleston and New Orleans, or the minstrel shows, which were still oddities at the height of their popularity.

But with the twentieth century there came a new manifestation of Negro music—jazz—which has certainly been the most powerful, even if not the most permanent, influence upon American music. True, the minstrel shows contained songs of a comic nature that could easily be pigeonholed as jazz, and surely the earliest blues singing was not much less advanced than the blues singing of today, but the important factor was not so much jazz itself, but its sudden and unrestricted popular spread.

Now, why has this left such a definite mark on the serious music of American composers? If we are true to our conviction that the music a man produces is the sum total of all his experience—conscious and subconscious, prenatal, amatory, social, visual, to say nothing of musical— then we are necessarily led to acknowledge that a composer who hears a certain kind of music around him all the time will show the effect of this force in his own music, regardless of his attitude toward it. Jazz in the twentieth century has entered the mind and spirit of America; and if an American is a sensitive creator, jazz will have become an integral part of his palette, whether or not he is aware of it.

At this point it becomes necessary to define and differentiate the particular species of jazz that we are speaking of. We are not referring to popular music as a whole. There have always been popular songs for the public, and as we know too well, they have rarely represented a progressive musical current. The popular song in the twentieth century is a more or less stale and stereotyped melody set over a 4/4 accompaniment, plunged usually into a ternary form (strain and repetition, release,* and strain). It has never yet dared to advance harmonically further than Schubert.

But we are speaking of something far different, a kind of popular music which has come along simultaneously with Tin Pan Alley, and has gained attention and strength steadily since the War, to the sorrow of the Alley. Long before it was called "swing" and had permeated our colleges and high schools to an extent where it too has almost become stale, this Negro jazz was *the* American music for those who were not impressed by the imitative output of the so-called serious composers. (Naturally, the more significant composers had pitifully few performances then.) In Europe it was hailed and imitated as America's contribution to music. In this objectification of Negro art, therefore, America had found her chief influence. But the healthy thing now was that America did not have to go out and *find* it; it came upon her.

This species of jazz (which we must call "swing" for lack of a better term) makes use of five constituent elements: Negro melodic peculiarities, Negro rhythmic patterns, Negro tone color, the 4/4 base, and (though not in all cases) a contrapuntal approach. It is a kind of improvisation upon stereotyped harmonic progressions by solo instrumentalists or vocalists in the Negro manner. It is very often the case that these improvisations are florid variations on the output of Tin Pan Alley, but the Negroid ornamentation of these uninteresting tunes is actually so far from the original that unless one knows what tune is being "swung," one has difficulty in deciding. Furthermore, the improvisor does not keep the *melody* so much in mind as the *harmony*, or the basic harmonic skeleton; and after all, harmonic skeletons are so alike in this business that they tend to become formulae.

From this we learn two things: one, that even this kind of "variation swing" is almost completely independent of the theme varied; and two, that harmonic background has very little importance in this art. More and more we find

* "Release" is the term applied by jazzmen to the middle section of a popular song.

wait 'tel Rock!

the rhythmic section serving as the whole supporting body, while the interest remains purely rhythmic or melodic. (This is a natural result of using chordal sequences which in time become so repetitious and banal that they do not even have to be sounded.) With a consequent increase of emphasis on the melodic aspect of this music, a new contrapuntal interest was almost inevitable. Thus arose the "jam session" (an outgrowth of what is now loosely termed "Dixieland" style), in which the members of a band improvise *simultaneously* upon a conventional harmonic pattern or in a conventional form such as the blues.

This contrapuntal tendency also has its rhythmic aspect. While the 4/4 meter is still the rhythmic basis of swing, the collective improvisation above it offers variety amounting to polyrhythms, so that the 4/4 rhythm is relegated to a comparatively unimportant position. The result of this weaning from the 4/4 bass is seen in the newer kinds of social dancing, where it is no longer necessary to follow a repeated pattern of four beats per measure; the dancing is dependent, in the final analysis, only on the alternation of a strong and a weak beat in no prescribed metrical grouping. Thus, along with the harmonic banality, we find the rhythmic banality disappearing.

Let us, then, sum up in the light of the above discussion the really active forces of swing: the Negro scale, or scale variant, and the Negro rhythms (these are the two main items); supporting them, Negro tone color, and the contrapuntal feeling applied both melodically and rhythmically.

2: The Negro Scale

The Negro scale variant, as it appears in its jazz manifestation, is identical with the Occidental diatonic major scale, but for three accidentals which may or may not be used:

The three flatted degrees of the scale are used almost exclusively, as might be expected, in descending figures, e.g.:

The flatted seventh, for instance, is never used melodically as a leading tone; that would occasion a modality far removed from this one. But this seventh is often found sounded melodically against the leading-tone seventh in the harmony,

producing a cross-relation that is one of the platitudes of jazz. As to the flatted fifth, it is used mainly as a kind of *appoggiatura* to the fourth in descending figures. The flatted third gives a strong minor quality to the music; but a minor of a special nature, since it is used melodically against a major harmony. (Of course, if the harmony is minor, the Negro poignancy is not particularly different from, let us say, the Spanish.) It is this major–minor conflict in the cases of both the third and the seventh that imparts the special Negro flavor; for, in point of fact, the actual note of the scale is somewhere between the natural tone and the flatted tone.

As a matter of strict record, none of these three alterations of the major scale can be notated absolutely correctly. They are dependent on the Negro *timbre*; that is, they are almost purely a matter of intonation (very much like certain notes of the Hindu ragas). It is for this reason that when swing is played on the piano—which, being a mechanically exact instrument, cannot produce quarter-tones and the like—the pianist must resort to such impressionistic approximations as:

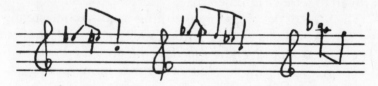

Obviously, music based on this scale sounds most authentic when sung by a Negro voice, although such instruments as clarinet and trumpet in the hands of a man with "feeling"—usually a Negro—can come very close to the vocal execution.

There are two restricting features involved in the use of this scale: one, its highly characteristic flavor, which creates such stereotyped formulae that it becomes almost unlistenable after a while; and two, the inevitable fact that it is entirely limited to diatonic music. Of the first it may be said that the influence of this scale on American music was consequently a temporary one, which had its heyday in the postwar jazz craze and ended suddenly, to all intents and purposes, in 1929. But in those ten years the experiments with this material left us some things which may still be heard with pleasure, despite their dated quality.

The second restriction—that this scale is inevitably limited to diatonic music—has resulted in the fact that only such conservative composers as George Gershwin were able to make unqualified use of it. No disparaging attitude toward Gershwin is here implied; he was extremely fertile, with always new and engaging material, at times displaying sheer genius; but he was only beginning to understand *composition* in its literal architectural sense when he died. He has left music none of which is dull, much of which is mediocre, and some of which is imaginative, skillful, and beautiful. There is rightly much controversy as to its lasting value, but there can be no doubt that it is highly significant and important in the history of American music.

The function that Gershwin's music fulfilled—the symphonization of jazz—was a small and thankless one, and has never been fulfilled as adequately as it was by him. But he suffers from sameness (we have spoken of the restricted possibilities of this music). The same chords, the same figures, the same general qualities appear again and again, all woven together *à la* Tchaikovsky, Puccini, or Ravel.

The type of developmental writing used so consistently by Tchaikovsky is evident throughout Gershwin's works. The *Rhapsody in Blue*, the *American in Paris*, the *Piano Concerto* are, for example, full of figures in mounting sequences, attaining fulfillment in the great *fortissimo*. In the *stretto* section of the exciting "Wintergreen for President" we find the same kind of menacing advancing of the thematic figure

from the Nibelheim of the bass to the final brass recapitulation, all over the usual crescendo tremolo in the timpani. This same kind of analysis would bring out similar imitations of Puccini and Ravel.

But these remarks, of course, are ultimately ridiculous; influences are much too easy to find. Reverting to our idea —now almost a slogan—that a composer's music is the sum of all his experience (including musical experience), we cannot deplore influences as such. These observations concerning Gershwin's models are not accusations; they are meant only to show that Gershwin did not try to reconcile a "modern" idiom with the diatonic Negro scale. He simply remained steeped in nineteenth-century methods and made the most of them. Again, his influencers are not necessarily Tchaikovsky, Puccini, or Ravel; these are only names intended to represent the *kind* of harmony or dramatic form that Gershwin used; hence, Gershwin's aesthetic. One might as easily call his influencers Dvořak, Massenet, and Charles Wakefield Cadman. The important point is that Gershwin's music *was* the result of all his musical experience; but that experience was limited to the older music—an inevitability, since that kind of music tied up so much better with the material he had to use.

If we carry this point through—and it is an important one for our investigation—we find that Ravel in his turn was influenced by Gershwin (again keeping in mind that Ravel represents a generic concept—one kind of French music—and that Gershwin represents one kind of American music). Between 1918 and 1929, Europe was intrigued by American jazz, and such people as Stravinsky, Milhaud, Honegger, Ravel, Tansman, and Hindemith used it freely. Thus we find all the features of our Negro scale appearing here and there throughout their music. In Ravel, for instance, appears the use of the natural seventh against the lowered seventh:

(*Alborada del gracioso*)

In Milhaud, we find the conflict of the major and minor thirds, with the typical descending minor third as the melodic figure:

It is interesting to note that this example comes from the fourth of the *Chants Populaires Hébraïques,* and not from a consciously Negroid work like the *Création du Monde.*

This whole discussion, then, shows that the least universal and most restricted feature of Negro music, the scale, has had a considerable effect upon American music, and has been used successfully and artistically by at least one major composer, Gershwin. Further, we find an interesting reflection of Gershwin in some of the music of many European composers; and this is important because it was the first influence European music has ever felt from America.

But a discussion of Gershwin is still far from the end of this investigation. There have been composers in America who were not content to use the old methods, who were averse to writing in the nineteenth-century idioms, who felt a new kind of spirit; but who still wanted to employ in their compositions whatever they could of the Negro scale, diatonically restricted as it was. Aaron Copland, for instance, who has been very sensitive to American jazz, has used the melodic idiom in both shorter and larger works: in the *Ukulele Serenade* for violin and piano, in *Music for the Theatre*, in the *Piano Concerto*, and in several shorter pieces. It was necessary for Copland to reconcile the scale with his own advanced style. Here a problem which Gershwin never had to face is met squarely and competently by a man who showed what could be done in the way of musical compromise.

Let us take the *Piano Concerto* as our point of departure. It was written in 1926, at the height of what is now called the "jazz age"—the days of the postwar boom. We have pointed out before that it was in this period that jazz was exploited to its fullest by serious composers, often in the form of little novelties, and most often partaking not a little of sensationalism. The Copland *Concerto* stands, however, as a work of skill, structural merit, and great contrapuntal interest.

The compromise in this "symphonization" of jazz lies in the fact that it is essentially both harmonic and contrapuntal. The harmony is mainly triadic, but polytonal, so that the harmonies arising from the Negro scale can be kept intact, while at the same time Copland's own idiom is ensured.

In the first part of the piece, for example, there occurs a

harmonic progression which is so overused in jazz as to be perfectly trite:

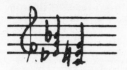

This arises, obviously, from the actual modifications inherent in the Negro scale. But the banality is removed very subtly by the imposition of suggestions of other harmonies above the progression:

The style is further ensured by the contrapuntal approach; as, for instance, when several melodic lines are going simultaneously over harmony which may be appropriate to only one of them. This ties up securely with the contrapuntal tendency in swing, which we have referred to above as the "jam session." It is interesting to find this truly twentieth-century feeling in popular music; it enables Copland to combine swing elements and his own style with complete authenticity. In these two ways, then—the polyharmonic and the contrapuntal—the dialectic between swing and the modern idiom has been effected.

The *Concerto* contains several themes of Negro character. Let us take some of them, for illustration, and see what happens to them in development. The first occurs in the opening slow section and is itself a development of the bold initial motif which follows:

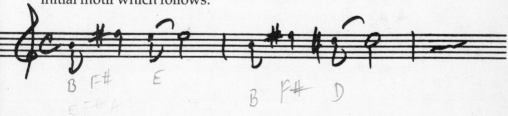

The implied tonality is obviously E; but when the phrase
reaches the D natural, the Negro character of the lowered
seventh is immediately perceived. Next we hear the theme
as a whole, in the solo horn:

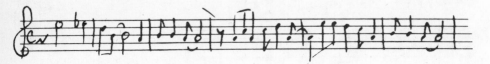

Above this, we hear the second Negro theme in counterpoint:

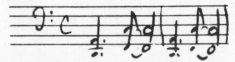

These themes are both in D. The supporting harmony is
also D:

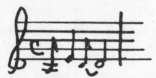

But simultaneously there is going on above a figure recalling the opening motif:

Now, all these elements are in D; yet the total result is
anything but conventional in sound, as can be seen by a
mental juxtaposition of the four staves above. (This, in fact,
is one of the simplest and clearest passages in the *Concerto*;
at other times the simultaneous themes collect so profusely
that it is almost impossible to follow them all, and the result
is sometimes cluttered up. But even this is skillfully amelio-
rated by orchestration varied enough to let the ideas stand
out in relief against each other.)

In the fast section, which is the main body of the piece,
the Negro themes accumulate rapidly. The first motif employs the device mentioned above, of sounding the flatted

third together with the semitone directly below it, to produce the feeling of a tone which is not on the piano:

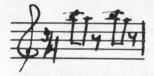

This is again a jazz banality, but again Copland rescues it
by suggesting the tonality of F in the left hand, while the
right is in A, so that the total effect is fresh and interesting:

Thus another harmonic solution aids the compromise.

Over and over again we find this method used—the setting of a jazzy tune in one tonality over harmony of another. Here is another example of an idea just saved from
triteness:

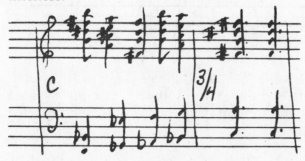

A good example of counterpoint to the rescue is found in
the entrance of a theme admittedly based on the "St. Louis
Blues" but combined with the rhythmic motif which has
just preceded it. This tune (in E) is purposely accompanied
by a very conventional pattern in the same key, for the
burlesque imitation of 1926 jazz bands; but here again the

whole is relieved by contrapuntal imitations both of the "St. Louis" theme and of the rhythmic motif. Thus we have the following simultaneous elements:

the theme:

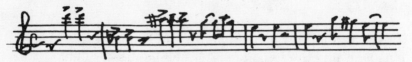

the imitations:

a)

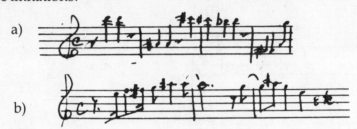

b)

the accompaniment:

Later on, this same "St. Louis" theme is free of any contrapuntal interference, but the platitude is this time avoided by having the harmony dexterously shun the expected chords at each cadence:

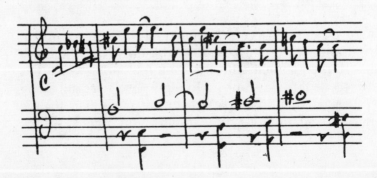

These are certainly enough examples for the adequate demonstration of what was done by such a first-rate composer as Copland in order to accomplish a satisfactory combination of certain jazz elements with his own idiom. And we find a perfectly natural, unforced, spontaneous, successful result. If the music is dated—as it is—it is nonetheless important as a monument to the days when composers had their fling with jazz—one aspect of the second stage of self-conscious American music.

But I do not want to give the impression that this influence is over. It is true that the Negro scale has ceased to affect American writing, except for purposes of out-and-out jazz imitation; but we have yet to investigate a much more far-reaching and complicated contribution of Negro music—that of the rhythms.

3: Negro Rhythms

The earliest adaptations of Negro material by American composers made use of the rhythms, above all. The scale variant, which we have been discussing, was not looked upon in the nineteenth century as typically Negro, since there were so many other scales used by the Negroes that none of them could be called really characteristic. In Dvořak's *New World Symphony*, for instance, the Negro themes used—and Dr. Dvořak called them authentic—range from the pure diatonic major:

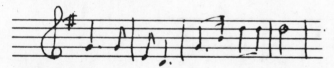

to the Dorian mode:

(Nowhere in this work does our scale variant make an appearance. It was not until Negro music had reached its peak of integration—in jazz—that its most characteristic mode became its predominant one, and the one destined to have the greatest effect upon American music.)

As a result, the truly distinguishing feature of these themes was the rhythms. Like the scale, these rhythms have since found expression in both conservative and more advanced uses; in certain cases, in fact, the development has advanced so far that the rhythms have practically lost all their Negro quality, and have become something typically and wholly American. It is this development that we shall try to track down.

The basic feature of Negro rhythms is syncopation, which we must define very broadly as a special accentuation of the weak beat. A conventional and more literal definition, of course, would involve the use of terms like "shortening" or "cutting off"; but it is obvious that this operation is effected by accenting weak beats, through the apparent omission of a weak beat as such.

Syncopations in their more elementary forms have been employed for centuries, independently of the Negroes. We can easily find them in Bach; and there are those who argue that they are everywhere in Josquin and Palestrina. There is really no rebuttal to this; every time a weak final beat is tied over the bar line, a syncopation has occurred, at least in theory. There is no need of elaborating upon the use of syncopation throughout the eighteenth and nineteenth centuries; it is obvious and ubiquitous. The favorite accompaniment to a romantic *con moto* melody has been:

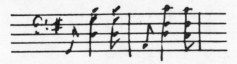

The Negro species of melodic syncopation is not fundamentally different from any other—from the much-talked-of "Scottish snap," for instance, or the typical Spanish folk figure:

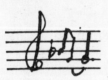

The only distinguishing trait one might point out is one of feeling. It is difficult to convey in words, but may be approximately described as follows: The Scottish and Spanish figures are amost like accented grace notes (*acciaccaturas* with an *appoggiatura* feeling) very often preceding a cadential note. The Negro syncopation is actually more rhythmic; that is, less arbitrary and more conclusive in the time continuum. For example, the Spanish figure quoted above is, in execution, rather free in time; and the two notes come so closely together in relation to the whole measure that the *appoggiatura* feeling is made very apparent. The Negro syncopation, on the other hand, is a decisive one, relying for its effect on the sense of beat underneath:

Even in music slower than the *Golliwog's Cakewalk* by Debussy, this is felt; as in "Nobody Knows de Trouble I Seen":

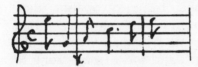

We might say that the Negro syncopation is a more organic one, whereas the others are primarily ornamental.

Now, this rhythmic device, simple and restricted as it is, has many possibilities of extension and development. For out of it can come the rather more complex devices of beat-group distortions, such as the demarcation of three-beat groups within four-beat measures:

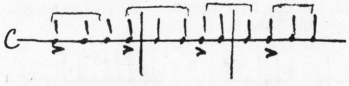

or even five-beat groups:

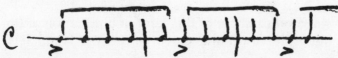

A second distortion is the diminution of the beat groups:

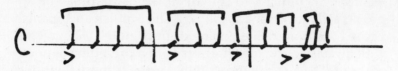

or, conversely, augmentation in the same way:

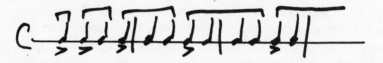

A third (really an extension of the second) consists in the diminution or augmentation of a rhythmic figure:

(diminution)

These are all simple extensions of the syncopation idea, and are entirely dependent on it. For it is easily seen that these rhythmic distortions have no syncopative value without the shifting of accents back and forth from strong to weak beats.

The earlier American composers used Negro rhythms just as they were, without these distortions. This seems to corroborate our feeling that the rhythmic developments came only with jazz. And here I should like to forestall an obvious objection: namely, that European composers have been using rhythmic diminutions all through the last two centuries. But it should be plain that a Tchaikovsky diminution, for example, is dependent on the duple integral, and therefore occasions no syncopation:

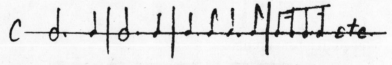

There is a good example of this kind of diminution at the beginning of the fourth movement of the *New World Sym-*

phony. This, of course, simply cuts the beat in two, and doubles the pace. There is no shifting of emphasis to a weak beat. Even the offbeat orgies of Beethoven do not approach the kind of syncopative extension that we are dealing with.

But with jazz the new feeling was brought into American music, making for new rhythmic variety with a flavor all its own. Again, the composer who used these rhythms most openly, and with intentions most closely resembling those of jazz itself, was Gershwin.

Gershwin's rhythms depend almost entirely on the 4/4 beat, with melodies employing the simplest syncopative devices. But accent as such upon a weak beat is not the only syncopative method. It is well known that accent can be produced in more ways than by merely giving a note more volume. A note of longer duration than its immediate neighbors—a sudden skip to a note—a sudden skip from a note—the top or bottom notes of a melodic line—a suspension—all these will give very considerable accent. Thus we find that melodic syncopation in jazz often takes advantage of these devices rather than purely dynamic accent.

The *Rhapsody in Blue*,* taken as a typical work, is just one series of themes made in these ways.

Following are some examples:

1)

2)

* And in our haste to condemn this preponderance of attention to Gershwin, let us not forget that even if we tend to relegate him to some very special but less important niche in the Hall of American Composers, he does occupy a place which is tremendously important, not only *per se*, but as an influence on others, and as a startling sociological document of his time.

Or, in slower tempo:

3)

It will be observed that in the first two examples the syncopations occur on the weak *half* of the weak beat; whereas, in the third example, it occurs on the weak beat itself. This is a distinction which is usually found between fast and slow syncopations, respectively. An example of the first type in extremely quick time is found in the *agitato* theme appearing toward the end of the piece, where the accent is very marked, owing to its coming on such a quick note:

This, in fact, is a simple *rumba rhythm*.

The importance of the rumba rhythm in American music cannot be overemphasized. We have spoken of the mixed musical nationalities which have imposed themselves upon Negro music during its history. One of the most telling has been that of Latin America, where there are great numbers of Negroes. Through these interrelations, some of the features of Cuban and Mexican music have entered jazz along with the Negro music; and it is surprising that people tend to think of all these influences as mutually independent. We have witnessed a tremendously popular wave of Mexican and Cuban bands throughout America; they have become almost as indispensable to the public as the swing bands themselves. And yet the obvious interdependence of these types is rarely observed. The racial integration of Negro and Latin American, in fact, is remarkably advanced; and it is therefore no wonder that the Negroes themselves have introduced the Cuban and Mexican rhythms to America.*

We do not contend, however, that the Rumba (capital

* N.B. (1982). At this moment, most Jamaican-style "Reggae" would sound Afro-Cuban if sung in Spanish.

R), as it came to us from the Latin American countries, is in itself a great influence. The basic features of the rumba are certainly inherent in Negro rhythms themselves, and it is therefore difficult to decide upon priority. We shall use the word "rumba," therefore, with a small *r*; that is, we shall think of it in terms of its rhythmic characteristics, rather than its origins.

To return to Gershwin, then, we have found the rumba rhythm in the theme quoted next above. The eight equal notes of each measure are divided into three parts: the first containing three notes, the second, three, and the third, two notes:

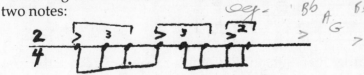

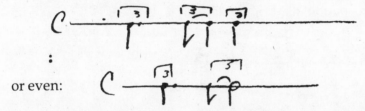

This is the <u>standard rumba count</u>.* It may be found in various other forms, such as a simple suggestion of it:

or even:

It therefore becomes clear that many themes in the *Rhapsody in Blue* are merely slow versions of the rumba rhythm:

1)

2)

* There is an interesting version of this rhythm in *El Salon Mexico* of Copland, where he is imitating the Mexican style:

This would achieve in a symphony orchestra a result obtainable from a jazz band with a much simpler time signature.

A common distortion of the rumba count occurs when the *last* note of each group is accented, rather than the first. This is eminently comparable to the difference between playing a German waltz in the village-band style:

and in the more sophisticated Viennese style:

Rather than a distortion, it is a refinement. Since the first beat of any group is the natural one to accent, sophistication will dictate an accent on a less important beat. In the case of the rumba, this amounts to a syncopation within a syncopation, as will be seen:

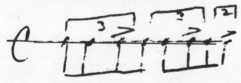

And this is exactly the rhythm used by Gershwin in the *agitato* theme we have been speaking of:

As a matter of fact, we have witnessed this very refinement in the last two decades, right here in the case of our own jazz. The postwar (twenties) kind of jazz (which is now deplored as "corny" by our present swing authorities) seems to have been at fault for being too obvious; that is, putting the accent where it would naturally come—*on* the syncopation:

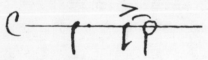

whereas our present-day jazzmen let the syncopation slip by unaccented, thereby creating an unexpected and satisfying effect:

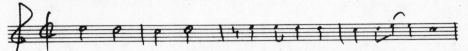

This is "good taste." We might draw another analogy between this kind of thing and the Chopin pianists, who go suddenly *pianissimo* on a note that wants accent—a device which has come to be standard excitement material for romantic hearts:

(The "good taste" here involved is a highly debatable matter.)

The point has probably been pressed more than enough; but I think rightly, in that it is a phenomenon occurring in the *performance* of music which eventually influences the writing and musical taste of an era. Such refinements are not possible, for instance, until enough time has passed to allow the obvious thing to become so natural to the public that a departure from it has significance. One might almost write a history of music in the light of this one point.

We have so far accounted for the most elementary kinds of syncopations, and for the influence of the rumba, using Gershwin as our model. We now have before us the more advanced uses of these rhythms, as they grow away from a purely and deliberately jazz idiom into an American style ultimately independent. Roger Sessions, for example, is a composer who has never been bothered by the jazz idiom, and who has rarely, if ever, tried to use it as such in his music. Yet we find many instances, throughout his work, of syncopations arising directly from jazz, but imbued with a highly individual flavor. The following excerpt from the Allegro of his *Piano Sonata* (1931) is full of such syncopations:

I have quoted so much of this because it is interesting from several points of view. The first thing that we notice about the music is the unique and Sessionsish approach to the rhythms—a kind of ponderous, "sit-on-it," almost German feeling infusing the fundamentally American quality of the music. It is heavily accented, not too fast, full of octave chords, constantly *forte,* and orchestral in feeling. It is an offshoot of jazz that finds few, if any, prototypes in jazz itself: that is, it has none of the racy, precipitate quality of jazz.

The rhythms themselves are very simple, using the most elementary syncopative devices. The three-beat group in the four-beat measure will be immediately observed. We find this device even in Sessions' sober *Three Chorale Preludes for Organ*:

 (no. 3)

Again, in the same Chorale Prelude, we find the diminution device used in addition to the basic syncopations:

Another interesting feature is the constant placing of accent *on* the syncopation, rather than in an unexpected place. According to our analysis of this question (pages 69–70), this music would fall into the category of *early* jazz—the kind that does not take advantage of the unexpected, since the syncopations, in themselves accents, are further accented by the left-hand chords:

(*Piano Sonata,* meas. 7)

But this method, in the *Sonata*, is anything but "bad taste."
It adds to the heavy, rather immobile character of the
music, which is, after all, the total effect; and so finds its
place. It is relieved from time to time, however, by punc-
tuating chords which accent the strong beat *after* the syncopation, with the result that the whole is not monotonous:

(meas. 8 and 9)

Again, we find the device of diminution of beat groups,
which we mentioned at the beginning of this discussion of
rhythms, where, by the constant subtraction of one note
from each succeeding group, a great syncopative effect is
obtained:

(In this same passage, a fine polyrhythmic effect is
achieved by the contrasting beat groups in the left hand.)

As far back as 1927, in the very heart of the jazz age,
Sessions already showed the elements of this style in his
Symphony in E Minor. The "heavy" feeling is made even
more explicit and cogent to the performer by the inclusion

of a parenthetical 4/8 time signature after the usual 2/4. By this Sessions means to convey to the conductor his wish that each note be "sat on." The syncopations are similar to those of the later *Sonata*; that is, regular elementary syncopations ultimately reducible to the underlying 2/4 count. The opening of the *Symphony* follows:

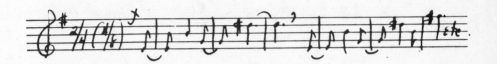

In Sessions, then, we find a genuine and important adaptation of rhythms primarily Negro, received through the medium of jazz, and combined with an intensely personal and highly developed style totally independent of jazz.

The other great development of Negro rhythms by an American into an independent idiom is to be found in the work of Aaron Copland.*

There have been two stages in this development, which seem to fall almost too neatly into the pre-1929 and post-1929 periods. It is unfortunate to have to divide people into periods—especially contemporary people; but in Copland's case there seems to be a great break in the vicinity of 1929, and for purposes of analysis this cannot be disregarded. Let us take as our two examples the *Piano Concerto* of 1926 (which we discussed above in relation to Negro melody) and the *Piano Variations* of 1929.

The *Concerto* serves as a kind of rhythmic preparation for the *Variations*. In it Copland has gone two steps beyond Gershwin: first, as with the melodic material, he saves the jazz rhythms from banality by rhythmic counterpoint; and second, he elaborates the rhythms themselves so that new ones are achieved.

---

* It is too bad to restrict our illustrative material to the same composers again and again, but it is in these composers that one finds the material we are dealing with most clearly and fully outlined, and most consistently used. It would be mere tautology to examine works of other composers who have done, from time to time, more or less the same things with the jazz idiom.

Examples of the first method are numerous indeed. The very opening bars of the *Concerto* contain a motif in imitation by two voices, with acute punctuations:

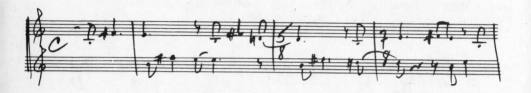

Let us examine some other themes, noting their syncopations. In the first (slow) section:

(simple syncopation)

1)

2)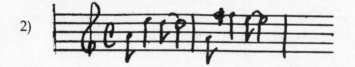

3)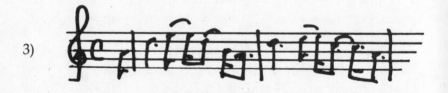

In the third example we observe syncopation within syncopation, in order to render the "loose" character of the Negro performance. The tune would be more simply notated:

4)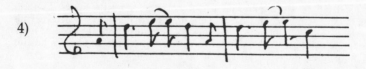

And from the *allegro* section:

5)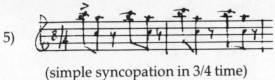

(simple syncopation in 3/4 time)

6)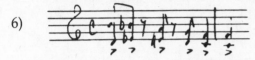

(relay of accent from strong to weak beats)

7)

Here we find diminution and augmentation in new forms. From a regular syncopation of four-beat measures into three-beat groups (meas. 1, 2, and 3) the figure is compressed into two beats (meas. 4), thence reduced to one and a half. Up to this point all is regular. But whereas in the first few measures the *measure feeling* of 4/4 had been practically destroyed, it suddenly pops up again in measure 4, with the preceding one and a half beats acting as *Auftakt*. Thus, measures 4 and 5 *feel* like 4/4 time. Copland then takes advantage of this by steadily equalizing, in the following two measures, the five tones in measure 4. This amounts almost to an augmentation, inasmuch as the previous eighth notes are now quarters. But the syncopative feeling is preserved by the simple device of having five quasi-equal notes contained in a four-beat measure:

8)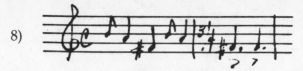

This is another "rumba" theme, the first measure of which
is strictly rumba rhythm:

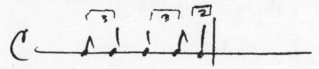

The second measure is a simplification of the rumba idea,
which we noted in connection with Gershwin's use of
rhythm.* Copland has left off the last beat in this measure
for the sake of rhythmic variety, but the essential feeling is
still very prominent. The "Charleston" rhythm is later used
as an *ostinato* figure in a long *stretto* section.

9)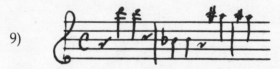

(three-beat groups within 4/4 measures)

This theme again exemplifies the use of rhythmic counterpoint. It finds its imitation thus:

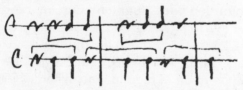

* This particular rhythm became very popular in the twenties as the "Charleston"
—accompanying a ballroom dance of the same name:

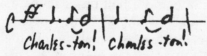

This, of course, with much snapping of fingers and coy lifting of skirts. It is a
typical bit of postwar jazz, highly accented, naive, full of life, yet pedestrian. It is
perhaps this attribute which makes the *Concerto* sound dated; but is this not, after
all, natural, when we consider that it is based upon a very special and dated
musical idiom? The *Concerto* has absorbed the jazz of its time, and held it fast, like
rings in petrified wood.

Even in the imitation, the three-within-four idea is still preserved.

And now we come to Copland's second method of rhythm-making in the *Concerto*—the actual development, extension or distortion of the basic jazz rhythms. His essential practice is to contradict the 4/4 beat in the case of those themes which are primarily based on it. By this means he not only obtains variety and relief from a very stylized kind of rhythmic system, but also achieves entirely new rhythms, which are the training ground for the even more advanced rhythms we shall find in the *Variations*. These *Concerto* rhythms are to be found predominantly in the *allegro* section, since it is really in the faster kind of jazz that the composer runs the danger of falling into banality. Slower music, obviously, offers more opportunity for extensional devices within a regular beat, since one beat can be redivided so many times that new patterns are freely established against the old ones.

From the *allegro*, then, let us extract a few themes, and notice the changes they undergo.

The opening motif is in 3/4 time—a relief in itself:

When this is recapitulated by the orchestra a little farther on, it remains 3/4, but assumes new proportions:

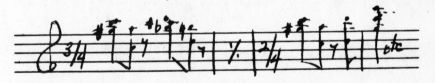

These three measures, amounting in all to eight beats, can be easily construed as two simple 4/4 measures, or one 4/2 measure, divided again into the rumba pattern: 3-3-2. And indeed, that is the very effect obtained: that of an *augmented rumba*. Thus we have here rather a simplification of the opening theme.

Another early figure of the piece is:

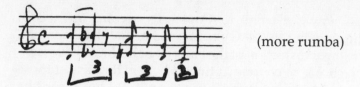

(more rumba)

This figure becomes very important in development, and undergoes many distortions:

Supporting this in the bass, we find the same figure, more regular, and in augmentation:

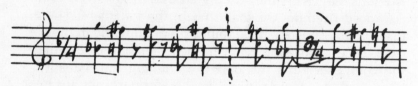

The three-in-four kind of syncopation is very apparent.
One of the most elusive distortions occurs much further on:

(The bass contains the same figure again augmented in groups of three.) The beat groups indicated are subtly arranged, their syncopative feeling being dependent upon the little eighth rest inserted between the groups. The whole would otherwise sound like a stodgy succession of 1-1-1-1-, etc.; the eighth rest serves to throw each group off the established beat. Even this analysis, however, does little good for the hearer, who feels it only as a violent, jerky, syncopated passage, with no particular measure beat. The only straw at which the hearer might grasp is the steady three-beat group in the bass; yet he cannot possibly hear the whole in three because of the contradictions in the right hand. For instance, Copland cleverly starts the three-beat groups one measure after the right hand has begun, so that the cross-rhythm effect is ensured. Couple with that the inner syncopation at the end of the passage, making three simultaneous planes of syncopation—and you have a complete distortion of the original stylized jazz rhythm.

Approaching the *stretto*, as the "Charleston" figure returns, Copland faces another stylistic problem of the same kind—avoiding jazz-band regularity. The method is simple: the first time the figure occurs, it is given two introductory measures in the solo trumpet, before the piano enters above it:

But the second time we hear:

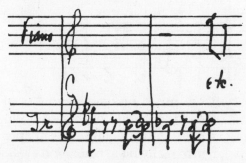

where two expected beats are deleted from the introductory bars.

One more example should be sufficient to establish the significance of this point. In the cadenza, the piano develops a theme which has previously appeared as:

But it now takes the following form:

where, by the addition of beats (and even measures), another distortion is obtained, which is, however, kept in check by the recurring triple beat in the accompaniment.

All these deviations from the monotonous regularity inherent in most jazz pave the way very solidly for a new system of rhythms, having little to do with jazz itself, yet directly derivative from it. Let us see exactly what they are, and what accounts for their American style, using the *Variations* as our model.

Again we must look to the *allegro* sections of the work for our examples, although even in the slower parts we find much syncopative writing mixed with the basically declamatory style. In the coda, for instance, there appears the following:

But the feeling is not one so much of syncopation as of chords in no particular rhythmic pattern, for there is nothing in the passage to give a rhythmic feeling. It is "paper syncopation," not tonal; hence really no syncopation at all.

Let us then take our themes from the *scherzo*-like section beginning on page 7 of the score and winding up just before the coda on page 16. Here at last we shall find the ultimate extent to which the development of simple jazz rhythms has taken us; and we shall be able to see that the feeling of these examples is in no way Negro, but peculiarly and unquestionably *American*.

There is something about 5/n and 7/n rhythms which, practically defying description, makes them particularly adaptable to American music. Certainly, these rhythms have been and are in use all over the world; they have abounded in Russian music, in Balinese music; and they are used by almost all contemporary composers. But the American use is quite different in feeling from any of the others. The Russian 5/4 (as in Tchaikovsky's *Sixth Symphony*) divides naturally into 3 and 2, or into 2 and 3:

Hindemith uses the 5/8 in his *Third Quartet* with equal accentuation:

In Stravinsky, these rhythms are usually a matter of convenience, incidental to a continuous 1-1-1-1- beat. But even when Stravinsky uses the 5/n as a basic pattern, there is a natural division into its smaller groups, as in the Dance of Glorification from *Le Sacre*:

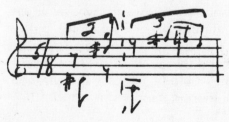

Again, the Hindu 7/8 usually divides into 2 and 5 (a strange division, and one suited to the nicety of Hindu dance movement):

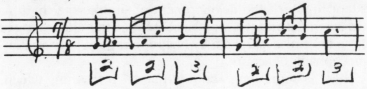

(*Danse Hamachandra*: repertory of Shan-Kar Co., arr. by Vishnunuss Shirali)

It will be noticed that even the five-beat groups divide naturally into twos and threes.

We conclude, then, that in most of the uses of these meters outside of America, they divide quite naturally and regularly into the more common beat groups of two and three, unless they are all equally accented, as in the Hindemith example. This is, after all, a natural phenomenon, taking for granted the elemental importance of duple and triple meters. We feel, also, an instinctive inclination to put our downbeat on the first beat of each of these subgroups; and in fact, this accent is often inherent in the music itself, as in the Stravinsky example. In the Hindu piece, again, there is a little bell that punctuates the seven beats on the first and third.

With these remarks in mind, let us see what differentiates the American 5 or 7 rhythms. First (we shall proceed by advancing the argument before the examples) there is no tendency toward a downbeat on the beginning of each subdivision. I say downbeat rather than accent, because in the preceding examples each beat group might be conducted by itself, and each beat of the group represented by one stroke of the baton. That is, in the Tchaikovsky excerpt, for example, one feels the count as 1, 2, 3: 1, 2—1, 2: 1, 2, 3; in the Stravinsky, as 1, 2: 1, 2, 3; in the Hindu piece, 1, 2: 1, 2: 1, 2, 3. In the American 5 or 7 meter, we feel *accents* here and there at the beginning of each subgroup, but we do not feel a *downbeat*; that is, we feel no *upbeats* on the intervening notes. Perhaps this is because the tempo is faster; but that argument would be begging the question, since non-American composers simply do not use these rhythms in this quick, precipitate way. In America the accents come out according to the melodic structure, and that may be anywhere. In other words, we have been talking about one more manifestation of that rockbound foundation of American music—syncopation.

We can see all this more clearly by establishing the vital connection between these rhythms and the basic syncopations we discussed earlier in the paper. It is both safe and convenient to take as a representative syncopation figure the rumba, whose omnipresence and flexibility we have noted again and again. The main idea of this pattern is the *close and rather rapid juxtaposition of groups of two and three notes.*

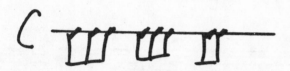

Out of this pattern, then, come the combinations of duplets and triplets which eventually go to make up the 5 and 7 rhythms characteristic of the Copland *Variations.* It is obvious that (were this orchestral music) no conductor would perform eight indications per rumba measure. He might conduct it in four, or in two, or even in three (with the first two strokes an eighth beat longer than the third); but never in eight. That is, it cannot be conceived of as 1, 2, 3: 1, 2, 3: 1, 2. This would be a flagrant falsification of the rumba feeling, which is based on the syncopative surprises of accents.

We have witnessed at last the most recent development of the originally simple Negro rhythms. Out of them has emerged a new system, with a new quality that is peculiarly American. The basis of this system, while not necessarily quintuple and septuple rhythms, is at least the new relationship of duple and triple figures, a relationship born of and nurtured by Negro jazz.

I hope that any remaining confusion or doubt will be cleared up by the following examples from the *Variations.*

It should not be necessary to make many remarks about them; I hope they are self-explanatory in the light of the foregoing discussion.

1)

2)

3)

Let us perform a simple experiment, which may prove to be a final hammer blow to this point. If we put example 3 over a 4/4 meter, we obtain the following result:

which does not look very different from many sections of the *Piano Concerto*! Yet the total feeling is a more elusive one, and certainly independent of any ostensible Negro affiliation, though there is blood kinship.

This is a veritable rumba—yet as far from the jazz-band variety as César Franck. And observe the right hand, lying in the bosom of the dead Charleston—a new and vital creation:

4)

Besides the more obvious accents on the short notes, there is the interesting throwing off of meter as illustrated by the dotted line:

5)

Here we observe the earliest syncopative device of three-beat groups in four-beat measures, used so often by Copland in the *Concerto*.

6)

Example 7 is an instance of a constant, steady syncopation, which (as so often with Schumann) should not be recognizable until we feel the missing beat at the end:

7)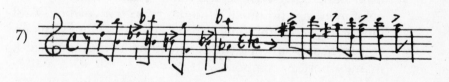

Yet the syncopation is felt all along, perhaps because the strong-beat notes are fortified by the octave, and are reached, moreover, by a sudden skip upward. This establishes the *regular* beat, so that the accented syncopation is felt.

And following climactically upon this, a simple but magnificent syncopation effected by the mere addition of an eighth rest:

New music—a new sound—a new feeling—an *American* feeling; but the old jazz is still the father of it all, and unfortunately, a too-little-honored progenitor.

To sum up, then: American music owes one of its greatest debts to the Negroes, not only for the popularly acknowledged gift of jazz, but for the impetus which jazz has given to America's art music. This incentive has come in two ways—melodically and rhythmically—with further support from tone color and contrapuntal feeling. Both the scale patterns and the rhythm patterns, as first manifested in jazz itself, were used freely in symphonic composition by men like Gershwin. With more advanced composers or with composers in a more advanced state, this initial use—especially of the rhythms—has grown into a new style, which might be called the first tangible indigenous style that can be identified in American music.

4: The Integration of New England and Negro Strains

The only other racial strain that can be said to have reached any universality at all is what we have called the "New England" music. Our definition of this term has taken us from the original hymns and folk music through their development as the musical literature of the cowboys and mountaineers to the final "spiritual" state, where this literature has become a feeling characterizing the art music of many American composers.

Very often this New England style is combined with certain features of the Negro—again, naturally and inevitably. And it is amazing that these two extremely different racial arts should blend so well and easily. But this kind of combination is always possible in America, where so many various racial tributaries come together and grow into a stronger, more unified current.

The three composers most representative of these standards are Roy Harris, Roger Sessions, and Charles Ives. Harris is a product of westward migration; he represents the New Englander transplanted and transmogrified. Sessions and Ives are thoroughgoing New Englanders. Each of the three achieves a completely personal and unimitative style, mutually independent, yet commonly dependent upon their ultimate origins.

Harris' *a capella* choral work *A Song for Occupations* is a case in point. Here he has taken as text the poetry of a great American (Whitman)—with emphasis on *American*. Through it Harris achieves a glorification of the American language—the *staccatos* and irregular accents of American daily speech; the glorification of American labor, of American progress. These are purely extramusical matters, but are inseparable from the music itself; and only naturally so, since vocal music must, to all intents and purposes, have a program or literary connotation of some kind. Thus, when we hear words like "development," "possibilities," "goods of gutta-percha and papier-mâché" machine-gunning out at us, we become aware of the fact that along with the American language, the music is sharing in an exaltation of America itself.

As for the purely musical features of the work, they are easily tracked down, but named with difficulty. The basic generality of the piece is the chorale. The opening is a veritable hymn tune:

Here we find all the chordal, diatonic, Lutheran squareness and solidity of *"Ein feste Burg,"* made even harder by the bareness of the triads (there are no thirds in the first two chords). This fourness (or twoness) of meter is common to the whole work, even when the time signature is actually a triple one:

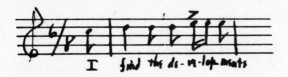

Of course, it can be argued that this distortion is only the result of the word settings; that an accent *must* fall on the second syllable of "developments." But that does not refute the contention that it could all have been written in duple time to begin with:

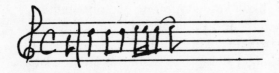

where it would be quite natural and unsyncopated. But the feeling Harris intends is one of 6/8 time (for he has established it regularly in the preceding section) so that the shift of accent is felt as syncopation. Whereupon we are suddenly conscious of the fact that the effects of Negro music are again present. The work is full of this kind of syncopation:

An even more complicated expression of these rhythms is found later on in the piece, where Harris combines counteraccents by means of a 6/8–3/4 dialectic, at the same time keeping the regularity of his chordality hard as nails:

This is the "style" that holds the work together (and I hope that by this time the process of emergence from material to spiritual, particular to universal, specific to general has become clear). Following are two passages which might be designated as the norm of the work. They are rhythmically very involved; but the most remarkable thing is the appearance of pure rumba, of the kind we have noticed throughout our discussion of Negro rhythms (measure 2 of [a] and measure 3 of [b]):

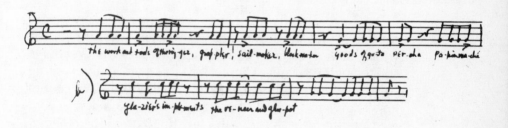

Yet we could never mistake these passages for Copland, for instance. The constant combinations of twos and threes are the basis of much American music, and yet conform to each composer's personal style in an unconfusable way. The difference lies, I think, in the regularity of Harris' fundamental beat, and the spasmodic irregularity of Copland's —a difference analogous to that between Oklahoma and New York City. More tangibly, the Harris could conceivably be conducted in eight counts per measure, with one indication for each note (though probably no conductor

would do so); while the passage from the Copland *Variations*

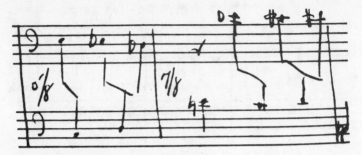

defies beat-for-note conducting.*

At any rate, Harris has shown that one kind of American
spirit can be infused into his writing, mixing successfully
with racial influences other than his own. It may seem unfortunate to use so little of his music as illustration, but any
more quoting would act only as repetition, and would result in a groping for more synonyms for *hard, square, solid;*
or for banal analogies with the brooding grandeur of the
Grand Canyon, or the ineffable infinitude of the prairies.

We have already observed (in the section on Negro
rhythms) that particular phase of Roger Sessions' music
which makes use of Negro rhythmic patterns. We have
spoken of the peculiar character of this syncopative writing
—the heaviness, almost *anti*-jazz quality of it. We cannot
go so far as to say that this is an American quality, even if
we can trace it back through New England to the stolidity
of the Lutheran chorale; but we can suggest it. Sessions is
not a Westerner; his Americanism is therefore based on
stern and aristocratic New Englandism. But he completed
the circle by spending years in Europe, absorbing the influence of Germany and its teachers; so that if his music out-
chorales the chorale, so to speak, it is not to be wondered
at. There is a bit of Teutonic atavism here. But his music is
not necessarily German; suffused by the rhythms of America, it becomes American. After all, how often does Wagner
sound particularly German? And how often Debussy's *Pel-*

* Cf. pp. 83–85.

léas sounds like sheer Wagner! These national boundaries are unsafe, in music as in politics; we cannot be dogmatic. We can only suggest, not force, certain reasonably logical developments in American music. Sessions does not always sound categorically American; but neither does Copland or Harris; or, indeed, Gershwin. We can merely point to signs which in turn point in the direction of a healthy and nonimitative art in our country. For example, we find that Sessions has written three chorale preludes. The choice of *form* is, shall we say, German–Protestant–New England. Here is one indication.

Then upon examining the music itself, we find the following lovely chorale,* with its typical five- and four-beat combinations:

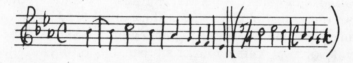

A little further on, we suddenly come upon it in a new form, colored by typically American syncopations:

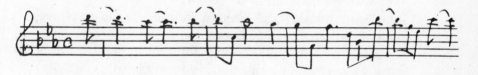

The same features characterize the accompaniment, quoted on page 71.

We are confronted with a chorale "jazzed up." But the effect is not that at all; it is as far from the ludicrous as the original chorale sung in 1550. The two currents merge quietly and fluently, making not a bizarre effect, but a new, clear, concise, and original one. This effect, it would seem, can reasonably be called American. It ties up with the whole logical progression of American music, and leaves no loopholes.

The same is true of Charles Ives. Here is another full-fledged New Englander who thinks philosophy as he

---

* A favorite with Brahms, who also wrote a beautiful chorale prelude for organ based on it *(Lo, How a Rose E'er Blooming).*—L.B., 1982.

writes his music. His style is a most universal one: it ranges from simple triads through to chords of almost every note in the harmonic series; from the easy to the unplayable; from Germanic solidity to French impressionism.* But again these criteria are meaningless; he is an American. He has written at least one large work worthy of respect—the second *Sonata for Piano*. It is difficult, obscure, and philosophically programmatic, being a *study* in four aspects of transcendentalism in Concord, Massachusetts, from 1840 to 1860. These aspects are exemplified by Emerson, Hawthorne, the Alcotts, and Thoreau. It is tiring, overlong, and a fierce challenge to any pianist.†

Now, if Ives is American, is his music so? In a large sense, of course; but we are trying to find instances in the *Concord Sonata* of definitely American features, based upon America's own musical experience. The extramusical Americanism is obvious—the program glorifies an American philosophical school, four or more members of which have become American institutions. But the music?

Certainly, if any racial style can be called predominant, it is the German. Very well; we have already linked the German and the New England styles when speaking of Sessions. But further, the chorale influence is everywhere evident. Mighty organ chords, pompous, slow-moving. There is a certain ruggedness belonging somehow to this music alone; a quality far removed from the supposed ruggedness or "bleakness" of Sibelius. This is as far as words will take us, without involving us in a meaningless rhapsody of false criticism.

The beginning of the third movement (the Alcotts) is sheer New England hymn playing:

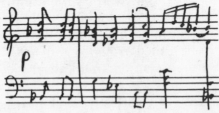

---

* Although he vigorously denied the latter, which he denounced as "sissy."—L.B., 1982

† At the time of writing, the Arrow Press is planning a republication of the *Sonata* with cuts, simplifications, and changes by the composer.

Our only tangible evidences so far, then, are the hymn-tune style and the general hardy quality of the music. Witness, for instance, the majestic opening of the first movement (Emerson):

But Ives, too, employs the American syncopative rhythms. It may be reasonably observed occurring in the Hawthorne movement, arising from Ives's conscious effort to suggest certain Negro episodes from Hawthorne; for we find in the preface to the movement the explanation that this section is

> an "extended fragment" trying to suggest some of his [Hawthorne's] wilder, fantastical adventures into the half-childlike, half-fairylike phantasmal realms. It may have something to do with . . . "Feathertop," the "Scarecrow" . . . or the concert at the Stamford camp meeting, or the "Slaves' Shuffle."*

But it matters very little in the end whether or not Ives was moved to these rhythms by programmatic impulses. The fact is that in the second movement there are frequent and extended passages of the following sort:

* Ives wrote a long dissertation entitled *Essays Before a Sonata*.

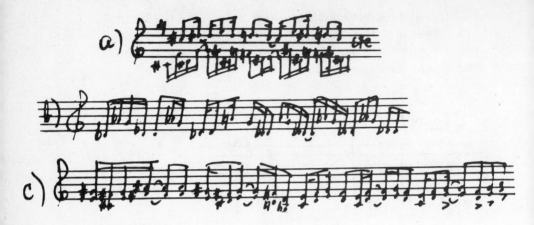

where all the fundamental Negro syncopative devices are very clearly in evidence.

But these rhythms are not restricted only to the Hawthorne movement. If they were, the programmatic argument would be greatly strengthened. Combinations of two- and three-beat groups abound in the piece, but in a manner different from any we have yet observed. The style is essentially unmetrical; not only is there no regular meter, but there is likewise no *irregular* meter of a constant kind. The *tempi* and dynamics change so frequently that any rhythmic intensity is virtually precluded. In this sense, the *Sonata* is really impressionistic. It is therefore difficult to find the kind of rhythms we have remarked in Copland and Sessions; but the rhythms are there, and are recognizable as such. The result is that we have again discovered a personal and genuine use of the Negro rhythms.

In the third movement (the Alcotts) these rhythms appear from time to time. This is strange, since the character of the movement is one of peaceful meditation alternating with a sort of ecstatic declamation—hardly the kind of music in which one would expect to find Negro rhythms. In the preface to this movement Ives speaks of "the broadarched street . . . the old elms . . . the little old spinet-piano . . . on which Beth played the old Scotch airs, and played at the *Fifth Symphony* . . ." and on the other hand,

of "the self sacrificing part of the ideal . . . Beethovenlike
sublimity . . . strength of hope that never gives way to despair. . . ." And yet in all of this domestic quietude or transcendental exaltation, with its *Fifth Symphony* motif
running all through it, there appear passages like the following (and it is interesting to note that they appear in the
transitional or developmental sections, where the style is
most personal, and where the hymns and Scottish airs are
temporarily dispensed with):

Despite the lack of bar lines, and the complicated temporal
pattern, it is very easy to detect the syncopative devices.
Besides the juxtaposition of twos and threes, Ives uses
counterrhythms in all three of the "chordal voices." If we
add arbitrary bar lines where the breathing spaces occur,
we should get something like this:

This rather complex analysis serves to show that various
beat groupings arising from triple and duple combinations
have been set together to produce a total syncopative ef-

fect. The jazz element has been strengthened—voluntarily or not—by the characteristic interval of the descending minor third, so typical of jazz; and further by the simultaneous sounding of E-flats and E-naturals in the tonality of C; and yet further by the G-flat which is another feature of the Negro scale variant. Add to this the inner syncopations in each chordal voice, as, for instance, in voice A:

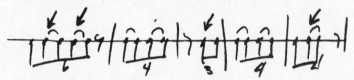

and you have practically a piece of jazz. Yet never does this music sound like jazz; never does the thought of it even enter the hearer's mind. But the *American* quality does; it *feels* American. For Ives has used these rhythms only in connection with his basically New England style (combined with his Beethoven obsession); and the combination results in a most personal sound, different from the musical expression of any other composer we have discussed. Ives could never be confused with Sessions, for example; yet they share exactly the same ingredients of Americanism.

5: The Tempering Force

There is one more consideration in respect to the usage of racial elements: the usage of these elements *as such*, without any admixture of other elements, and without the Americanizing influences with which we have been concerned. That is, we are considering Scottish, English, or Irish material, for instance, quite apart from any New England influence. This usage is not nearly so common today as it was before the war, when, as we have seen, so many attempts at nationalism were made. It is a reversion to the old method of using racial substance—the "material" method, as opposed to the "spiritual." But as it is done now, it is not necessarily predestined to failure as in the old days, simply because the attitude has changed. Our composers are not *attempting* nationalistic music; they are merely taking advantage of their heritage quite naturally, and with no artificial racial thesis. This change in approach is clearly authenticated by the rarity of appearance of characteristic *themes*; the racial element is no longer *cultivated*. (None of this applies to the Ives *Sonata*, where in the Alcott movement an old Scottish song is simply and gently brought in; this is only pictorial, as Ives points out in the preface to the movement; see page 95.)

Roy Harris, for example, often turns out something Scottish in character. Whether or not it is consciously Scottish is not our affair; we are not even worried about whether the *tune* is actually Scottish or not. Our interest lies in the two facts that it *sounds* Scottish, and that Harris has Scottish blood in him. There are jigs in the *Piano Quintet*, for example; and the same work often uses musical ideas of a pentatonic nature. Again, the fugue subject in the *Concerto for Piano, Clarinet, and String Quartet* could be said to be Scottish in feeling, by virtue of the much-talked-of "Scottish snap":

This use of racial elements is common to composers of other racial extraction. There are those who find an abundance of Hebrew elements in Copland.* Here and there it is possible to point to passages in the *Variations* which may be interpreted as having a trace of the Hebraic about them. But further than this trace—which we could identify only by words (*declamatory, chromatic, anguished*, etc.)—there is nothing actually identifiable as either Hebrew or Jewish. It is easily understood that a composer who is a second-generation American, whose parents were immigrants, still maintains a close contact with the old racial traditions. If these traditions are part of his childhood, they are inevita-

---

* Paul Rosenfeld on Copland: ". . . like the harsh, brooding sentences of the rabbis." Discarding this kind of generality, we can point to at least one work by Copland that is based on Jewish themes—the piano trio *Vitebsk*.

bly part of his life. But the social phenomenon of assimilation is ultimately the stronger force. The country of birth is the determining factor—the basic material; the ancestral tradition is the tempering force. Thus, whatever there is of the Hebraic in Copland's music is embodied subordinately within the fundamentally American personality of the music.

Even with Bloch, who writes music programmatically and deliberately Jewish, that racial element is not *musically* the primary factor, but is immersed in the post-Romantic style that permeates the music as a whole. But for the program booklet, we might as well be listening to a symphony of Enesco or Samuel Barber. Except for such pieces as *Schelomo*, where actual Hebrew themes are used, Bloch's Hebraism is all in the program notes. Thus, with Copland, it is fair to say that if it were not known that he is of Jewish descent, the Hebraic element would probably be unnoticed. As a matter of opinion, certain themes of Roy Harris sound almost more Hebraic than the avowedly Jewish themes in *Vitebsk*.

The circle closes, then, with the return to our introductory assumption concerning the graduation from the *material* to the *spiritual* usages of racial elements. These elements are soluble, adaptable; in heterogeneous America it is their delicate balancing which determines the composer's particular, personal Americanism. The only really universal racial influence in America has been the Negro, and in some cases, the New England. Negro through its countrywide manifestation in jazz; and New England because it is the music of the races that form the sociological backbone of the country. With one or both of these influences the composer of yet another racial extraction blends his own heritage, unconsciously or not. The confluence of these three streams has become the mighty American river which is now, for the first time, pouring its fullness—a genuinely indigenous contribution—into the sea of world music.

LEONARD BERNSTEIN, '39

Part Two
POSTWAR
MEDITATIONS

1946–1957

STATEMENT: CONDUCTING VERSUS COMPOSING

It is impossible for me to make an exclusive choice among the various activities of conducting, symphonic composition, writing for the theater, and playing the piano. What seems right for me at any given moment is what I must do, at the expense of pigeonholing or otherwise limiting my services to music. I will not compose a note while my heart is engaged in a conducting season; nor will I give up writing so much as a popular song, while it is there to be expressed, in order to conduct Beethoven's *Ninth*. There is a particular order involved in this, which is admittedly difficult to plan; but the order must be adhered to most strictly. For the ends are music itself, not the conventions of the music business; and the means are my private problem.   □

From "Music and the Dance"
Dance Magazine, *June, 1946*

"FUN" IN ART

I remember giving an interview to a New York newspaper in which I replied to the question "Which of your different interests will you eventually choose to follow?" by saying that I wanted to do the thing which seemed most like fun at the time. This elicited a furious letter from one of its more articulate and choleric readers, upbraiding me for my "light" attitude toward music, and for my apparent lack of social responsibility in giving my art insufficiently serious thought. These paragraphs are meant as a rebuttal to that letter of long ago. (That I did not rebut at the time stands as mute testimony to the fallibility of man and the power of the press.)

The main trouble with these remarks is that the word "fun" is going to appear far too often. The fact of the matter is that the word has no single synonym in our present use of its meanings.

If we add up "sense of rightness," "tranquillity," "balance," "catharsis," "expressivity," we begin to approach the meaning of "fun." Add to these "participation," "creativity," "order," "sublimation," and "energy release," and you almost have it. Fun is all the things we find it impossible to say when we hear the Opus 131 quartet, or witness *Letter to the World*. (Beethoven and Martha Graham must have had this kind of fun *making* those works.) Fun is the final goal of the collected aesthetic searchings of David Prall, Dewey, Richards, and Santayana. Fun is the "x" of the equation that tries to solve the riddle of why art exists at all.

To the normal American mind, "fun" carries with it the connotation of a "good time," a party, a relaxation, diversion, a roller-coaster ride, a thriller on the screen, a hot dog. There is no Dreadful Dichotomy here; we must simply refer

1945

these phenomena to the field of art, deepening the experiential values, solidifying the transience to continuousness, even to semipermanence. (Analogously, construe the difference between Love on the Run and Love Eternal. They are not opposed to each other, as some would have us think. They are separate manifestations of the same phenomenon, with different motivations, and different results. And they can both be fun.)

Does it seem strange that a musician, of all people, should be discussing these matters in, of all things, a dance magazine? Not at all. For what other two arts better exemplify this concept of *fun* than do music and the dance?

Basically, the only split that occurs in the various art media is that which divides the representational from the nonrepresentational. Whatever the technique used, or the medium engaged in, all art is one except for this distinction. It is this which often makes it difficult for the writer to comprehend the basic aesthetic impulses of the musician, and vice versa. It is this which gives rise to the interminable discussions on technique versus content, form versus functionalism, Marxism versus Ivory-towerism, style versus prettiness.

In the case of music, we find that its inherent meaning, from any of the above points of view, is purely a *musical*

Ca. 1980

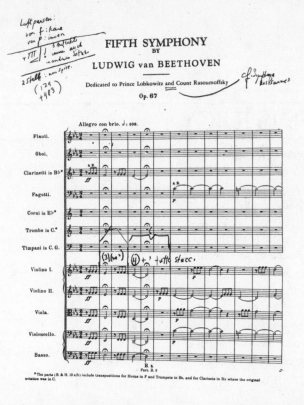

FIFTH SYMPHONY
BY
LUDWIG van BEETHOVEN

Dedicated to Prince Lobkowitz and Count Rasoumoffsky

Op. 67

meaning. Give it what titles you will, add copious program notes, and you still have only a series of notes, arranged in certain orders and patterns. Call the opening of Beethoven's *Fifth Symphony* "Fate Knocking at the Door," or "The Morse Code Call to Victory," and you still have three G's and an E-flat. That's *all* you have. Through some freak in the human animal, these four notes, in their particular rhythmic pattern, have the power to produce a substantial effect on us. Isn't that funny? Exactly: funny.

Certainly there is infinitely more profound searching to be done in any one aspect of this tangled question. These remarks are merely teasers. Only think, for example, of the idea "representational" in terms of the subtle psychic life of the artist: what an unexplored field lies there! Perhaps one day we shall attain to a new meaning of Meaning, in a new frame of reference which is intangible to us now. But for the present we "abstract" artists, we musicians and dancers, have this to say to ourselves: Relax. Invent. Perform. Have fun. □

Written in a cottage
on the mucky shore of
Lake Mah-kee-nak
Stockbridge, Massachusetts
2 July 1947

LIFE IS JUICY

Life begins in the waters—
   Not the deep, but the borders of land:
   The stagnants that nourish the sterile earth
Like a juicy gland.

Life is the seed of the marriage
   Of liquid and solid events.
   In the coves, in the swamps, in mysterious pools,
Our heartaches commence.

Life is the pulp and the slime,
   The marshmallow bellies of frogs,
   Their thyroided eyes, their eggjellies caught
On the rotting logs.

Life is the algae, the roe;
   The army of maggoty breeds
   Devouring the corpse of a very old perch
Adrift in the weeds.

Life is the plasm, the cells,
   The fat symbiotics in pairs;
   The ankledeep fungoids which darkly provide
The crawfish with lairs.

Life is the scaly and scummy,
   The poisonous green without breath;
   The marinal maze whose only solution
Is ultimate death.

For Death is the crisp and the clean,
   The fine oxidation, the rust,
   The spermless, the painless, the classic, the lean,
The dry, dry dust.

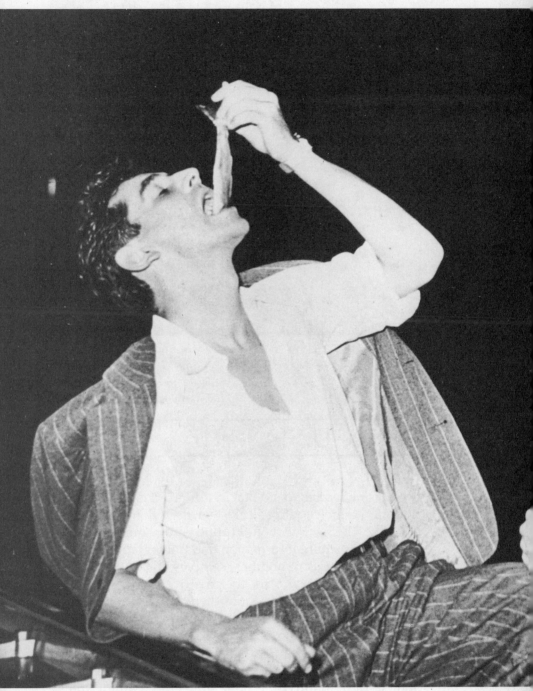

Holland, 1947

New York City, 1949

Written 8 July 1947
at the request of RCA Records
for publication in various newspapers
throughout the United States

MUSIC U.S.A., 1947

It seems incredible to me that in this era of lightning transportation there should still exist such a gulf in information and knowledge between Europe and America. Newspapers can acquire information and photographs in a telegraphic instant; commodities, samples, ideas, persons can be flown from New York to Paris overnight; and it is a comparatively short hop from there to Beirut or Tunis or Tel Aviv. And yet in each country, during my recent European tour, I have been asked the same old questions about life in each other country; I have met the same eagerness for information, the same naive credulity, the same intelligent spirit of inquiry, the same hunger of man for knowledge of his fellow man.

Much of this situation can be explained in terms of power politics, of "areas of influence," of continuing censorship, of "security zones"—in short, in terms of fear. The world seems to me, in the perspective of my three-month journey, a place of suspicion and hostility, of borders, barriers, and distrust.

There is a new rise of nationalism almost everywhere—including the occupied countries—from Holland to Egypt. In the breaking away of countries from the old empire pattern, new nationalist revolutions are in the making, and a new concentration upon local and state preeminence is all too discernible. And all this at a time when international cooperation and coordination are desperately needed as never before.

The symptoms display themselves in all fields; and since music has always served as a kind of barometer of social movement, the musical signs of the times are particularly clear. The Czechs still avoid programming German music —even to the point of proscribing Bach. The Dutch government clamors for the employment of only Dutch musicians, and is trying to ban foreign artists who have not previously appeared in Holland. Even in Paris, the cosmopolitan center of the world, there are rumors of pressure brought to bear in favor of French musicians. This activity is completely understandable from the point of view that each land is trying to protect the livelihoods of its own workers,

Vatican Rehearsal, 1973

through their unions; and we can sympathize with the Czechs' imposing their ban after their six years of nothing but German music. Yet it is undeniable that this activity contributes heavily to the general nationalistic world-fever.

In returning to America, I found much more general knowledge of Europe than I had found in Europe of America. We are awake at our cable depots; our newspapers have highly organized foreign services; and our musical programs are nothing if not international in character. But most important of all (to music, at least), we have a thriving, highly active recording industry. Through discs we can promulgate and perpetuate international art in the most effective way. But the essential thing is to make these recordings available to all the world. The business arrangements between American and European companies are so complicated that it would take far more than this brief glance to unravel them. There is an urgent need for such an unraveling, both musically and politically. European industry is in no position to lead in recordings. Discs are scarce, material difficult to obtain, prices prohibitive. America—to whom all the world now looks for leadership, in art, in design, in invention, in democratic organization of business methods—has this responsibility.

This is a plea for the execution of that responsibility. We can do so much to help our faltering, perplexed, emotion-ridden world. This is not Pollyanna altruism; it is our duty to ourselves, and our own crying need.   □

April, 1948

DIALOGUE AND . . .

Scene I

(Aboard the H.M.S. *Queen Mary*, docked in New York, one hour before sailing. Those readers who have had the experience of sharing a stateroom with an unknown roommate

Israel, 1948

will immediately recognize the keen, subtle flavor of this hour. The visitors—well-wishers, relatives, photographers —have gone; there is an endless succession of meaningless blasts which seem to come from whistles situated directly below the bed; and one is overactive unpacking grips for the voyage. The atmosphere combines elements of apprehension, loneliness, disappointment (that the roommate is not at least Henry Wallace or Jean-Paul Sartre), and tension over who will speak first. I sneak a look. The roommate is a tall, spare, fiftyish, intellectual type—horn-rimmed spectacles to boot—with personal accessories that seem somehow all wrong. There is absolutely no telling what he may be. He is probably French. He might possibly . . .)

L.T.: *Léon Trirème. Sociologue.*
   (I am taken aback at the sound of a voice. There is a
   second of silence and calculation.)
L.B.: *Enchanté, monsieur. Léonard Bernstein, musicien.*
   (Handshaking. Rapid return to the business of unpacking.)

L.T.: A musician, hm. You compose, you play?
(Damn. My accent must be a dead giveaway.)

L.B.: Yes—although my main function on this trip is to conduct around Europe.
(This could have been said infinitely more impressively.)

L.T.: (Suddenly talkative.) How lucky to have the chance so young to know the world! I have found in this last visit to America that the basic trouble with most Americans lies in their lack of international comprehension. Of course, the war . . .
(Whoosh, an intellectual. Put away the gift champagne: massage the brain cells for six days. It could be worse.)

Scene II

(The ship has sailed. We stand on the aft deck and watch the lights of New York die. Half the world's languages promenade past us, although there is an undeniable preponderance of British. A most elegant official, in white tie, stops and says, "My company wishes you a very happy voyage, Mr. Bernstein" and passes on.)

L.B.: Who told him to say that? I wonder.

L.T.: That, my friend, is a representative of the Cunard Line, and you, my friend, are on what they call the "Commend List." You will have to get used to it.

L.B.: I wonder how he'd feel if he knew that I had just accepted artistic directorship of the Palestine Symphony Orchestra. Might the words perhaps stick a bit in his throat?

L.T.: Don't tell me! What an internationalist you're turning out to be! American, citizen of the world, tying up with the most nationalistic movement on earth! Are you a Zionist?

L.B.: Not with a capital Z, at any rate. But I can't think of anything I feel more strongly about. It took me a good long while to make up my mind, I admit. . . . It meant giving up . . . well, I won't bore you with details. But in the end I couldn't resist it any longer.

Israel, 1948

L.T.: Resist what?

L.B.: Resist the temptation of being able to help. That's a weakness we all share—the desire to go where we're really wanted and needed.

L.T.: But help how? You're not going to shoot—

L.B.: No. To help morale, to help in the development of Palestinian music, to help a new civilization come through.

L.T.: Does this mean you are going to live in Palestine?

L.B.: Not at all. They have been most understanding over there. I shall open the season, conduct for two months, make artistic policy and overall program-ming, and then be free to go elsewhere. It's a kind of remote-control directorship, I guess.

L.T.: Let me understand you. We have been talking for

about two hours, and we know a little about each other. You can certainly see from what I have told you that as a sociologist I am a liberal, and as a mathematician I am a music-lover. Since I fought with the French Resistance movement, I have had some practical experience. I am certainly no anti-Semite—in fact, I had a Jewish grandmother. I think I should be equipped to understand your problem; and yet I don't. First I should like to know how you can reconcile your feeling of international progressivism with so local and nationalistic a movement.

L.B.: Don't think for a moment that I have had no problem here. It is a conflict many of my Jewish friends have shared with me; and some of them have come out with altogether different solutions. I have learned to reconcile the opposing factors, and it wasn't easy to do. But it can be easily stated.

L.T.: Okay, fire away. You see, I've picked up some American slang.

L.B.: (Maintaining seriousness, come what may) First of all, I am no nationalist—not by a long shot. I have felt for years that if all symptoms of nationalism in the world could be abolished, we might have a start toward living as a human race, instead of as factions. I would love to see all borders and boundaries done away with; I long for the end of passports, permits, declarations, tariffs, inspections, and flags. I want what Willkie called One World, what the Church calls Universal Brotherhood under God, what Communists call The International, what industrialists call Free Trade, what democrats call Full Equality, what Yogis call being part of the All. I think everybody wants this in some form, but fear is very much in the way. And, at the moment, fear seems to be here to stay.

Okay. Having accepted that, we find we are living in a world of nations, like it or not. There is one exception—only one ethnic group which has no real nationality—and that is the Jews. It is a question of living on somewhat equal terms with the rest of the world—a question, almost, of survival. There you have it.

L.T.: But my dear boy, don't you think that the Jews can do a far better job being a force for internationalization, as long as they are in this position anyway? It certainly seems to me that if you believe in the growing together of peoples, you would want to support and further that end, rather than simply contribute to the status quo. It is almost reactionary of you.

L.B.: I see what you mean. Are you trying to explain to me the common conception of the alliance of Jewry with Communism?

L.T.: In a way, yes. It would be very strange if there were not such an alliance. Yet you—

L.B.: Yet I reject it. I don't think there's much time left in which the Jews can acquire the dignity they need to balance themselves in the world.

L.T.: And you think Palestine will do it?

L.B.: I think . . . Palestine will do it.
(New York is gone. And there is nothing more international than the uncluttered ocean.)

Scene III

(Back in the stateroom. We have disappeared into our respective beds, those incredibly deep, downy beds which give you each night the sensation of a heavenly dying. There is a thick, rolling darkness which helps this illusion.)

L.T.: One last word. Something you said earlier troubles me. You spoke of helping in the development of Palestinian music. I take it that in this respect you are again a nationalist? You want to help build a national art, after all. Isn't this directly opposed to your social philosophies?

L.B.: (It's a bit late for this sort of thing. However . . .) No, I shouldn't say so. Don't you recall the great Soviet slogan in the thirties: "Cultural nationalism—political internationalism"? I'd say they had something there.

L.T.: Except for the fact that Russia is perhaps the most nationalistic single power on earth today.

L.B.: *Touché*. But that doesn't deny the formula. For a mathematician, you're being very hard on the abstract.

L.T.: In other words, you think it's taking a healthy direction to foster a local music in Palestine? I can't help thinking—

L.B.: (I switch on the berth light and rear up as well as I can in that quicksand bed.) Look. Neither I nor Beethoven nor you nor God nor the Irgun can create a nationalistic music in Palestine. Nor can the composers themselves. Either it will grow, or it won't. It will grow as the national community grows, as the integration of their society progresses. Otherwise it won't. And that's a mathematical formula.

L.T.: Haven't I heard of a new movement in Palestinian music? I think they call it the "Mediterranean Style." That certainly sounds to me—

L.B.: But—

L.T.: You always interrupt. I said, that certainly sounds to me like a conscious movement, apart from the social integration of the community. If you go to help music there, you must inevitably help this school. No?

L.B.: No. One cannot help a school. Especially this one, where Palestinian composers, mostly German-bred or -influenced, are consciously using Arabic thematic material. What you really have is Max Reger trying to write cooch dances.

L.T.: But this is rather a special case. After all, Palestine is primarily a society of refugees . . .

L.B.: It's not without precedent. Palestine isn't the only new, artificially created country in history. America too was a land of refugees, who arrived full-grown with their own traditions and training. During the nineteenth century our "nationalistic" composers had their own epidemics: Indian operas, and Negro quartets. Where are they now?

L.T.: Obviously, in the public libraries or buried in institutional archives.

With Felicia Montealegre Bernstein, Israel, 1953

L.B.: Exactly. Purely reference works. Only because they were so artificial. Neither the composers nor the audiences were either Indian or Negro. It was simply a decision, consciously taken, to be "American." Being American meant building on the folk music. To some that meant Indian chants, to others Negro spirituals and cakewalks, to others Baptist hymns. But it all turned out to be exotic in the long run, because the composers themselves were disciples of Brahms and Liszt.

L.T.: Then there isn't any such thing as American music?

L.B.: Of course there is, just as one day there will be a Palestinian music after the conscious attempts have died down. It is only in the last twenty-five years that American music has begun to acquire a flavor of its own, largely through the influence of jazz. That's one folk element that is really common to all American lives. But even the jazz influence was a perfectly conscious one in the initial stages, and was just as mixed up with other styles as were the Indian influences. Even in Gershwin's—

L.T.: Ah, your Gershwin! *Ça, c'était un maître!*

L.B.: If you mean as a maker of melodies, yes, *maître*. But you wouldn't call him an integrator of styles, would you? Is it masterly to take an inspired jazz tune and dress it up in Tchaikovsky sequences and Debussy harmonies? I think not.

L.T.: *D'accord*. But then, what composer *has* integrated jazz with his personal styles? I've never heard it.

L.B.: Now, there's where the case becomes subtle—or at least subtlish. The jazz influence has crept into serious music by a kind of osmotic process, whereby you can't even recognize the jazz anymore. Yet there's a quality of "Americanism" in the music which is intangible but undeniable; and close examination reveals that jazz lurks somewhere behind it, though transformed by the composer's personality. You'll find it in Piston, for example—the top internationalist!—and in Copland—

L.T.: And in Bernstein?

L.B.: I think so. The Scherzo of my *Jeremiah Symphony,* for example, is certainly not jazz; and yet I'm convinced I could never have written it if I had not had a real and solid background in jazz. It's a funny thing to observe one's own music. Self-analysis—

L.T.: You're wandering. What has all this to do with Palestine?

L.B.: You're right; one does wander at three in the morning. What I started to show was the parallel in Palestinian music with what we've experienced in America. They have the same problems of conscious nationalism, and will flounder and experiment until the society is sufficiently integrated to allow the osmosis I referred to before. It's wonderfully exciting to watch it happen.

L.T.: I'm disappointed in you. You sound more and more like a nationalist with every word. Why do we need any national music anywhere? That was fine in the nineteenth century, when countries were very much aware of being themselves, when they were growing and unifying themselves, when Bismarck was making Germany and capitalism was starting its industrial race. But now countries are so interpenetrable, so interdependent! Recordings and wireless throw the styles around like pollen in the air. Why shouldn't a German seed take root, say, in France?

L.B.: It does, of course. Look at the new French composers: so many of them writing twelve-tone music, which is really a Viennese idea. Look at the influence of Shostakovich on the British boys, and on us, particularly. Of course we're headed in an international direction; but there's got to be nationalism first before these styles are crystallized enough to join together. You can't add A and B unless you have first defined them exactly, can you?

L.T.: That's good sense and bad mathematics. But let's not wander. It seems to me, *en somme,* that you haven't really resolved your conflict. You're an internationalist who believes in the necessity of nationalism in our time, both musically and politically—am I right?

You're an American with one foot in Palestine. You're a conductor with one eye toward composing. You're like the Passover Seder they're holding on the ship tomorrow night—you must see it! All of them praying *à l'anglaise*, in dinner jackets!

L.B.: (Very sleepy by now) Well, that sounds as international as anything I've heard.

L.T.: Not so much international as confused. But that's only right. Wouldn't it be odd if you were all settled and figured out at thirty!

L.B.: Twenty-nine! Don't rush me.

L.T.: I doubt if you'll see it any more clearly by thirty. Anyway, it's just as it should be. Faust feeling for the answers. Hamlet writhing in doubt, convinced he's right in each contradictory soliloquy.

L.B.: (Almost asleep) You flatter me. (The blast again from under the bed.) That did it. The final comment is always made by a third party.

L.T.: Very well, *fini*. Shall we sing the "Internationale" and go to sleep?
(Lights. Queasy stomach. And somewhere deep in the sleepy brain, addled by talk and the rolling of the sea, there is a real conviction that only the nations themselves, after all, can achieve international cohesion; and that Palestine will one day stand as a bright symbol for that end.)

. . . ENCORE

Scene: The "greenroom," that den of guile and ego-bathing, where L.B. is receiving well-wishers after a passably well-played but enthusiastically received concert. L.B. is moderately happy, though knifed by the contrasting knowledges that 1) he has failed to do what he wanted with the music, and 2) he will be heartily congratulated. But the uplifted state persists; the adrenaline is still pouring, to say nothing of the perspiration.

Tel Aviv, 1947

Mrs. Francisca Ffin is a lady of a certain age who fancies herself an intimate of the conductor. She has long since joined the orchestra's Women's Committee. Mrs. Ffin has her own greenroom technique: she waits until the "others" have finished their congratulations (Dear peasants!) before addressing herself to L.B. She obviously has something special to say, something that will stand out as a monument among all the other conventional attestations. Leave the shibboleths for the masses, says Francisca Ffin; the intimate have their own wondrous speech. So she stands, secure and sublime, letting the slogans bounce off her ears: "Bravo!" "Truly a German performance of Brahms!" "I have rarely been so moved!" "I love the third movement like that—good and fast!" "It was like hearing it for the first time!" She has heard all these before: they are not for F.F. But the moment is here.

F.F.:   Lenny, dear. (She whispers.) If you insist on cutting your hair so ridiculously short, nobody is going to care how you conduct! (She winks with both eyes, and is gone.)

FAST CURTAIN   □

Written 1948

N.B.: This is the beginning of what was conceived as a long Audenesque poem (Letter to Myself), never finished. I gave it up with the final line that appears here, "We've just begun," having suddenly realized that I had become a very-well-behaviorized chimpanzee. But Auden influence or no, I find enough personal declaration here to retrieve it from the flames, or the eternal Bank Vault. (L.B., 1982)

LETTER TO MYSELF

Prologue (San Francisco)

Insidious golden rust begins to form.
The gaping eyes of new decay appear.
Open, slow, ashamed, consumed with fear,
The elegant construction rots away.
The happy empty rooms are drowned in day,
And yet there's been no storm.
Oh, who was there to see my old house fall?
To bless the dry old boards with one bright tear?
Or was there one constituent to cheer?
No, one is rarely seen here anymore,
Except the workmen ripping up the floor,
And field mice in the wall.
Unwitnessed, then, I take me by the hand
And seek my newest castle in the sand.

Salutation (London)

I mean to write my fight with Time
in all its phases; Now, Not Yet,
Tomorrow, Since, Before, and While.

I may, as I am apt to do, slip into rhyme,
invent a stanza, add a foot, perhaps forget
to keep a strict tetrameter, or guard my style.

I use this kind of changing verse
to be not chic, but, rather, terse.
E.g., my secretary knows
my life in dull and battered prose;
my friend-confessors have to hear
my problems once or twice a year;
my lovers come to know the facts
in terms of secret, awkward acts;
my critics seem to know so well
the springs that make me tick, and tell
them quite without persuasion, while
they slyly tap their nose, and smile.
It seems, to make a summary,
that everybody knows but me.
I write myself this note, therefore.
If it becomes a gangling bore,
or fails in a constructive sense,
it's I who must do penitence.

For I am hid away, and there
is no one else to tell me where.
I mean to hunt myself, and find
myself, and, finding, be defined,
and, in defining, reexpress
the nature of my singleness.

Chapter One (London) (Before)

When first I sensed a greening field,
a gaudy garden, I rebelled.
What was it that my vision held,
or, say, connected with? A field?
A sight? A photo? Did I own
what lived before me? Lived, indeed?
And after, where did seeing go?
The field of sense, remembered sense?
To what extent could I ally
sensation and experience?

Consider this bold barrier, this
successless search for realness, this
remembered dark rebellion, this
forgotten heap of answers. What
wild warfare can consume more blood
than that which draws sensation's own?
What injury more raw than that
which comes of hanging feeling out
upon the twisted wire? I
have come the longest way about,
by day increasingly alone,
by night with those who ask a lie,
but then forbid reply. And now
I find myself upon this hill,
making my dull rebellion still.

This is a time to fuse the dream,
remember all of it, and try
one meaning with another. I
must gather up the weapons which
I used before—and find some more.

Oh, that was a different time, Before!
Then someone taught me to be clean,
and someone to be still and wait.
And everyone became a friend
who knew a way. But less with more
became a paradox too lean
to bear with. Always in the end
the barrier rose, barbed wire and all,
between the seeing and the seen,
the hearing and the call, between
sensation and experience.
The hurt renewed, the hurt renewed
itself from day to day. And now
I find myself upon this hill,
seeking the first connection still.

Paris, 1958

I suddenly recall a burning night
of sour sleeplessness. There was a train,
and in it I was flinging back the earth,
extended stiffly in my upper berth.
I can remember raising up the shade
to find a million stars upon a plain,
then closing it again in sudden fright,
and snapping on the light. The stars
had been too bright. They were not mine.
They hurt my eyes and heart, like someone
dead with dreams, who never can
belong to those around him. So
the stars did not belong to me,
nor I to them, nor any man.

Another unslept night comes back to me,
when, flying, later on, across the sea,
we felt a sudden want of oxygen.
And then the stars put on their act again,
pretending to reach down below the plane
in universal circularity.
Ecco, I thought, my first specific truth:
here I belong, and nowhere else at all.
For where is up, now; what is east or south?
Now cross me your two axes on the chart!
Now find me X, where intersections fall!
For I, and all of unbelonging men,
have found our place, adrift in oxygen.
Where all there is exists, there too must I;
where time needs no support from X and Y,
where love's asleep, abed with neuter Z,
which once we thought hostility to be!
How vain was I to wish for more than this
upon my little hill! *And yet*
I did reach Paris (cruel noon),
and did touch earth, and stood in line
to pass the customs, wondering how
the whole thing happened. Well, and now
I'm back upon my ancient hill,
planning the weary warfare still.

I find there is a sharper sting
than that of failing in one's art,
or being lonely in the spring.
The pain is this: to make the fight
with Time, to tell the days apart,
advance, seek answers, muddle through,
make love, feel growth—and find that you
have finished where you made your start.
As Alice found, you have to run
as fast as you can run, to stay
exactly where you are. So I,
high in my plane, remain in the train.

Well, chalk it up; at least there's one
small thing we know: We've just begun.

With his bride, Felicia Montealegre Cohn (L.B. is wearing Koussevitzky's suit), 1951

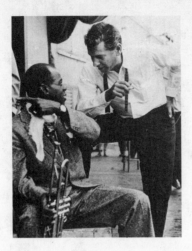

With Louis Armstrong at Lewisohn Stadium, New York, ca. 1956

Remarks on the occasion of the "We call it Jazz!" concerts in Minneapolis December, 1947

EVERYBODY'S SOUP

My only regret is that I must leave Minneapolis before this jazz concert on Sunday. But before I go, may I exhort you, as an intelligent public, to listen to this magic in a most serious way? It is certain that you will have fun; but try to remember that this is also a rare opportunity to make a serious investigation into the roots of American music.

Remember that there have been many attempts by American composers to create schools of American music. Some, headed by MacDowell, thought that Indian folk material provides the true basis; others, like Henry F. Gilbert, relied on Negro material. All the schools have failed, because Americans are not Indians all, or Negroes all, or Irish all; and any special folk school will always sound exotic to most citizens.

But jazz belongs to everyone. And when, after the First War, jazz began to penetrate all serious American music, it was a real influence, because it was unconscious, it was in the air, it was everybody's soup. And from this beginning, for less than three decades, our American music has been growing. Jazz was the real beginning.

So remember to be serious. You are listening to the authentic roots of a great new culture. I wish I could join you. ☐

ME COMPOSER—YOU JANE

I suppose that any composer would define his aims as being an ultimate personal expression. I imagine that the various elements of my background which contribute to the "personal" quality or nature of my music will soon be integrated; at the moment, they are not.

One thing I have already discerned, however. I have a basic interest in theater music. Most of my scores have been, in one way or another, for theatrical performance, and the others—most of them—have an obvious dramatic basis. I rather glow with pride at this discovery, rather than feel vulnerable, since I count such masters as Mozart, Weber, and Strauss (even Bach!) as similarly disposed. Where it will lead I cannot tell; but if I can write one real, moving American opera that any American can understand (and one that is, notwithstanding, a serious musical work), I shall be a happy man. □

With Betty Comden, Adolph Green, and Jerome Robbins, 1944

TWO LETTERS
TO HELEN COATES

Munich
8 May 1948

Dear Helen:

Letter #2 received, and I hasten to answer because I have to tell you about the Bavarian Alps, since I know how you feel about Alps. We drove to Garmisch yesterday, and went up to the Erbsee, a fantastic mountain lake resort halfway up to the Zugspitze. We couldn't get to the top because the cable cars weren't running (it being a German holiday). But what a country! One forgets in America that Germany is a land of beauty, and comes to think of it as a steel-clad place, like Mars, with everyone in steel helmets forging weapons. Not at all! And Bavaria is a dream-world. God, there's so much beauty and joy—why can't there be some peace? Must people go on plotting, being opportunistic, making war, being afraid?

Tomorrow is the concert, although it was nearly canceled because of a streetcar strike. But the Joint Distribution Committee (for Jewish Displaced Persons) will provide transportation* for the whole orchestra! I think that's the greatest story of all time. Jews helping out the Germans in this time and atmosphere! I think that's one for Leonard Lyons!

The orchestra seems to "love me," despite the three strikes on me of being under thirty, American (which means no culture to them), and Jewish. One violinist told me at this morning's rehearsal that there were maybe two conductors in all Germany who could do Schumann as well as I, and they were both over eighty! My biggest compliment to date. That from a German!

The concert is tomorrow, barring further strikes. You can never tell over here. But I've already had my triumph in conquering that orchestra.

---

* Sixteen trucks, formerly used to transport Jews to and from unmentionable places.—L.B., 1982.

Monday I will give two concerts for D.P.'s in two camps—Landsberg and Feldafing. That will be exciting. You should see the posters! I'll bring one home.

I wouldn't have missed all this for the world. And I've been so lucky to be quartered here in Geiselgasteig (Munich's film center), eating like a king, and with hot water all the time, personal maid service, and the works—amid all this misery.

I cabled you today about the Mahler program.

Thanks for all the news. I feel wonderful, if somewhat on edge all the time, and am learning almost more than I can absorb. It's a great experience, but unbelievably complicated. I can't tell it all in a letter—it must wait till I return. But it certainly makes America seem like a big, stupid, efficient, dull place. I may change my mind by the time Budapest comes around.

Helmut Grohe (manager of the orchestra there) is a complete idiot, and bungles everything. Thank God for Moseley.

Till Milan,

Love to everybody,
L

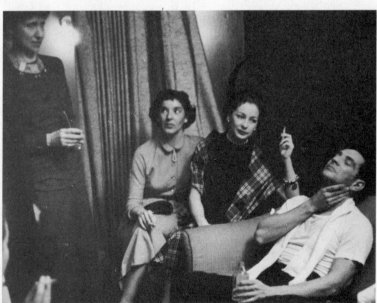

With Helen Coates, Shirley Bernstein, and Felicia Montealegre Bernstein, 1951

Verona, Italy
11 May 1948
2:30 A.M.

Dear Helen:

Here I sit, reeling with fatigue, in this rotting railroad station between trains (three and one-half hours' wait!) drinking marvelous Italian coffee, and full of the greatest train ride I've ever had. It was a warm, heavenly day, and we went from Munich through those fantastic Bavarian Alps, the Tyrol, Austria, to the Brenner Pass, and then a headlong plunge down the mountain into Italy. It's been fantastic, but when I'll get to Milan is an unknown factor. It's worth it, though, despite the fatigue. I shall never forget it.

The Munich concert was the greatest success to date. Especially because I had three obstacles to overcome—youth, Americanism, and Jewishness. And what a riotous success! There's nothing more satisfying than an opera house full of Germans screaming with excitement. I wish you could have been there. It means so much for the American Military Government—since music is the Germans' last stand in their "master race" claim, and for the first time that claim has been exploded in Munich.

Almost more exciting were the two concerts in D.P. camps yesterday (Monday). I was received by parades of kids with flowers, and the greatest honors. I conducted a twenty-piece concentration-camp orchestra (*Freischütz*, of all things!) and cried my heart out. And the entire (all-Nazi?) Munich orchestra journeyed out to fill the front rows, bouquets in hand, at *both* concerts. I can't tell this to you now—it's too deep and involved—and my train is due.

I've walked for two hours in Verona, which is crumbling with age and still breathing Dante. It's all amazing and horrible and beautiful and ugly and messy and inspiring.

Love,

L

You will receive by airmail a package containing a real concentration-camp costume which they gave me. Be particularly careful of it—it's a great (if slightly odorous) possession. □

Theatre of the Absurd piece
Written sometime
in the mid-1950s

SOUND EFFECTS: A TINY CHINESE OPERA

Two characters, X and Sound-effects Man (Chinese), latter seated downstage Right, torso only visible above percussion instruments, in semicircle. Directly before him is a record player. He putters on instruments.

Scene: Zoo. Not a soul about. Cages empty.

X rushes in, runs from cage to cage (during Prelude), slowing down gradually till he is strolling.

SOUND-EFFECTS MAN: What are you doing here?

X: I always come here; well, often, anyway. Except on Sundays.

SEM: Why do you come?

X: I'm unhappy.

SEM: Does the zoo make you happy?

X: Yes. I like crowds and the society of beasts. It's cheering.

SEM: But there's no one here. The cages are empty.

X: That's why I'm unhappy.

SEM: A further complication. Weren't you unhappy before you came?

X: I told you, that's why I came.

SEM: What makes you unhappy?

X: One thing only. I have a bad habit.

SEM: What is your habit?

X: I can't tell you.

SEM: Is it heroin?

X: (*piano*) No.

SEM: Do you stutter?

X: (*forte*) No, no.

SEM: Is it liquor?

X: (*fortissimo*) No.

SEM: What then?

X: (*pianissimo*) I can't tell you.

SEM: Oh, I see . . . it's mastur—

X: (*fortissimo*) No!

SEM: What then?

X: (*piano*) I'm too shy to say. (Suddenly *fortissimo*) All right!
(*pianissimo*) I . . . (*pianissimo*) crack . . .

SEM: Speak up! They can't hear you across the footlights!

X: I crack my knuckles!

SEM: Goodness!!

X: But it's my only vice, my very only vice!

SEM: And that makes you unhappy.

X: (recovering himself) Oh, so very. Otherwise I am in great shape—only this one miserable addiction.

SEM: You're sure there is no other reason.

X: None. I have everything. Money, flowers . . . I have girls, an erector set, a jade inkwell. I have remarkable luck.

SEM: To have is not to be.

X: To have is to be. To have good health is to be healthy. To have money is to be rich. To have talent is to be gifted. He who hath a goodly wife, he is blessed. He who hath, is. He who hath not doth not. But I have; ergo, I do, I be. Only I crack my knuckles.

SEM: Why don't you try to stop it?

X: I have tried. I have prayed. I have visited five psychiatrists for two years each. That makes ten years, one year for each finger. The first psychiatrist for my left forefinger, the second for my right ring finger. The third for my left ring finger, the fourth for my right thumb, and so on. But then I discovered that each finger has three knuckles. That makes thirty knuckles, thirty years on the couch. No—not quite right: the thumb has only two knuckles. That makes only twenty-eight knuckles in all. But you understand that I cannot spend twenty-eight years with psychiatrists, neither with seven psychiatrists for four years each, nor four psychiatrists for seven years each, nor even fourteen psychiatrists for two years each. I haven't the time.

SEM: But I thought you had everything?

X: *(fermata)* Not time. *(fermata)* Time, no. *(fermata)* That is one thing I have not. You are right. (Kneels.) *(fortissimo)* Oh, God, I don't have time!!
(Suddenly SEM puts on record player, from which issue crowd noises, animal noises, carousel music. The cages fill up with animals. Crowds enter Right and Left, very gay—children with balloons, hot-dog vendors, etc. A hurdy-gurdy man. The beasts howl, the crowd babbles and shouts. Beasts and people cross from R to L and vice versa, mingling, then exiting in the opposite directions until the stage is empty again. The noises do not diminish gradually with the grand exit, but stop suddenly, at full volume, the moment the stage is bare, by SEM's taking off needle. During the mass crossing, X has crouched down as low as he can get, shielding his face and head with his arms, like a fetus. He remains so after the noises have stopped, for a long pause. X then looks up slowly, and says in a trembling voice:)

X: I don't have time.

SEM: To have is not to be. Only not to have is to be. Since you do not have, you are. Since you do not have time, you are timeless. You may take my place.
(Slowly, they change places. As SEM leaves his position for Center Stage, we see that his lower half, hitherto concealed by the percussion apparatus and record player, is that of a hairy beast with a long tail and obvious genitalia. He stands, Center, on all fours, while X moves to drums, seats himself, and begins to putter.)

SEM: O people, let us pray. O beasts, pray with me, for the timeless one who cracks his knuckles. Let him be pacified; let all his twenty-eight knuckles know lasting joy:
(He shits on the stage.)
Second joint, right ring finger.

(X ticks on wood block.)
Third joint, right index finger.
(Ditto. He steps four-footed slowly off stage during this litany.)
First joint, right pinkie.
(X ticks.)
First joint, right ring finger.
(Tick.)
Third joint . . .
(Exit.)
(X goes on ticking, with other figurations creeping in between ticks, and on the twenty-eighth tick the curtain falls swiftly.)   □

With Stephen Sondheim. NYC, 1962

22 March 1957

FOR STEPHEN SONDHEIM

(an acrostic on his birthday)

Stephen Sondheim is a maker and solver of puzzles:
The jigsaw of his mind, the crosswords of creation, and
Especially the cryptologies of the heart.
Puzzler-poet of word and note, puzzled by some, puzzling to others,
He will (may), like his work-puzzles, inch apart, just
Enough to reveal the delicate cracks between:
Next moment the pieces magnetize and spring together with jolting
   rightness.

Stephen Sondheim loves Christmas: not
Only for the joy of giving the precisely definitive gift,
Not, certainly, for the getting; but for the ritual,
Decembral restatement of warmth and remembrance.
He is compulsively loyal,
Even to friends who are disloyal to one another, which is loyalty
Indeed. Puzzler, poet, friend, riddle,
Musician.

January, 1954
Asked, along with many others
(including Eleanor Roosevelt),
to write a credo
for a book entitled:

THIS I BELIEVE

I believe in people. I feel, love, need, and respect people above all else, including the arts, natural scenery, organized piety, or nationalistic superstructures. One human figure on the slope of an Alp can make the Alp disappear for me. One person fighting for truth can disqualify for me the platitudes of centuries. And one human being who meets with injustice can render invalid the entire system which has dispensed it.

I believe that man's noblest endowment is his capacity to change. In this he is divine. Armed with reason, he can see

NYC, 1954

Leonard Bernstein

two sides and choose: he can be divinely wrong. I believe in man's right to be wrong. Out of this right he has built, laboriously and lovingly, something we reverently call democracy. He has done it the hard way, and continues to do it the hard way—by reason, by choosing, by error and rectification. Democracy is being achieved only by democratic method. There are far easier methods—swifter, more impressive, apparently more efficacious. But they ultimately achieve nothing as compared with the difficult, slow method in which the dignity of A is acknowledged by B, without impairing the dignity of C. Difficult indeed, with two billion A's, B's, and C's to be considered; but whatever cherished steps we have taken on the long road to the democratic ideal have been taken in this way. Man cannot have dignity without loving the dignity of his fellow.

I believe in the potential of people. I cannot rest passively with those who give up in the name of "human nature." Human nature is only animal nature if it is obliged to remain static. *Human* nature must, by definition, include among its elements the element of metamorphosis. Without growth there is no godhead. If we are to believe that man can never achieve a society without wars, then we are condemned to wars forever. This is again the easy way. But the laborious, loving way, the way of dignity and divinity, presupposes a belief in people and in their capacity to change, grow, communicate, and love.

I believe in man's unconscious, the deep spring from which comes his power to communicate and to love. For me, all art is a combination of these powers; art is nothing to me if it does not make contact between the creator and the perceiver on an unconscious level. Let us say that love is the way we have of communicating personally in the deepest way. What art can do is extend this communication, magnify it, and carry it to vastly greater numbers of people. In this it needs a warm core, a hidden heating element. Without that core, art is only an exercise in techniques, a calling of attention to the artist, or a vain display. I believe in art for the warmth and love it carries within it, even if it be the lightest entertainment, or the bitterest satire, or the most shattering tragedy. For if art is cold it cannot communicate anything to anybody.

I believe that my country is the place where all these things I have been speaking of are happening in the most manifest way. America is at the beginning of her greatest period in history—a period of leadership in science, art, and human progress toward the democratic ideal. I believe that she is at a critical point in this moment, and that she needs every bit of belief in her and in her goals that we can offer. We must believe strongly, more strongly than before, in one another—in our ability to grow and change, in our power to communicate and love, in our mutual dignity, in our democratic method. We must observe taste in not exploiting our sorrows, successes, or passions. We must learn to know ourselves better through art. We must rely more on the unconscious spirit of man. We must not enslave ourselves to dogma. We must believe in the attainability of good. We must believe in people. □

Playing Mozart's piano, Salzburg, 1975

LETTER
TO MARTHA GELLHORN

Dreamgirl:

I ran into a character whose nickname was actually Sim or Shim, and so I immediately reread *Weekend at Grimsby* and find it to be a real story, deeply moving, and stylistically and formally exact. Therefore my great and abiding pleasure to hear from you that you are banging away again, mammoth dreck though you may think it to be. One of these days you are suddenly going to stumble on the core of it all. Of course, there it was all the time, right in this little backyard of my cranium, you will say, and then all hell will break loose. Not that this will happen without a hell of a lot of mammoth dreck first. But oh, God, how you need continuity of work: take it from one who needs it more than you do. I do the family bit too (though not as intensively or dramatically as you), and I have my small life-kitchen, and two or three other careers to boot, and I know what a horror it is to confront the one thing that makes sense, creating, after not having done so for ages, and wondering who one is and how one ever came to the notion that one could create anything at all except babies. So I

Martha Gellhorn, 1943

With Alexander Bernstein. Italy, 1967

too have started to improvise great derrickloads of dreck, and one of these days something is going to come out of it. This is to be a composing year; little if any conducting, no Europe, all winter on 57th Street with my ever-widening family circle; a new show (tragic this time) and rewriting the old show (the interminable *Candide*) and a big orchestral work for the Boston Symphony's 75th Anniversary, and etceteras I shall not bore you with. This is it; critical; if it doesn't work this year, I shall join you in endless walking tours of Scandinavia forever.

But Alexander Serge Leonard B!! What can I say of this glory? He is certainly destined to be our first Jewish president: he already looks exactly like Rutherford B. Hayes without the beard. (And without eyebrows or lashes or head-hair either.) He is manly, nay, manlissimo; fat, serious, a great eater and screamer. I feel so close to him: how can I tell it? He is familiar in a way that makes me think he has always been around; unlike Jamie, who will always have something a bit special and exotic about her for me. Perhaps what I mean is that Alexander looks like a Bernstein—like my father when he takes his teeth out at night, or a little like brother Burtie when drunk—whereas Jamie looks like a princess, namely Felicia, and is unutterably blond and delicate and fey. Can it be that these are the factors which determine one's ultimate relationship to one's child, and eventually send him or her shrieking to the analyst's couch? That is one of the most agonizing things about having children—that you really don't know what you are doing to them all the time that you are loving

Felicia Montealegre Bernstein, 1952

them madly and watching them like hawks and hoping and praying for them. But somehow I feel Alexander is stronger than all of this, and that by the time he makes the valedictory at Harvard at the age of 8 I won't be able to hurt him anymore. He has such lovely bowels, and a great crooked smile. Jamie is afflicted with the expected sibling rivalry (what a good name for a character in a Restoration play: Sir Sibling Rivalry), and she sometimes comes dangerously close to stuffing his pacifier down his throat, the while murmuring sweet nothings into his ear; but that is a normal abnormality, they say, and I am sure she will come out of it if we all live that long.

Fely has never looked more beautiful. She made a fantastic recovery, so much so that barely a month after producing the bairn she was playing a ravishing Communist spy on Kraft Cheese Television. Her hair is short and her chin is high, and I do believe I have a most attractive family. I am now in the horrid process of unwinding in the bosom of same, after a terribly hardworking year, and it turns out that unwinding is harder than staying wound. All those little and large ills and ailments that remain mercifully suppressed while one is working take hold the second work relaxes, and so one cannot relax at all. But the country here is so beautiful, and everyone has thankfully gone away but the frogs and the birds and us. Two more weeks here, and then back to the factory. Burtie comes for a 20-day leave this weekend, and we are all breathless with excitement. Did I tell you what happened to him? He was made, through no intervention on anyone's part, PIO of all the Antilles, and though still a private, is having a great time owing to the PIO armband, which entitles him to a car and chauffeur (who is a sergeant) and free air trips to St. Thomas to cover July 4th parades, etc. What a joy of a Cinderella story. He is the playboy king of Puerto Rico, whatever that may mean. So everything is lovely; and the big outstanding problem is whether to reduce Alexander to Sandy or Andy or Sascha or Alex or Lex or Aly or Lumpy (which is Jamie's last suggestion). If you see Flavia, our love to her, and our condolences. I never did get to see her in Rome, and feel abashed at the thought, but that doesn't mean we don't love her as much as always. I hope you made Italy all right, and that the *solitudine* continues to work, and produces work. Keep writing, because in a way, I live on your letters. Will we ever meet again? Love to Omi and Tom and Sandy from us both. I think of you every day.

An enormous hug.

Lenny

P.S. The thesis of your married-couple series is pablum to this kid. Remember *Trouble in Tahiti*?
P.P.S. I was 37 last Thursday. Good God. □

EXCERPTS FROM A
WEST SIDE STORY LOG

New York, Jan. 6, 1949. Jerry R. called today with a noble idea: a modern version of *Romeo and Juliet* set in slums at the coincidence of Easter-Passover celebrations. Feelings run high between Jews and Catholics. Former: Capulets; latter: Montagues. Juliet is Jewish. Friar Lawrence is a neighborhood druggist. Street brawls, double death—it all fits. But it's all much less important than the bigger idea of making a musical that tells a tragic story in musical-comedy terms, using only musical-comedy techniques, never falling into the "operatic" trap. Can it succeed? It hasn't yet in our country. I'm excited. If it can work—it's the first. Jerry suggests Arthur Laurents for the book. I don't know him, but I do know *Home of the Brave,* at which I cried like a baby. He sounds just right.

New York, Jan. 10, 1949. Met Arthur L. at Jerry's tonight. Long talk about opera versus whatever this should be. Fascinating. We're going to have a stab at it.

Columbus, Ohio, April 15, 1949. Just received draft of first four scenes. Much good stuff. But this is no way to work. Me on this long conducting tour, Arthur between New York and Hollywood. Maybe we'd better wait until I can find a continuous hunk of time to devote to the project. Obviously this show can't depend on stars, being about kids; and so it will have to live or die by the success of its collaborations; and this remote-control collaboration isn't right. Maybe they can find the right composer who isn't always skipping off to conduct somewhere. It's not fair to them or to the work.

New York, June 7, 1955. Jerry hasn't given up. Six years of postponement are as nothing to him. I'm still excited too. So is Arthur. Maybe I can plan to give this year to *Romeo*— if *Candide* gets in on time.

Beverly Hills, Aug. 25, 1955. Had a fine long session with Arthur today, by the pool (He's here for a movie; I'm conducting at the Hollywood Bowl). We're fired again by the *Romeo* notion; only now we have abandoned the whole Jewish–Catholic premise as not very fresh, and have come up with what I think is going to be it: two teen-age gangs, one the warring Puerto Ricans, the other self-styled "Americans." Suddenly it all springs to life. I hear rhythms and pulses, and—most of all—I can sort of feel the form.

New York, Sept. 6, 1955. Jerry loves our gang idea. A second solemn pact has been sworn. Here we go, God bless us!

New York, Nov. 14, 1955. A young lyricist named Stephen Sondheim came and sang us some of his songs today. What a talent! I think he's ideal for this project, as do we all. The collaboration grows.

New York, March 17, 1956. Candide is on again; we plunge in next month. So again *Romeo* is postponed for a year. Maybe it's all for the best; by the time it emerges it ought to be deeply seasoned, cured, hung, aged in the wood. It's such a problematical work anyway that it should benefit by as much sitting time as it can get. Chief problem: to tread the fine line between opera and Broadway, between realism and poetry, ballet and "just dancing," abstract and representational. Avoid being "messagy." The line is there, but it's very fine, and sometimes takes a lot of peering around to discern it.

New York, Feb. 1, 1957. Candide is on and gone; the Philharmonic has been conducted; back to *Romeo*. From here on nothing shall disturb the project; whatever happens to interfere I shall cancel summarily. It's going too well now to let it drop again.

Three production stills of West Side Story

Oliver Smith's rendering of "The Rumble" finale of Act I West Side Story

New York; July 8, 1957. Rehearsals. Beautiful sketches for sets by Oliver. Irene showed us costume sketches: breathtaking. I can't believe it: forty kids are actually doing it up there on the stage! Forty kids singing five-part counterpoint who never sang before—and sounding like heaven. I guess we were right not to cast "singers": anything that sounded more professional would inevitably sound more experienced, and then the "kid" quality would be gone. A perfect example of a disadvantage turned into a virtue.

Washington, D.C., Aug. 20, 1957. The opening last night was just as we dreamed it. All the agony and postponements and re-re-rewriting turn out to have been worth it. There's a work there; and whether it finally succeeds or not in Broadway terms, I am now convinced that what we dreamed all these years *is* possible; because there stands that tragic story, with a theme as profound as love versus hate, with all the theatrical risks of death and racial issues and young performers and "serious" music and complicated balletics—and it all added up for audience and critics. I laughed and cried as though I'd never seen or heard it before. And I guess that what made it come out right is that we all really *collaborated*; we were all writing the *same* show. Even the producers were after the same goals we had in mind. Not even a whisper about a happy ending was heard. A rare thing on Broadway. I am proud and honored to be part of it.

Part Three

THE NEW YORK
PHILHARMONIC
YEARS

1959–1967

With Olga Koussevitzky at Tanglewood, 1953

152 • *Leonard Bernstein*

LETTER
TO OLGA KOUSSEVITZKY

Dear Olga,

Today everything seems to bring S.A.K. to my mind, in a focus of extraordinary sharpness: the place; the date; the desert air; this tragic, stony, desert mountain. On a day like this (almost nine years ago), in a setting like this (his home in Phoenix) we sat and contemplated a similar mountain. He had only a few more months to live, although neither he nor I knew it. But he knew *something* was ending; he spoke with sweet resignation about time and timelessness, as he saw it in that dry, dry mountain; not sadly, but beyond sadness, just as the desiccated mountain was beyond weeping, purged of grief by centuries of suffering, aridly tranquil. He knew something was ending, because he was subtly and quietly assigning charges to me—dreams to be realized, responsibilities to be shouldered, standards to be guarded. He spoke constantly of Israel. That was another desert, and I remember him just as sharply against the tragic hills of Jerusalem, dry beyond even the weeping of Jeremiah. I remember his proud humility as he spoke of King David, musician; and I was aware of his struggling personal emotions as he looked at the city, torn and bleeding in the name of Faith.

Almost nine years. Music has changed in that time; there is so much more of it, so many more people listening to it, and listening differently. Works that were still thorny and forbidding then are everyday classics now. And so largely owing to him, to his stubborn insistence on commissioning them, and on playing them, as he would say, *coûte que coûte*. Bartok, Stravinsky, Copland.

Copland: today, curiously enough, is his birthday. It is hard for me to see his face in my mind without seeing the face of Koussevitzky behind him—my two deepest teachers, together, neither of them primarily a teacher by profession, yet both great teachers by their natures, generously inspiring, communicating, sharing with love their love of music and of

With Tod Penny, Aaron Copland, and Olga Koussevitzky at Tanglewood, 1974

enlightenment. This time I see them against another mountain, a green, fertile, wooded mountain of youth and joy, in
the glorious summer dream we called Tanglewood.

Today is also another, personal anniversary: sixteen years
ago this afternoon I made my sudden, frightening debut with
the New York Philharmonic. S.A. was not there; he had had
nothing to do with my appointment as assistant conductor; he
knew nothing of the emergency occasioned by Bruno Walter's
illness. But he was with me note by note, bar after bar, charging me with the authority I needed, goading my imagination,
shaping and controlling my passions. I still hear him: "When
you come to the *orchestre*, you stand straight, like a great tree
in the sun. You look the *orchestre* every one in the eyes, everyone, slowly, until you *have* them. Then very very slowly, you
raise the *baguette*, and you begin. You come to the *orchestre* a
magician, to unlock the secrets of the composer. . . ."

And now I recall another desert, this time in Mexico, June,
1951. I have given up conducting for an indefinite period; I am
writing music, alone, quietly. The telephone: S.A. is in the
hospital, "for tests." In two hours I am on a plane; that night I

am at his bedside. More charges, dreams, standards to be guarded. The next day he is gone.

Almost nine years. Music has changed, yes; and something basic has fallen out of it for me. Can I name it? Glamour? Guidance? Gala? Is it only that I miss my musical father? Or the festive spirit that surrounded his concerts? Or the sense of revelation I experienced in our discussions? All of this; but more—yes, I think I can name it: an Importance is gone. When Koussevitzky stepped out on the stage, made his deft right-face to the podium, marched to it as to his destiny, raised his *baguette* (very slowly—it was *important*): no matter what the music was going to be, it was going to matter, because he was performing it. Nobody in his audience could fail to perceive that, and you listened in a heightened way, as though you had eaten peyote, to each strand and caress and inflection and breath of the music. Nobody else (except Dinu Lipatti, and he too is gone) has ever made me listen to music in that way.

The sun is almost out of sight behind the arid mountain; there is a sudden chill, and I must go inside to study. Next week I shall be conducting again; Bartok's *Concerto for Orchestra* lies open on my desk, waiting. A Koussevitzky commission. It is all one; the thread continues to spin.

Affectionately,
L.B.

Remarks written in October, 1959.
This speech not given,
L.B. speaking extemporaneously instead.

SPEECH TO THE NATIONAL PRESS CLUB

The thought of addressing the National Press Club freezes me with horror—first, because I tread in the steps of my predecessors, and secondly, because I have been really thrown as to a subject. Of course, the subject usually requested of me these days is my impressions of Russia—

which sounds depressingly like the title of a seventh-grade English composition. What's more, you have heard and read so much on that subject lately that I thought I'd limit my Russian remarks to saying that I came out of the Soviet Union with the same feeling I had going in, only multiplied and in spades. I have always liked the Russian people and equally disliked the Russian regime, and I came out of Russia loving the Russian people and loathing the regime. Therefore, I have no changes of heart to report, and I thought I would talk to you about something you probably want least to hear discussed: the press.

On a tour such as we have made, which included seventeen countries and twenty-nine cities and fifty concerts in two and a half months, there is bound to be a lot of press, both local and American. We have all struggled through reviews in Swedish and Finnish and Serbo-Croatian and Russian, trying to make out whether they thought we were great or gruesome. I must say modestly that it usually turned out that we were not gruesome—but then, you can't trust my Swedish. We did have warm, wonderful receptions everywhere. Of course, there was a particular significance in our Russian visit, which lasted three weeks, in itself. We gave eighteen concerts in Moscow, Leningrad, and Kiev to what might be described as fanatic audiences. I spoke of particular significance because Russia, of course, was our most (as local officialdom would say) "sensitive area." It was here that our mission of friendship—which is, after all, what we were on, besides being on a highly complicated concert tour—had to work. We just had to be good. Therefore, it was of the utmost satisfaction to have Russian audiences that screamed and stamped and all but tore the seats out of the floor.

I would come out from the concert hall sometimes after midnight, an hour or more after the concert had been finished, and find one hundred or so people standing in the Leningrad rain (which can be very, very damp), waiting for a chance to touch us, to embrace us, even to kiss my hand; and I have a feeling that this was not only in tribute to the musical standards we represent but also to us as Americans. There is a very strong attraction to things American in the Russian cities, in spite of all their conditioning since childhood through their press and schooling and radio—conditioning that would have them think of America as a kind of Hades, riddled with lynching and exploitation and unemployment. I firmly believe that deep down they don't really believe this, even though they may mouth it at us as dutifully as they have to. I also believe that these contacts we make with them on so deep a level as that of musical communication can tell them much more about us than their press can tell them. Besides, they really don't believe their press. Of course, a lot of us don't believe our press either, but at least we can pick up six papers in New York City and read six remarkably different accounts of the same

Moscow, 1959

incident and we have a choice, and choice means freedom. You can usually piece together a fairly true picture by montaging these six incidents on top of one another. But in the Soviet press, there is no choice at all. All the papers say the same things, which are official things and which very often contradict that which the public knows and feels to be true. Try to think of yourself as a Russian to whom it was suddenly revealed some years ago that Stalin's regime had been one of unspeakable crime and duplicity. You would suddenly get the idea that not all was rosy with Soviet officialdom, and this doubt would inevitably begin to apply to the present regime as well; and with Khrushchev's subsequent liberalization policy, the skepticism has begun to grow. For example, if one thousand people witnessed an event in the street, such as the stoning last year of the U.S. Embassy, and then read in the official press a report that the Embassy was politely visited by three delegates who left a note on a silver tray, then there are at least one thousand people who won't believe that report; nor the report in the adjoining column; nor, ultimately, their press in general.

Also, since the line changes so often, they get confused and don't know what to believe. We made friends with a charming young woman in a highly official capacity with whom I argued day and night, and who all too frequently was bereft of any final argument except tears. I once asked her what she had been taught about the rift between Lenin and Trotsky, and she answered that she had been taught so many things that she didn't know which was true. She had had two versions under Stalin and a third one since. She also had no idea Trotsky was dead, to say nothing of the fact that he had been murdered, but had some vague notion that he was living in darkest Brazil. I then asked her point-blank how she could possibly believe anything she was taught in the face of this shifty history, and she calmly replied that she didn't believe anything. Of course, that was my moment to counter with "Then you don't believe *in* anything, do you?" to which she replied, "No." I pursued with "Not even Socialism?" to which she replied, "No." She just wanted to be let alone. Those were her words.

Even Party patriots can be broken down in this way. An American friend of mine had a rather extraordinary exchange with a young Russian on the subject of elections. "Why do you need two parties?" said the Russian. My friend carefully explained our democratic thesis that without choice there is no freedom and that it is this very opportunity to choose which entitles us to use the word "democracy." "But," answered the Russian, "there is only one freedom"—which had my friend stumped for the first three seconds, because this is the kind of empty slogan that can be very impressive at first onslaught and then crumbles upon any examination. Within a couple of minutes the Russian knew that he had only been mouthing an empty slogan. One can only hope that this constant, if slow, liberalization and the growing awareness that there are choices to be made in the world will continue. And one has to pray hard that the Russian people, having gotten a little taste of freedom and naturally wanting more, will not bring the Iron Fist crashing down on them again as it has so often before.

I worry about this almost more with regard to the Poles. They have gotten almost reckless in their freedom, such as it is. They like to think they can say anything they want, paint any pictures they want, write poems as "mad" as those of our own beatniks. One young Pole said to me, "In Russia, nobody can open his mouth except Khrushchev. In Poland, everybody can open his mouth except Gomulka," and they glory in this. Again, we can only pray that this trend can press ahead in the right direction and doesn't get slapped down.

Back to the press. In Russia, I found myself becoming a wildly chauvinistic patriot about our American press, owing to the sheer, astonishing contrast with what I found there. You see, the main trouble with the Russian press, apart from its enslavement, is that it is boring. There is no variety of any sort. As I recall it, page after page, there is nothing to read about except that the production of Bulgarian tractors is up ten percent—that, of course, being page one news; or something similar about Romanian wheat or that the Chinese are our brothers, or that America is Rome dying all over again, or that Socialism is Socialism is Socialism. You can never read, for instance, that a house burned down on the corner of Something Street, or that "X" was divorced, or that Protocol made a *faux pas* and invited the wrong Mr. Morse to a Khrushchev dinner. After a workout or two like this, you just long for a little rape story, or at least a ten-liner about two cars colliding; but no such thing. There are no fires, no collisions, no *faux pas*, no rapes, no divorces, because after all, Socialism is Socialism is Socialism.

And so I found myself reading whatever I could get hold of from the American press with more than usual avidity. I found that in general, the United States reporting of our tour was marvelous, not only because it was so copious and complimentary, but because it was on the whole so accurate. Now, this is harder than it would first appear. When a reporter like Franklin or Carruthers in Moscow is called upon to report on music, you can't really expect him to get everything right. He has enough trouble learning what he must learn about political and social matters without also being capable of distinguishing between Starokadomsky and Dargomyzhsky or between *andante* and *adagio*; and yet they were both magnificent—no gaffes, no boners —and almost all the reportage I saw was accurate and fair.

I say "almost" because there were some exceptions— and I speak of them not in any way to discredit, but in order to sermonize, if I may for a second, on the huge responsibility of the press in delicate matters within that so-called "sensitive area." It is precisely because the American press is free and because journalism is generally of so high a level in our country that we must make doubly sure not to fall into errors that can be said to resemble certain patterns of an unfree press.

Opinion is, of course, the lifeblood of journalism, and I say *"Vive la différence!"* But opinion not based on fact, or fact made to conform to opinion, begins to have the very quality we are constantly deploring in the Soviet press.

For example, I don't know if you are familiar with a small incident that occurred in Moscow during our tour—an incident that ended up being reported in the Russian press in such terms as "Bernstein rows with Moscow critics." In

Бетховен	— VIII симфонія	Россіні	— Увертюра до опери „Облога Корінфа"
Барбер	— Роздум Медеї і танець помсти	Даймонд	— „Мир Пауля Клее"
Чайковський	— IV симфонія	Стравінський	— Сюїта з балету „Жар-птиця"
		Вагнер	— Увертюра до опери „Тангейзер"
			Вступ та Смерть Ізольди з музичної драми „Трістан та Ізольда"
			Подорож Зіґфріда по Рейну з музичної драми „Загибель богів"

ДИРИГЕНТ

НЕДІЛЯ 6 вересня 1959 року

ЛЕОНАРД БЕРНСТАЙН

ПОНЕДІЛОК 7 вересня 1959 року

П Р О Г Р А М И

6 вересня 1959 р.

Барбер	— Другий етюд для оркестру
Бетховен	— Концерт для фортепіано, скрипки та віолончелі з оркестром
Берліоз	— Фрагменти з драматичної симфонії „Ромео і Юлія"

7 вересня 1959 р.

Бетховен	— Увертюра „Леонора" № 3 VII симфонія
Копленд	— Сюїта з балету „Парнишка Билли"
Гершвін	— Рапсодія в стилі „Блюз"

соласти:

ЛЕОНАРД БЕРНСТАЙН (рояль)
ДЖОН КАРІЛЬЯНО (скрипка)
ЛАСЛО ВАРГА (віолончель)

соліст

ЛЕОНАРД БЕРНСТАЙН

Початок о 8 год. вечора

Soviet Union, 1959

the first place, there was no row. In the second place, the incident involved one critic, not plural. And in the third place, the critic in question was not even functioning as a music critic. Let me tell you what happened that fateful night and clear the record. We were playing that night a special program which included two works by Stravinsky, whom I consider the greatest Russian composer of the century, but one whose works are frowned upon in his native land. One of these works was the great ballet *The Rite of Spring*, which local musicians told me had not been heard in Russia for more than thirty years, and the other was his *Piano Concerto*, which had never been performed in Russia. The program, moreover, contained a work by Charles Ives, an American, of whom we are justly proud. This was a curious little piece called *The Unanswered Question*—written in 1908, before modern music had really been heard on this earth, and which nevertheless anticipates many of the most modernistic trends of our time. Because of all this and the fact that there was no time for program notes to be printed, I decided that I would have to make a few remarks to the audience about these three special pieces. The public's reaction was tremendous. In fact, they kept calling me out for bows over and over again after the Ives piece and had begun that insistent rhythmic clapping which in Europe means "Encore." So that I finally said to them in my dreadful Russian, "You mean you really want to hear that piece again?" At which they thundered their affirmation, and so we played it again. There were equally rousing receptions for the two "Sovietic" Stravinsky works. The only sour note of the evening issued from the Minister's box in the form of grunts and other protesting sounds—which came, I believe, from the Minister of Culture—when I spoke of Stravinsky's being unplayed and of Ives's having invented a kind of modern music in Danbury, Connecticut. The next day the reviews were all marvelous—including the one in the official paper of the Ministry of Culture, *Literaturnaya Gazeta*. But underneath that review there appeared an additional little article with this critic in question deploring my immodesty at choosing to speak at a concert, as though they were provincials who knew nothing about Stravinsky —which, of course, they were. But none of this upset me. What did set my teeth on edge was his statement that despite a small, polite ripple of applause after the Ives, I had insisted on inflicting the piece a second time on the audience. This really got me, and I made a boiling-mad statement about it to the press.

It was all a negligible affair, and I regret now that I reacted so strongly. It was not worth even that one moment of anger—but I was angry, and that's that. The next day I wasn't angry anymore, nor am I now. Well, it is understandable that the official publication of the Soviet Ministry of Culture might employ such below-the-belt tactics; but what's a bit hard to take is the snowball that ensued, the teapot tempest in the American press, plus, of course, a certain amount of editorial snowballing in the *Saturday Review of Literature*.

Luckily, that was a highly unimportant incident; but just think of what could have happened along these lines, with a little piece of misinformation being magnified and distorted into really harmful results. I am thinking particularly of the night of our farewell concert in Moscow, at which the great Boris Pasternak was in attendance. He came backstage during the intermission to congratulate me and spoke with me. Now, there was a good deal of world press around that night, because it was our final concert and because Shostakovich was present to hear his *Fifth Symphony* performed. When the press realized that Pasternak was there too, and in my dressing room, they all swarmed in with cameras, notebooks, and microphones akimbo. He was charming to them—unruffled, warm, and simple. But at one point, while trying to pay me a compliment about the Beethoven symphony he had just heard, he said, "It is hard for me to express what I mean. Even in Russian, the words would 'lack' me." When he had finished, a reporter pounced on him asking, "What was it you said before about March tenth?" Pasternak was utterly bewildered. So was I. The reporter insisted, "Didn't you say, 'On March tenth even the Russians would like me'?" He didn't reply, naturally, not knowing which of his sentences had been misconstrued. He seemed like a puzzled, trapped animal, finding no exit from this absurd situation. At which point I got scared as I heard the various reporters pressing him with "What is going to happen March tenth?—Will a new book appear?—Will you make a statement?—Are you

Embracing Boris Pasternak (with Jack Gottlieb and Felicia Montealegre Bernstein), Moscow, 1959

planning an apology?" It all seemed so unfair; but luckily, Pasternak himself realized in time which of his phrases had started this nightmare—namely, "Even in Russian, the words would 'lack' me." But neither he nor I could figure out the original phrase from which "March tenth" had sprouted. So it was cleared up; but I was left with a feeling of horror at how close we had come to a situation that could be harmful for this brave and noble man, just through the misunderstanding of a phrase in broken English in a small, crowded room. Those reporters behaved with integrity. As soon as Pasternak had explained, they were satisfied that they had misheard; but what if he had not had the brilliance to realize which of his actual words had been misheard? I leave it to your imagination.

None of this is particularly amusing—and I have been told that it is customary for luncheon speakers at the Press Club to be wildly amusing. I am sorry that these are not joking matters; but these are the matters that occur to me when facing the National Press Club. I would like to leave you with what I consider a real shocker along these lines— an example of angled journalism that does exactly what we tend to accuse the Russians of doing. During our Moscow visit, it had been suggested to me by a Deputy Minister of Culture that we might play our final farewell concert in a big sports stadium for a hundred thousand people—an idea I took very kindly to. As it turned out, the weather suddenly grew cold and the plan was no longer feasible. A simple tale with no undercurrents of meaning. Now listen to how it was reported in one instance to the American public.

"For a time in Moscow, it looked as if Soviet musical strategy had worked. When the Russians agreed last Spring to play host to Leonard Bernstein and the New York Philharmonic for three weeks this summer, they thought they had prepared for everything. Well aware of the crowd appeal inherent in the dynamic conductor's podium acrobatics, the bureaucrats at the Soviet Ministry of Culture refused Bernstein's pleas to play one or more concerts for the massed thousands who could be accommodated in either the 10,000 seat Sports Palace or one of the city's

With Mstislav Rostropovich, Washington, D.C., Ca. 1980

parks. Instead, they decided to keep Bernstein and his Orchestra confined to the Grand Hall of the Tchaikovsky Conservatory of Music (Capacity—1,100)."

I read this in Moscow and was filled with shame. After all, there we were on a United States Presidential mission under the wing of the State Department, standing for everything good and true about America, and this kind of thing didn't help me in the least to feel good and true, being on about the same level as the Moscow critic who recorded that the audience had applauded only politely for the Ives. I take all this so seriously because we cannot afford this kind of thing if we are to succeed in convincing the Iron Curtain peoples of the values in our way of life. This is my bit of sermonizing, for which I humbly beg pardon. Please always remember that as the free press of the United States, you have a responsibility that is almost sacred in these times. And you must double your effort and magnify your guard to keep it exemplary, honorable, and proud. ☐

*Speech given at honor ceremony of
the America-Israel Cultural Foundation
for contributions to the cultural interchange
between Israel and the United States
2 February 1959*

THE WHOLE MEGILLAH

Let me say, first of all, that I am moved by your tribute beyond any verbal expression. As an American, I treasure the gesture of our President; as a musician, every note of this musical offering has been dear to me; and as a Jew, the words of Ben-Gurion, to say nothing of what you all have done and said, will always remain to warm my heart.

But more important, I wonder how many of you know Samuel J. Bernstein? He is the president of the Samuel J. Bernstein Hair Company, a small but energetic enterprise in the city of Boston; he is also a lovely man; and he is also a great Hebrew scholar. He has one fault only: whenever he has to make a speech—in fact, even when he doesn't have to—he always resorts for his text to the Bible or the Talmud. At his knee, I learned my lesson well—I'm a chip off the old Tanach—especially when honors are being offered; then I turn to him: for in turn, it is I who must honor him.

And so, being the son of Samuel J., the appropriate Biblical texts come leaping to mind tonight. Thirty years ago, I stood at the annual Purim play and sang *"Va-y'hi bi'meei Ahasueroth,"* which is the opening of the lengthy recitation we have come to know and avoid called "The Megillah"— *die ganze Megillah.* But in recalling all that monotonous chanting of what is actually a charming and gripping novella, the Book of Esther, I am most impressed by the following brief section:

(Esther, VI, 2–12)
2 *And it was found written, that Mordecai had told of Bigthan and Teresh, two of the king's chamberlains, the keepers of the door, who sought to lay hand on the king Ahasuerus.*

Ca. 1921

3 And the king said, What honour and dignity hath been done to Mordecai for this? Then said the king's servants that ministered unto him, There is nothing done for him.

4 And the king said, Who is in the court? Now Haman was come into the outward court of the king's house, to speak unto the king to hang Mordecai on the gallows that he had prepared for him.

5 And the king's servants said unto him, Behold, Haman standeth in the court. And the king said, Let him come in.

6 So Haman came in. And the king said unto him, What shall be

done unto the man whom the king delighteth to honour? Now
Haman thought in his heart, To whom would the king delight to do
honour more than to myself?

7 And Haman answered the king, For the man whom the king
delighteth to honour,

8 Let the royal apparel be brought which the king useth *to wear,*
and the horse that the king rideth upon, and the crown royal which is
set upon his head;

9 And let this apparel and horse be delivered to the hand of one of the
king's most noble princes, that they may array the man withal
whom the king delighteth to honour, and bring him on horseback
through the street of the city, and proclaim before him, Thus shall it
be done to the man whom the king delighteth to honour.

10 Then the king said to Haman, Make haste, and *take the apparel*
and the horse, as thou hast said, and do even so to Mordecai the Jew,
that sitteth at the king's gate: let nothing fail of all that thou hast
spoken.

11 Then took Haman the apparel and the horse, and arrayed
Mordecai, and brought him on horseback through the street of the
city, and proclaimed before him, Thus shall it be done unto the man
whom the king delighteth to honour.

12 And Mordecai thereupon returned to the king's gate. . . .

It's a wonderful and exciting passage, and a beautifully
ironic variant on the idea of doing honor to a man. But what
impresses me most of all is that last line: "And Mordecai
thereupon returned to the king's gate." You see, that was
Mordecai: a little exiled Jew, sitting in the king's gate, waiting and hoping for something good to happen. And here
am I, like Mordecai, feeling the strangeness of royal apparel, the king's horse, the crown—in short, being honored. But ultimately, I am little old Mordecai, who goes
back after all the shouting has died down, to sit, and hope,
in the king's gate. In some very important part of me, I will

always be that exiled, frightened little boy of ten, singing the Megillah, and praying for a chance to make music in my lifetime.

Last night at dinner, Samuel J. Bernstein was talking of honors, of honor, of being honored. And in appropriately true style, he reminded me of a deeply touching moment in the Book of Kings, when God appeared in a dream to King Solomon in Gib'on, and wished to honor him. "Ask what I shall give thee," He said. And Solomon answered, among other things, "Give thy servant an understanding heart, to discern between good and bad." My father quoted justly and wisely; because that is indeed my prayer, keeping Solomon as my model:

LB

> *To be strong of will, but not to offend;*
> *To be intimate with my fellow man, but not to presume;*
> *To love, but not to be weakened by loving;*
> *To serve music, but not to forget humanity for the music;*
> *To work, but not to destroy oneself in working;*
> *To rest, but not to be idle;*
> *To be a proud and grateful American, but also to be a proud and*
>   *grateful Jew;*
> *To give, but also to receive;*
> *To create, but also to perform;*
> *To act, but also to dream;*
> *To live, but also to be.*

This is not an easy undecalogue. My prayer is for the wisdom to observe it; and to be worthy of your most deeply cherished honor. □

INSOMNIAD

There once was a bully
Named Raymond Bonelli.
Much older than us:
He could hardly subtract,
And had been left back.
He had him a gang,
Who were always along
And he swaggered to school
With his hair like coal,
And his eyes were of coal.
It was said of him, hushed,
That he once took a cup,
Masturbated into it
And then cut his finger
And mixed the two liquids
Together, and stirred it,
And strained it, in hopes
That real skin would result.
One day he loomed near
With his gang in the rear
And the gang held his arms
So that he couldn't strike:
He was raging and black,
And his gang held him back.
And to me he approached
(Not to Melvin or Sid,
But to me:) and his mouth
Opened wide, to let out
The most horrid pentameter
I've ever heard.
I remember each word:
"What's the idea of laying Millie Long!?"

I was stunned. No reply.
I turned to a friend,
And shakingly asked him
The meaning of lay.
When he told me, I died.
For of all things on earth
I did love Millie Long. (She sat in the seat
                 Just in front of me, there
                 In the lonely sixth grade
                 Of Miss Donnelly's grace.)

I didn't! I didn't!
You did; *I saw you,*
Through the downstairs window,
On the living-room floor,
And you laid her last night.
I didn't   I didn't:
I wouldn't have, either,
Or thought of it, even.
Much less do it.
I did love Millie Long.
The school bell rang;
The moment was saved.
But that night in my bed
I knew very hard
That I loved Millie Long
No longer.

Address introducing
Lillian Hellman
for the Brandeis Creative Arts Award
at the Tenth Annual Banquet
of the Fellows of Brandeis University
10 June 1961

AN OLD-FASHIONED ARTIST

Dear President and Mrs. Sachar, distinguished Fellows, honored guests, and friends of Brandeis University:

The public presentation of awards is not always the pleasant duty and privilege that I have tonight. How often have we sat through these rituals, so facile, so poorly motivated, that the honorific value is often reduced to a minimum, in favor of attracting public attention to the award-giver.

But tonight I rejoice in my duties, for three reasons: first, because Brandeis University has been, from its first moment of breath, keenly conscious of the creative arts, and unfailingly active in encouraging them; second, because the juries that have selected the recipients are year after year blue-ribbon grand juries; and third, that the recipients being honored here tonight are themselves truly honorable.

Let me say just one word about what I mean by *honorable*. Today, more than ever, the talk in art circles is about the newest, the latest, the way-outest, the beatest, the sickest, the cliquiest—all of which is to say the most dated. Nothing dates so fast as exteriorized experiments, or willful shocking of the bourgeoisie. Don't misunderstand me: I am all for shocking the bourgeois of the world, for stirring up discussion, and provoking controversy; but not when it becomes a primary artistic goal. Such goals float away in a half-decade, down a brackish river; and the moment we take artistic stock—even with the tiny perspective we have about our own century—we find that all the durable art has been made by old-fashioned artists. I am proud, and

With Lillian Hellman at Wolftrap, Va., 1978

pleased, that all the artists being honored tonight are old-fashioned and honorable; and that Miss Hellman, who will accept the awards on behalf of all the recipients, is possibly the most old-fashioned of all.

I have worked with, fought with, and loved Lillian Hellman for about fifteen years; and basing my thoughts on that lengthy and instructive relationship, I would like to recite for you a litany defining my idea of an old-fashioned artist.

First, and above all, a fiercely hard worker, an agonizer, never satisfied, yet always rewarded by the simple act of creating.

Second, an extender of tradition, acutely aware of roots and lineage, who extends these by measuring them incessantly against the future; therefore, of course, an insatiable progressive.

Third, an inward-looker, a self-searcher, a soul-picker, who will spare no part of his body or spirit to achieve expressive cleanliness, stylistic rightness, and moral truth.

Fourth, a socially oriented conscience, a society-lover and implacable critic; therefore, of course, a persistent radical.

Fifth, a fountain of humor, of laughter, be it savage, snide, or shy; a sport, in love with the very athletics of creating art.

And *sixth*, an experimentalist; but one who experiments with personal, interior materials. Which, in fact, sums up all the elements: you cannot make this kind of inner experiment without the agony of labor, the respect for tradition, the sense of future, the self-searching, the direct wire to human society, or the gift of laughter which protects against every undue pomposity and solemnity.

This is the artist who will cackle and hoot if you call him dedicated, and rush off in a fit to create a very old-fashioned thing which men still call, in their fumbling, old-fashioned way . . . beauty. □

*Speech made in Boston
at a dinner honoring his father
1 January 1963*

TRIBUTE TO S.J.B.

Let me start with a confession: I have been trying to write this little speech for ten days. It's not easy to stand up and assess your father, especially in retrospect from the solemn occasion of a seventieth birthday. From what point of view should he be described? Childhood? Adolescence? Adult-

174 • *Leonard Bernstein*

With Samuel J. Bernstein

hood? It has to be all three; because a child is not aware of his father as a separate person: he always sees his father in relation to himself and his own needs or desires. But there comes a moment, usually in adolescence, when he may suddenly realize that his father is an individual in his own right; and that is a new view of him.

But the real understanding of one's father comes in adulthood, after one has himself become a father. And so it is only in the past nine years, since I became one too, that I have begun to have some real idea or appreciation of the complex phenomenon that is Samuel Bernstein. And he *is* complex, because he is a great and multifaceted man. And so I hope you'll forgive me if I speak seriously about him, or even didactically.

What is a father, in the eyes of a child? The child feels: My father is first of all my Authority, with power to dispense approval or punishment. He is secondly my Protector; thirdly my Provider; beyond that he is Healer, Comforter, Law-giver; but finally, and principally, he is the Creator, because he caused me to exist. This is the child's conception; but we immediately realize that this is a perfect image of God. Authority, protector, provider, healer, comforter, law-giver, creator. To the child, the father is God, the model to be followed, in whose image he was created. And as the child grows up, he retains all his life, in some deep, deep part of him, the stamp of that father-image whenever he thinks of God, of good and evil, of retribution.

For example, take the idea of defiance. Every son, at one point or another, defies his father, fights him, departs from him, only to return to him—if he is lucky—closer and more secure than before. Again we see clearly the parallel with God: Moses protesting to God, arguing, fighting to change God's mind. So the child defies the father; and something of that defiance also remains through his life. For instance, I was reading excerpts from the Kaballah the other day, and was suddenly aware of a strange, hidden memory that this was in some way a forbidden book; and I went on reading it; and I came across something that added a new dimension to my father-thinking. In the revelation of Rabbi Shimeon it is pointed out that the total manifestations of God are to be understood as Wisdom, or *Chachmah*, but that this cannot exist except in the dual form of male and female; and so *Chachmah* is the Father, and *Binah*, or Understanding, is the Mother. But the two are not separate—that is the mystical necessity; they are indivisible; and Rabbi Shimeon even proves it by making an anagram of *Binah*: *Ben-Yah*, the Son of God. What a marvelous paradox, and so typically Jewish: the mother is, after all, a Son of God, just as the father is: therefore, they are one.

And so I discovered through this *Pilpal* that perhaps the chief quality of a father is the mother; and the deepest part of Samuel Bernstein is therefore Jennie Bernstein. And so whatever tribute I make to him, I make to her also.

I think that probably the greatest gift my father bestowed on us children was to teach us to love learning. He *was*, in our house, *Chachmah*; he was the flaming angel in charge of

". . . The deepest part of Samuel Bernstein is therefore Jennie Bernstein"

it. A child may or may not have Understanding, *Binah*, the more female, intuitive side of Wisdom; if he doesn't have it he will never have it, for it cannot be learned. But *Chachmah* can be learned, and I think that is probably the foundation of all Jewish living and culture—that learning can be learned; and it is certainly the sense in which I call my father a great Jew. He made it impossible for his children not to love wisdom, to love the actual seeking after it. Of course, he may have ruined our lives in the process, because, as we all know, it's the desire to know too much that starts all the *tsuros*. And yet, I wouldn't have it any other way.

I first became aware of my father as an individual—a man with his own life and problems apart from my own—

exactly thirty years ago, in 1932. That is a complete generation ago, but I can still remember almost the exact moment when I suddenly saw my father as himself. We had just gone through the worst year of the Depression; everybody was poor, jumping out of windows, selling apples; and that year my father, somehow, *auf tsaluchas*, got rich. Just for one year, mind you, and not *very* rich at that: but compared with the general economic state of affairs, rich. And in that year he built for us a house: for the first time in his life, at last, a house of his own. In fact, he built *two* houses—one in Sharon, for the summers. All in one year. And then he had no money left, and has never been rich since. But he was happy. Right then I saw him as an individual, with decisions to make. Ordinarily, when a man acquires money, he uses it to get more money. That, I believe, is called business. But not Samuel Bernstein. He had dreamed all his life of a home, a family shrine, an altar of *Chachmah* and *Binah*; and so he built it, and then he didn't need money anymore.

It was in that year also that I began to see him in his office, happily wasting time that he could have spent making money, discussing a situation for an hour with a customer by producing from his desk a well-worn Bible and giving a lesson in the fourteenth chapter of the Book of Judges. This is the way he has always run his business—with that book at his fingertips—and that's how he still runs it, I'm sure, since he still hasn't got any money.

That was a big year, thirty years ago, a good year. My brother was born in that year; I had just had my Bar-Mitzvah, at which I made not one but two speeches, one in English and one in Hebrew; it was the year I began to smoke in secret, the year the conflicting torments of the flesh and the spirit awakened me to the problems and challenges of life.

But perhaps my fondest memory of that year is of the night when I gave what I believe was my first public musical performance. It took place in the vestry of what was then Temple Mishkan Tefila in Roxbury, a building no doubt well known to you all. I don't think people listened very hard that night to what I played on the piano: for one

With Jamie Bernstein and friend, 1953

thing, they had all just eaten a big, heavy kosher meal; and besides, what I played probably wasn't very good. But I remember my own excitement very well, because I was playing a composition of my own. It was a series of variations on a tune my father was very fond of singing in the shower, and from hearing it sung so often I had gotten to be rather fond of it myself. So I composed variations on it —one in the style of Chopin, one as Liszt might have written it, and the third like Gershwin. I've completely forgotten them now, and the music is, fortunately, lost; but I know they must have been bad, because the tune doesn't suit those composers at all.

Well, Dad, in honor of your seventieth birthday—may you have seventy more—I have composed, thirty years later, a new variation on that theme, this time in the style of myself. It is called "Meditation on a Prayerful Theme My Father Sang in the Shower Thirty Years Ago."

And I offer you this gift with all my love, and respect, and thanks for having made it possible for me to write it.   □

*Facsimile of original shooting script
(with all cuts, revisions and additions)
for CBS broadcast of the first
New York Philharmonic Young People's Concert
of the 1963–1964 season
2 November 1963*

A TRIBUTE TO TEACHERS

New York Philharmonic Young People's Concert

339th Concert — 41st Season
(Founded by Ernest Schelling in 1924)

LEONARD BERNSTEIN, *Music Director*

Saturday, November 2, 1963, at 12:00 Noon

Leonard Bernstein, *Conductor*

"A Tribute to Teachers"

MOUSSORGSKY	Prelude to "Khovantchina"
THOMPSON	Scherzo, from Symphony No. 2
PISTON	Suite from "The Incredible Flutist"
BRAHMS	*Academic Festival Overture, Opus 80

Program subject to change

*Recorded by the New York Philharmonic

Columbia Records   Steinway Piano

The telecast of today's concert will be shown on CBS Television, Channel 2, on Friday, November 29, at 7:30 p.m., sponsored by Shell Oil Company.

Mr. Bernstein plays the Baldwin Piano

THE PHILHARMONIC-SYMPHONY SOCIETY OF NEW YORK, INC.
Philharmonic Hall, Lincoln Center, Broadway at 65th St., New York 23, N. Y.
Carlos Moseley, *Managing Director*   William L. Weissel, *Assistant Manager*

OPENING

FILM (WITH SOUND EFFECTS ON TRACK)

              ANNOUNCER (V.O.)

(ON CUE)

From Philharmonic Hall in Lincoln Center,

home of the world's greatest musical

events, the Shell Oil Company brings you

the NEW YORK PHILHARMONIC YOUNG PEOPLE'S

CONCERTS under the musical direction of

Leonard Bernstein.

CUT TO LIVE (ORCHESTRA TUNING)

(BERNSTEIN ENTERS) (ON CUE)

And here is Mr. Bernstein.

(APPLAUSE)

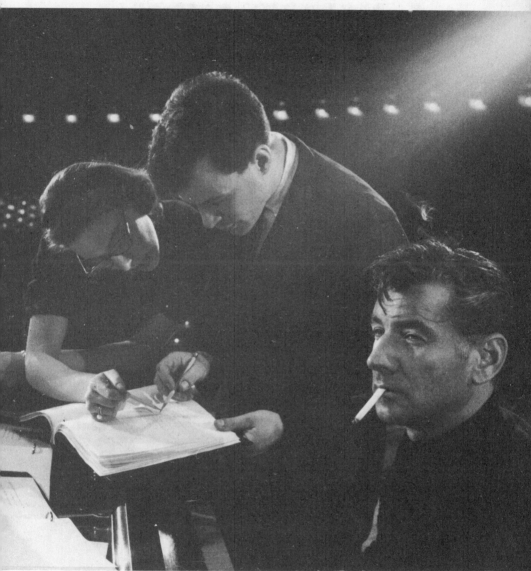

With Mary Rodgers and Roger Englander before the broadcast

BERNSTEIN

Welcome back to Phil. Hall

My dear young friends: [~~It is good to be~~
~~back with you all again for another~~
~~season of YOUNG PEOPLE'S CONCERTS here~~
~~in Philharmonic Hall.~~] You may think
it strange that I have chosen to open
this new season *of Young People's Concerts* with the subject of
teachers. After all, aren't these
programs always about music? And what
have teachers got to do with music?

The answer is: everything. We can all ~~think of painters as being completely~~
imagine a ~~self-taught~~ *painter, a self-taught writer,*
~~self-taught, and maybe some writers too,~~
but it is almost impossible to imagine
a professional musician who doesn't owe
something to one teacher or another.
The trouble is that we don't always
realize how important teachers are, in
music or in anything else. Teaching is
probably the noblest profession in the
world -- the most unselfish, difficult,
and honorable profession. *but* It is also the
most unappreciated, underrated, underpaid,
and underpraised profession in the world.

(MORE)

3

BERNSTEIN (CONT'D)

And so today we are going to praise
teachers. ~~Since we here are not in a
position to pay them higher salaries,~~ we
~~can at least pay them tribu~~te. And the
best way I can think of for me to do
this is by paying tribute to some of my
own teachers, who, over the last 30
years, or so have given me so much ~~musical~~ joy
and inspiration.

I want to begin with a teacher who is
still one of the strongest influences
in my life, even though he has already been dead
now for 12 years -- I'm referring to Serge Koussevitzky.
I am not sure how many of you young
people know that famous name, but you certainly
ought to. He was one of the greatest
conductors of all time, and for 25 years
led the magnificent Boston Symphony
Orchestra to a position where it came to be ~~was~~
known as the finest orchestra in the
world.

       (MORE)

PICTURE CARD
KOUSSEVITZKY

On top of that, he created the famous
summer school at Tanglewood, known as
The Berkshire Music Center; and it was
there, in 1940, *it's a long time ago* that I was lucky enough
to become his pupil, and eventually his
close friend. I would like to start
our music today with a tribute to his
memory. Koussevitzky was a Russian,
and he dearly loved Russian music. So
we are going to play a Russian piece
that was a great favorite of his: The
lovely, quiet prelude to Mussorgsky's
opera Khovanshchina. *Now* That's a long
name, but it's a very short piece; *which*

POSS. CUT

~~it~~ describes the sunrise on the Moscow
River: everything still and sleepy,
interrupted only by the occasional
crowing of roosters, and the booming of
bells from the Moscow steeples.) When
Koussevitzky played this music he *somehow*
managed to produce an almost magic spell,
curls around with us
which we, his students, still ~~have~~ in our
ears; and his performance remains a model
that we can strive all our lives to equal. Here
is the Prelude to Mussorgsky's opera
Khovanshchina.

2⁴⁵

MUSSORGSKY PRELUDE TO "KHOVANSHCINA" 5   SUPER TELOP *Matt card*
(ORCHESTRA)

(4:55 APPROX.)

(APPLAUSE)

BERNSTEIN

I wish you could all have heard that
beautiful little piece played by
Koussevitzky. *It was magical.* And the ~~same~~ magic, *that* he
brought to it he brought to everything
he did ~~and said~~, especially to his
teaching. He ~~got through~~ *taught* to his pupils
by simply inspiring them. He taught
everything through feeling, through
instinct and emotion. Even the purely
mechanical matter of beating time, of
conducting four beats in a bar, became
an <u>emotional</u> experience, *instead of* ~~not~~ a
mathematical one. I can *still* hear his voice
now, ~~showing me~~ *telling* how he wanted me to beat
a slow tempo of four beats, smoothly, or
as musicians say, <u>legato</u>. *He would say* "Von-end-two-
end-tri-end-four-end.... It most be
vorm, vorm like de sonn!" [Or if he
wanted, four beats played <u>staccato</u>, very
short, precise and light, he would say:
"Von-end-two-end-tri-end-four-end."] You
see, he couldn't dream of conducting four
dead beats, just lying there: 1, 2, 3, 4.

(MORE)

BERNSTEIN (CONT'D)

It was always a question of what

happened <u>between</u> the beats; how the

music moved from one beat to the next:

Von-end-two-end-tri-end-four-end...;

and the beats came to life. It became
    ^suddenly

an exciting experience just to beat time.

You see, teaching is not just a dry

business of scales and exercises; a
                            ^of etudes

great teacher is one who can light a

spark in you, the spark that sets you

on fire with enthusiasm for music, or

for whatever you ~~are~~ studying. ~~[Because~~
                 happen to be

~~it's only out of enthusiasm that~~   (POSS CUT)

~~curiosity comes; and you have to be~~

~~curious about things in order to want~~

~~to learn about them.~~ That's where real

knowledge comes from -- from the desire
         For instance,
to know. You can study the history of
              until you're blue in the face,
the Civil War ~~for a year~~, memorizing

battles and generals and dates and places;

but if you don't <u>care</u> about the Civil
                                   darn cut
War you'll wind up not knowing a ~~bloody~~

thing about it.

(MORE)

BERNSTEIN (CONT'D)

(POSS CUT)

But if you're lucky enough to have a
teacher who makes that war part of your
life, part of your country and your
~~past~~ ~~civilization, your problem and your~~
~~feelings~~ -- then you can drink in whole
gallons of dates and names and places,
and never forget them, because you
learned them out of enthusiasm, ~~out~~ of
~~the excitement of filling yourself with~~
~~new knowledge.~~) Koussevitzky was ~~such~~ *That kind*
a teacher. He lit those sparks. I
wish he were here with us today. But
we are privileged in having with us his
gracious wife, who is, in her own way,
just as inspiring as he was. ~~I wonder if Mme~~
~~Koussevitzky would grant us the pleasure~~
~~of standing up and talking to~~
~~(OLGA BOH)~~

Mme Koussevitzky, do you
remember the first piece I ever
conducted under your husband's
guidance?

(MORE)

I knew I'll never forget it, because it was the

BERNSTEIN (CONT'D)

~~The first work I ever conducted under Koussevitzky's guidance, (in fact the~~ first work I ever conducted in public at all,) ▄▄ the 2nd Symphony by Randall Thompson, the distinguished American composer who by a curious coincidence, was also one of my teachers. I had been studying orchestration with him at the Curtis Institute of music in Philadelphia; and I shall always be thankful to him for the insights he gave me into orchestration, how instruments work, blend, and combine into an orchestra. And so now I want to pay a musical tribute to Randall Thompson, ~~as well as a~~ **birthday** tribute, ~~because this season~~ he is ~~going to be 65~~ years old. We are ~~going to play~~ the 3rd movement from that same Symphony No. 2 that I conducted way back then in 1940. This movement is a wonderful sort of jazzy scherzo; and I'll never forget what a challenge it was to conduct it at the age of 21, (and it my first public concert!) -- because the rhythms in it are so tricky.

(MORE)

PICTURE CARD:
RANDALL THOMPSON

BERNSTEIN (CONT'D)

They go mostly in 7 beats to a bar,
which is unusual enough to start with.
(1 2 3, 4 5 6 7) And on top of that

Cut

basic beat, there are all kinds of
syncopations, changes and surprises, so
that the rhythm winds up pretty wild
(SING). But any of you who ever listen
to Dave Brubeck or Stan Kenton will
feel right at home in this piece; it's *tricky but*
it's great fun, and strictly American. Here
is the scherzo from Randall Thompson's
2nd Symphony.

4 15

Talk - 7
music - 13

Pt. I - 20

RANDALL THOMPSON   SYMPHONY #2   SUPER TELOP

(SCHERZO)

(ORCHESTRA)

(5:45 APPROX.)

(APPLAUSE)

COMMERCIAL

13

BERNSTEIN

You know, every grown-up can look
back and remember one or two of his
teachers with special affection;
everyone has had at least one teacher
he had a crush on, or one who suddenly
made algebra fascinating, or Egyptian
history, or whatever. But the moment
he thinks about it more deeply he is
bound to realize that there are many
more than one or two ~~now~~ who have had a
real, lasting influence on his life.

Out of all the teachers I've had in
my life -- and I'd guess roughly there
have been 60 or 70 -- there are at
least 2 dozen I would want to thank
for the excitement and inspiration they
brought me. Of course ~~we haven't time~~ I can't do that today;
~~There isn't time for anything like that today;~~ But
I would like to mention a few of the
most important ones, ~~just to give you an~~
~~idea of what I mean by a lasting~~
~~influence~~ so that I can share with
you my ~~eternal~~ deep gratitude to them.
(MORE)

BERNSTEIN (CONT'D)

PICUTRE CARD
DAVID PRALL

PICTURE CARD
EDWARD BURLINGAME
HILL

PICTURE CARD
HEINRICH GEBHARD

PICTURE CARD
ISABELLA VENGEROVA

For instance, there was the great
Professor David Prall at Harvard, who
taught me philosophy and aesthetics like
a blazing illumination; *There was* Edward
Burlingame Hill *at Harvard,* that fine American
composer, who first opened my eyes to
orchestration; Heinrich Gebhard, the
great piano teacher of Boston, who made
every lesson a ride on a magic carpet;
Isabella Vengerova -- oh, how I miss
that great lady, that adorable tyrant
who forced me to listen to myself when
I played the piano.

And so many others: Richard Stoehr,
Susan Williams -- I won't go on with this
list of names. But I'm happy to say that
some of them have been kind enough to
come here today and be with us: and
for that I feel proud and honored. ~~Here~~ *We have here*
in the hall, for example, ~~is~~ Philip Marson, who long years ago
at Boston Latin School drew back the
curtain for me on the wonders of
the English language, of poetry and
rhythm; *and* who through *his* love of words
made me fall in love with them too.

(MORE)

BERNSTEIN (CONT'D)

And here is Helen Coates, who 30 years
ago gave me my first really important
piano lessons; and who for almost 20
years has been my devoted and overworked
secretary.

And Renée Longy, who taught me the art
of reading orchestra scores at the
Curtis Institute, and shared with me
So many exciting new discoveries in modern
music.

And Tillman Merritt, whose brilliant and
original way of teaching counterpoint
and harmony I have never found equalled.
~~It always had to do with music, never
just with notes.~~ He was also my tutor
at Harvard, and I owe him a particular
debt of gratitude.

Mr. Marson, Miss Coates, *Mme.* ~~Miss~~ Longy,
Professor Merritt, would you do me the
honor of rising and accepting, in the
name of all teachers, everywhere, my
grateful tribute.

(APPLAUSE)

BERNSTEIN (CONT'D)

But Now I want to make a very special tribute
to one of the foremost composers of our
~~time and our~~ country, Walter Piston, ~~who~~ *because*

PICTURE CARD
WALTER PISTON
X
                this season *he* is celebrating his 70th
birthday. [It was Professor Piston who
made the study of so dry a subject as

cut fugue come alive for me week after
week, hour after hour.] Anyone who
has ever had the good fortune to study
                at Harvard College
with Piston, can never forget the deep
understanding of music he was able to
communicate, or the deep belly-laughter
                                    because
that went with all our classes; he is
certainly one of the wittiest minds ~~and~~
~~tongues~~ I have ever known. And in
honor of his 70th birthday, we are going
to play his most popular piece -- the
suite from his ballet The Incredible
Flutist. It's ~~a story-ballet, of~~
~~course, but~~ I'm not going to bother
you with ~~all the details.~~ *The story,*
Except to say that it's about a
circus that arrives in a

(MORE)

BERNSTEIN (CONT'D)

~~I think it's enough for you to know~~
~~that it all happens in the market place~~
~~of a~~ sleepy Spanish town, *and* that ~~everyone~~
one of the circus acts is a flute player who wakes the
~~lazily goes about his business, mostly~~ *town up*
~~dancing~~ tangos and fandangos, until
suddenly a circus arrives in town
(you'll ~~recognize that moment, I'm sure~~).
~~This circus contains, among other~~
~~things, an incredible flutist, who for~~
~~reasons I won't go into, leaves the~~
~~town a different place from the one~~
~~he found. But not before there has~~
~~been another series of delightful~~
~~dances — a minuet, a Spanish waltz,~~
~~a Sicilian dance, and a brilliant~~
~~final Polka for the whole company of~~
~~dancers. It really doesn't matter~~ why
~~all this happens~~; the music is what's
important, and it's a delight to hear.
And
~~But~~ even in this popular, gay ballet,
the brilliant technical mastery for which
Piston is famous shows through in
every note.

(MORE)

Well anyway,
Everybody dance
tangos, fandangos,
minuets & Spanish
waltzes & polkas.
And what not, but it really
doesnt matter
why.

BERNSTEIN (CONT'D)

Now here is Walter Piston's Ballet-Suite
<u>The Incredible Flutist</u>, which we are
playing as a birthday tribute to a
marvelous composer, a lovable man,
and an inspired teacher.

19

WALTER PISTON   "THE INCREDIBLE FLUTIST"   SUPER TELOP
(BALLET SUITE)
(ORCHESTRA)
(16:00 APPROX.)

That really is an incredible flute player, isn't it?

I have saved for last my greatest living

teacher, also probably the greatest

~~living~~ conductor in the world today --

PICTURE CARD:
FRITZ REINER

Fritz Reiner, who next month will be

celebrating his 75th birthday. For some

reason or other, all my teachers seem

to be having ~~special~~ *Round-number* birthdays this

season; and I wish them all long life.

But what can I say to this supreme

master of the baton, Fritz Reiner, who

gave me my first baby-lessons in

conducting? That a maestro of his

standing and distinction should have

spent tireless hours on a green, callow,

21-year-old boy who had never thought

of conducting before, and done it with

all his energy and heart -- it is almost

unthinkable. But he did just that --

because he is a great teacher, one of

the greatest I have ever known.

(MORE)

Reiner didn't use

BERNSTEIN (CONT'D)

~~His was never~~ the Inspirational Method

in particular

of Koussevitzky; ᶺthere were no poetic

of things like that

speeches about the **warm** sun; thereᶺ

was only hard work, impossibly high

standards of knowledge, and the

all-important law of economy; don't

waste a motion or a gesture; every

movement must be concentrated on getting

the orchestra to produce the sound

Things

you ~~want-ing the sound~~ the composer

~~wants.~~ *wanted,*

And so I want to pay my musical tribute

to Dr. Reiner by playing for him, and

for you, The Academic Festival Overture

by Brahms. ~~For two reasons: first,~~

~~because it is the first piece I think of~~

~~when I think of Reiner. I shall never~~

~~forget that first time we met, when I~~

~~came to Philadelphia to audition for his~~

~~conducting class.~~

(MORE)

Cut !

22

BERNSTEIN (CONT'D)

I was shaking with fright -- I had
never conducted before, or, as I said,
never even thought of being a conductor,
And what's more, I had a horrible case
of hay fever; I was coughing and
sneezing, and I could barely see out of
my eyes. And there stood this stern-
looking man, who peered at me over his
glasses and said "So you want to be a
conductor!" At that moment I really
wasn't sure if I did want to be. Dr.
Reiner then led me to the piano, where a
huge orchestral score lay open to the
middle pages. "Do you know that piece?"
he asked. I stared at the forest of
black notes and I admitted that I
didn't. "Hm," he said; "Do you think
you can play it on the piano?" I
shivered and said I'd try. I was lucky;
some heavenly fire took hold of me,
opened my hayfeverish eyes, and I played
it like a maniac. Suddenly I realized
I was playing a tune -- a folk-song --
that we had sung in grammar school years
ago:
                    (MORE)

Cut !

25

BERNSTEIN (CONT'D)

(SING)   What clatters on the roof
         With quick impatient hoof?
         I think it must be Santa
         Claus,
         Dear old Santa Claus,
         He's in his golden sleigh.

         I wonder what he'll bring!
         What bags of pretty things...

Something like that. And then something
clicked in my mind, and I remembered
hearing this piece on the radio many
years after grammar school, recognizing
the old tune, and hearing the announcer
say:
"That was the Academic Festival Overture
by Brahms." And so now, on that fateful
occasion, I was able to turn to Dr.
Reiner and say: "Of course I know this
piece. It's the Academic Festival
Overture by Brahms." And I was
accepted into his class.

                (MORE)

~~ALTERNATE VERSION — IF MONILO — IS CUT:~~

I have two reasons for choosing this
piece: one because it was with this
overture that I first auditioned
for Reiner, when I was trying to get accepted into his
conducting class at the Curtis Institute.
And so I always think of The Academic
Festival Overture whenever I think of
Reiner.

But the seond reason is more important.

(CONTINUE P. 23(new) LAST PARAGRAPH,
    "You see,.....)

BERNSTEIN (CONT'D)

I've loved ~~that~~ overture ever since.
Of course, now, years later, I know that
my little school-song about Santa Claus
is really an old German folk-song, that
every German student has known and sung
for 200 years:

(SING A BIT IN GERMAN)

And that brings us to the second and
main reason, ~~for choosing this piece.~~

You see, Brahms wrote this overture in
honor of a school -- the University of
Breslau, in Germany; and he even put
into it four famous University student songs --
all old favorites of the University
students, + I'm sure they'll all sound familiar to you too ~~as a way of honoring them~~
So the Academic Festival overture is
really a tribute to learning,
to students and to teachers, & to schools everywhere. And it is
in that spirit that we play it now;
to honor not only Fritz Reiner, but
all the great teachers on earth who
work so hard to give young people a world
that is a better, richer, and more
civilized place.

(MORE)

SUPER TELOP   BRAHMS   ACADEMIC FESTIVAL OVERTURE

                               (ORCHESTRA)

                               (10:05)

                               (APPLAUSE)

ANNOUNCER (V.O.)

From Philharmonic Hall in Lincoln
Center--another NEW YORK PHILHARMONIC
YOUNG PEOPLE'S CONCERT under the
musical direction of Leonard Bernstein
has been presented by the Shell Oil
Company.

This first program of the season was
titled "A Tribute to Teachers" and
featured works by Modeste Mussorgsky,
Randall Thompson, Walter Piston and
Johannes Brahms. The next in the Young
People's series will take place in four
weeks, on Monday December 23, at which
time Mr. Bernstein will present "Young
Performers."

The preceding program was prerecorded
and was produced and directed by
Roger Englander.

Starting Sunday afternoon, January 19,
Shell's "Wonderful World of Golf" returns
to the air featuring the world's
leading golfers playing the world's most
beautiful and difficult courses.

REVISED

NEW YORK PHILHARMONIC YOUNG PEOPLE'S CONCERTS #1

7TH SEASON   1963-64

WITH   *LB Final*

LEONARD BERNSTEIN

"A TRIBUTE TO TEACHERS"

Tape Date: Saturday, November 2, 1963
                      12:00 Noon to 1:00 p.m.

Air Date: Friday, November 29, 1963
                      7:30 p.m. to 8:30 p.m.

Originations: VTR Remote from Philharmonic Hall
                      Lincoln Center, New York City

PRODUCED AND DIRECTED BY: Roger Englander

WRITTEN BY: Leonard Bernstein

ASSISTANTS TO THE PRODUCER: Mary Rodgers
                              Elizabeth Finkler

PRODUCTION ASSISTANT: Robert Livingston

With members of the audience after the performance

With Serge Koussevitzky in New York City, 1949

Speech delivered at the
Plaza Hotel, New York City
23 May 1963

VARÈSE, KOUSSEVITZKY, AND NEW MUSIC

My dear friends:

Tonight we are paying homage to this memorable, extraordinary man Edgar Varèse, who has just spoken to us out of the rugged prime of his seventy-eight years. But at this ceremony we are also, inevitably, paying homage to another, utterly unique man, Serge Koussevitzky, who is as much with us tonight, in our hearts and words and motives, as if he were actually seated at this table. Without his vision, his stubborn insistence, his clarity of purpose, we would not be gathered here at all. It was in the shadow of his wing, in the glow of his radiance, that so many of us here came to know and love one another. It was at his feet that we learned contemporary music—more than that, that we learned to regard contemporary music as an indispensable part of symphonic life. He was the great educator, the founder of Tanglewood, of the Koussevitzky Music Foundation, of this International Music Fund. And through it all, he taught us one elemental and indestructible lesson: *The composer comes first.* In the beginning was the Note, and the Note was with God; and whosoever can reach for that Note, reach high, and bring it back to us on earth, to our earthly ears—he is a *composer,* and to the extent of his reach, partakes of the divine. This reach, this leap, aspiration, thrust—this is what Koussevitzky held most sacred; and he put all his vitality and concentration into serving it as well as he could. This meant not only conducting music, but teaching others to conduct it with the same blinding devotion; teaching the public to listen; and encouraging composers to reach high at every opportunity. He published new works, commissioned new works, and most important, *played* new works, with the same intensity, care, and beauty he lavished on the established repertoire.

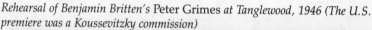

Rehearsal of Benjamin Britten's Peter Grimes *at Tanglewood, 1946 (The U.S. premiere was a Koussevitzky commission)*

Serge Koussevitzky knew that the supply–demand ratio had changed radically in the century following the death of Beethoven. He knew, as if by the sniff of animal instinct, that the concert hall was in danger of becoming a museum, a treasure-house of the past. And to maintain a healthy balance, he knew that there had to be constant prodding and priming, as in any free economy. He knew that modern audiences, left to their own devices, would never insist on hearing new music; they had to be taught to expect it, to regard it as natural, even to *demand* it. And so every Koussevitzky performance was just as much a gala, an event of celebration, for Copland and Schuman, for Bartok and Prokofiev, as it was for Mozart and Tchaikovsky. The composer came first.

Now, I must tell you that it's not so easy for a conductor to have this noble attitude; after all, a conductor is automatically a narcissist, like any other performing artist; he is an exhibitionist by profession—why else would he be a performer at all? He has a built-in suction pump attached to his ego, and no torrent of praise is big enough to slake his thirst. This, of course, is a highly generalized statement; and it is true that in a certain sense Koussevitzky was no exception. He had his share of vanity too, like all of us. I remember that when we were his students, twenty-odd years ago, at Tanglewood, we used to hear malicious rumors that he possessed upwards of ninety pairs of shoes! He liked to dress well, and look well; he did not disdain compliments in the greenroom. *But*—and this is a mighty conjunction—all of this was marshaled and harnessed to be at the service of music. He was simply taking all possible pains to make of himself the finest vessel for the composer's thought, the perfect instrumental link between composer and audience. You see, motive is everything. The difference lies between the conductor who is vain on his own behalf, and the conductor whose ego glories in the reflected radiance of musical creativity. Both conductors may appear to be narcissistic, but their motives are so different as to be exactly opposite. There is a simple test for this that anyone can try: ask a conductor about the sound of his orchestra—what distinguishes it from all others, what is its unique quality? If he answers anything at all

Leonard Bernstein

about *his* sound, or *its* sound, or attributes any special so-
nority to his orchestra, then you know he has base motives:
he is putting himself before the composer. Koussevitzky
could be justly proud of the glorious noises that came out
of the Boston Symphony during his regime; but he was
even prouder of the fact that those noises changed in quality from one composer to another, from one style or nationality or epoch to another. That is a true manifestation of
humble service, ego pumps to the contrary.

I bring all this up only to point out that it is not common,
or natural, or easy, for a conductor to be a devoted servant;
and it is all the more remarkable, then, to understand the
extent of Koussevitzky's humility, once we know these flagrant conductorial truths. If one had asked him, in a given

With, among others, Aaron Copland, Serge Koussevitzky, Roger Englander,
Seymour Lipkin, and Lukas Foss at Tanglewood, 1946

season, which mattered more to him, conducting his first performance of Harris' *Third Symphony* or his hundredth performance of Beethoven's *Ninth*, I don't think there'd be any doubt about his answer.

Now, exactly two weeks from tonight, it will have been twelve years since Serge Koussevitzky died. And in those dozen years, something has happened to modern music that even he may not have foreseen. There is a crisis in modern music, such as never before existed. Young composers are swayed one way and another, uncertain of their own terms. The paradox of music's being written for a public that moves further and further away from it has become so explicit as to constitute an anomaly. Can the twelve-tone system have come and gone so quickly? Is Darmstadt already passé, as Hans Werner Henze said to me last week? Is this world of NATO and Birmingham and the *Faith-7* a world in which a composer is forbidden to write a melody? Does anyone care anymore—really care—if any one of us here ever writes another note? You see, our crisis *is* different from the historical precedents: it is concerned with human expressivity, the mirroring of our inner lives in music. Are we still living in a world where an octave leap upward implies a sense of yearning, or reaching? Or is it become only an intervallic symbol? Do we still base our forms on the concept of struggle and resolution, or are we now condemned to reveal ourselves as forever unresolved?

These are only a few of the questions that rack the composer's soul today; our experimentation has acquired a sort of desperate quality, and we don't know many answers. But that is *precisely* the wrong reason—and this would be the wrongest possible time—to abandon the modern composer. Now, if ever, he needs all the encouragement he can get: stimulation, interest, commissions, performances. And the first one to realize this, to raise his voice, and to act, would be Serge Koussevitzky. God, how we need him; how we miss him. But we have his spirit with us; and we continue his work as best we can. The creation of this International Recording Award is one way, and a significant way, because it is not just a prize, or a token of esteem; it is a practical and pragmatic way of honoring a composer, and at the same time of disseminating his music, via score and disc, to the far corners of the world.

The *first* work to have been singled out and recorded under the auspices of the Fund was by our honored guest, Edgar Varèse—an extraordinary work titled *Arcana*. With all the mysticism that that name implies, I find that the strongest quality of the music is its defiance, its uncompromisingly rugged individualism. Varèse has said that what he deplores most in the world is mediocrity; and in his fiercely independent way, he has tried in *Arcana*—as in all his music—to reach out and up, with that *thrust* I spoke of earlier, to catch a star—to raise himself and his hearers above that mediocre level. I can't think of a better way to describe Varèse, or pay homage to him, than to play some of this *Arcana* for you; I wish I had that huge orchestra here, and could play it for you live; but I don't, and so you are now going to hear the last four minutes or so of the work as conducted by Robert Craft on the very recording the American International Music Fund has caused to be made.

And now, as you listen to these last minutes of the music, it may be rewarding to bear in mind the six-line epigraph, or motto, which Varèse has placed at the beginning of his score. The words are from the mystic astronomical writings of Paracelsus, the sixteenth-century scientist:

> *One star exists higher than all the rest.*
> *This is the Apocalyptic star.*
> *The second star is that of the ascendant.*
> *The third is that of the elements,*
> *Of which there are four;*
> *So that six stars are established.*
> *Besides these there is yet another star,*
> *Imagination,*
> *Which gives birth to new stars,*
> *And a new heaven.*

Now here is the music.   □

Washington, D.C., 1961

Speech made at United Jewish Appeal benefit
Madison Square Garden
25 November 1963

TRIBUTE
TO JOHN F. KENNEDY

My dear friends:

Last night the New York Philharmonic and I performed Mahler's *Second Symphony*—"The Resurrection"—in tribute to the memory of our beloved late President. There were those who asked: Why the "Resurrection" Symphony, with its visionary concept of hope and triumph over worldly pain, instead of a Requiem, or the customary Funeral March from the "Eroica"? Why indeed? We played the Mahler symphony not only in terms of resurrection for the soul of one we love, but also for the resurrection of hope in all of us who mourn him. In spite of our shock, our shame, and our despair at the diminution of man that follows from this death, we must somehow gather strength for the increase of man, strength to go on striving for those goals he cherished. In mourning him, we must be worthy of him.

I know of no musician in this country who did not love John F. Kennedy. American artists have for three years looked to the White House with unaccustomed confidence and warmth. We loved him for the honor in which he held art, in which he held every creative impulse of the human mind, whether it was expressed in words, or notes, or paints, or mathematical symbols. This reverence for the life of the mind was apparent even in his last speech, which he was to have made a few hours after his death. He was to have said: "America's leadership must be guided by learning and reason." Learning and reason: precisely the two elements that were necessarily missing from the mind of anyone who could have fired that impossible bullet. Learning and reason: the two basic precepts of all Judaistic tradition, the twin sources from which every Jewish mind from Abraham and Moses to Freud and Einstein has drawn its living power. Learning and Reason: the motto we here tonight must continue to uphold with redoubled tenacity, and must continue, at any price, to make the basis of all our actions.

It is obvious that the grievous nature of our loss is immensely aggravated by the element of violence involved in it. And where does this violence spring from? From ignorance and hatred—the exact antonyms of Learning and Reason. Learning and Reason: those two words of John Kennedy's were not uttered in time to save his own life; but every man can pick them up where they fell, and make them part of himself, the seed of that rational intelligence without which our world can no longer survive. This must become the mission of every artist, of every Jew, and of every man of goodwill: to insist, unflaggingly, at the risk of becoming a repetitive bore, but to insist on the achievement of a world in which the mind will have triumphed over violence.

To the beloved memory of John F. Kennedy

Kaddish
Symphony No.3

Leonard Bernstein

I
Invocation

*Chorus humming, sustained notes *ad lib.*, chosen arbitrarily by singers in low registers:

We musicians, like everyone else, are numb with sorrow at this murder, and with rage at the senselessness of the crime. But this sorrow and rage will not inflame us to seek retribution; rather they will inflame our art. Our music will never again be quite the same. This will be our reply to violence: to make music more intensely, more beautifully, more devotedly than ever before. And with each note we will honor the spirit of John Kennedy, commemorate his courage, and reaffirm his faith in the Triumph of the Mind. ☐

IMAGE OF CHILE

Mr. Secretary, Ambassador Gutiérrez, distinguished guests, and dear friends:

I am afraid that I stand here tonight in a rather oblique relationship to you all: my formal connection with the Image of Chile is a purely marital one. It is a curious experience for me to appear as a speaker-in-law, so to speak; but I do it warmly and willingly, because my affections for Chile have gone far beyond the confines of mere husbandly interest. Chile is a country that you love, that you cannot help loving, wife or no wife. Have you ever met a traveler returning from Chile who was less than in love with it? I haven't. There is a special charm in that country, and in its people—a mixture of Old World civility and New World freshness; a vitality born of that life-giving air and climate, together with the gentleness and peacefulness of a people snuggled into a sweet strip of earth between the Andes and the Pacific. It is a country wonderfully alive without being hectic; and that is a magic formula we *norteamericanos* may well envy.

The first direct news of Chile I can remember came from my friend Aaron Copland, our leading American composer, who in 1942 made a tour for the State Department of the principal countries of South and Central America—with an eye, of course, on what was happening musically in those parts. I will always remember the enthusiasm with which he returned: his excitement at finding new, younger composers like Blás Galindo and Pablo Moncayo in Mexico, Guarnieri in Brazil, Juan Orrego Salas in Chile, Hector Tosar in Uruguay—of course, that was more than twenty years ago, and there have been many new names in the meantime. But way back then those were almost like names from Mars; and when Mr. Copland subsequently brought a good many of these young composers to study at Tangle-

*With Felicia Montealegre Bernstein on South American
tour with the New York Philharmonic, 1958*

Chile, 1958

wood, where I too was working, one had the feeling at first of meeting Martians, who upon closer acquaintance turned out to be real, live, gifted, dedicated musicians, not very different from our own. Copland also brought back stirring tales of a frontier culture: of Indians playing Schoenberg; of German refugees playing Indian drums; of disappearing colonial social structures; of new nationalistic impulses. But what I recall most vividly of all his reports was his impression of Chile—warm, vital, *simpático*—so far away geographically, and so near to us in spirit and in humor.

My next brush with Chile occurred some four years later when I met Felicia Montealegre, who became my wife. In her I met that same warmth, vitality, *simpatía*; and through meeting her family and friends I began to be able to see and feel for myself the very special quality of that country.

But it wasn't until 1958 that I was finally privileged to *go* there. In that year the New York Philharmonic and I made an extensive tour—also under the sponsorship of the State Department—of every country in South America plus Panama and Mexico. It turned out to be one of the happiest and most exciting trips of my life, especially when I discovered the power of music in establishing friendships and lasting relationships on the widest basis. I am not speaking idly, or boastfully, or simply as a musician, but as a citizen of the United States, of the Americas, and, I hope, of the world. That tour happened to coincide with another South American tour which was being made by our then Vice President; and the coincidence yielded some striking observations, especially when the Nixon tour and the Philharmonic tour happened to intersect in Quito, Ecuador, where we exchanged notes. I reported to the Vice President tumultuous receptions; record crowds; cheering, stamping audiences; kisses; roses; embraces; while he reported to me the unpleasant, distasteful incidents of Caracas, Lima, and other places. Where *did* the difference lie? After all, we were both Americans, both on goodwill missions, and both vulnerable to the same demonstrations of anti-Yankee feelings, whether Communist-inspired or not. Where did the difference lie? In music: in the exchange of the deepest feelings and revelations of which man is capable—those of art. We had music on our side. In other words, if we are really serious about communicating with one another, about knowing ourselves through our neighbors—in short, about peaceful civilization—then we can never overestimate the good that comes from artistic communication. When we touch one another through music, we are touching the heart, the mind, and the spirit, all at once.

As you can see, our State Department has been aware of this truth for a long time, and has stood behind such tours as those I have mentioned by Copland, the Philharmonic, and others. But it has still not been enough; it can never be enough. And of late there has been something of a falling-off in this area, to say nothing of the paucity of artistic visits in the other direction—from South to North America. That is why this Image of Chile convocation is so important and necessary. There should be many more like it. I cannot stress strongly enough the need for constant artistic interchange—constant, not *de vez en cuando*. The cries of budgetary strictures are really not to be taken that seriously: if I am not mistaken, our entire tour of South America cost the State Department a great deal less than it costs to make one wing of an obsolescent bomber, and it accomplished a good deal more, if I may say so, in the matter of international understanding. Mrs. Rusk, please do persuade the Secretary of State to send us back to Chile! Apart from anything else, I long to sit again in a little room on the outskirts of Santiago and listen to the magical folk singing of Violeta Parra. I have always been a folk-music fan, ever since I can remember—any kind: Hindu, Swahili, hillbilly. But I must say I have never felt so close to a newly discovered folk music as I did to those heartbreaking *Saludas* and *Parabienes* that poured out of Parra's mouth and soul. I only wish she too could be here for this Image of Chile.

I had not meant to get so seriously involved in this subject tonight; after all, I am only a speaker-in-law, and I intend to leave the bulk of speaking to my dear wife, who will speak far more beautiful words than I can. But when I come near to this subject of cultural exchange, I can't help becoming a bit polemical; and I can't resist pressing home this one point: The future of our world is obviously an international one—or else it is a bleak future indeed. We have got to continue to know our neighbors better and better; the time of complacent isolation is over; and national boundaries must become, increasingly, purely geographical symbols. The road to peace is the road to universality; and this road is fed into by all kinds of smaller byways and avenues that come from self-knowledge, and knowledge of our immediate neighbors, growing into broad highways that lead to all parts of the world. But we must begin with ourselves; we must be exposed to images of all kinds—how interesting it would be now to have an "Image of Alabama," for instance!—and go from there to the great original concept of America—North, South, and Central, all together. History is rushing by; and self-knowledge has now become a hemispherical matter, at the very least.

I was startled into a reminder of this concept the other day while I was in the process of solving one of those tricky British crossword puzzles—in *The Manchester Guardian*, I think it was. The clue read: "Italian city starting in America"—answer in seven letters. After much brain-racking, I discovered the answer to be "Perugia": of course—an Italian city starting with "Peru." But is Peru in America? Of course it is! Only we North Americans still don't think big enough to accept that natural concept. And we must begin to think that way soon, before it's too late. This presentation of Chilean art and thought is a significant step in that direction; and I congratulate all of you who have helped it to come to be, and hope that it will achieve everything you expect of it—especially those deep, warm ties that arise from artistic communion, and that lead to a fruitful, peaceful life on this earth.

Thank you.   □

Two pieces for Marc Blitzstein:
"Reminiscences," a speech given for a memorial concert
2 April 1964
and "Letter to Marc,"
published by the National Institute of Arts and Letters
December, 1964

TRIBUTE TO MARC BLITZSTEIN

Reminiscences are at best difficult; precision of recall always suffers at the hands of subjectivity. Worse still is the unfortunate human tendency to lump our images of people together into labeled categories. This has never been more obvious to me than in these months after Marc Blitzstein's death. In "remembering" him with others who knew and admired him, I have found myself shocked more than once by the easy way in which people had consigned him to the file marked Urban, Radical, Bohemian, Angry—whatever. This is sheer laziness of mind. To whatever degree these

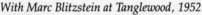

With Marc Blitzstein at Tanglewood, 1952

appellations were true, they do everything but describe the man I knew. My most vivid images of Marc are all connected with nature: by the sea, in the woods, on a boat, in the sun, in the snow. Marc swam as devotedly as he composed, and with equal discipline. He rose with the sun, swam before his spartan breakfast, was continually escaping from New York.

My earliest memory of him is in Cambridge, Massachusetts, where he had come to see my production of *The Cradle Will Rock* at Harvard in 1939. I met his plane in East Boston —it was still rather daring to fly then!—and I was amazed at the slightness of this man I had imagined, through his music, to be a giant. He attended our dress rehearsal that morning, and then we walked, all afternoon, by the Charles River. Now that image leaps up in my mind: Marc lying on the banks of the Charles, talking, bequeathing to me his knowledge, insight, warmth—endlessly, with endless strength drawn, like that of Antaeus, from his contact with the earth. And gradually he became a giant again; and so he continued to be whenever he touched earth, sea, woods, snow. That was the secret of the giant who had written those notes which seduced my soul, those thousands of special, mysterious notes that can never be forgotten.

Santiago, Chile
23 December 1964

Dear Marc:

For almost a year now they have been telling me you are dead. And now the National Institute asks me to write a commemorative tribute. It is macabre. All right, we'll play it through, like one of our gallows jokes. And anyway, I'm always glad to write you a tribute.

Gallantry, vitality. Wry, Talmudic humor. A fresh, slanted view of everything. A secret affair with wordnotes. Loyalties of improbable intensity, in unlikely places. Endless affection, grace. Endless capacity to suffer through quarrel, to find truth, or if not, to invent it. All these have been yours.

With Marc Blitzstein, Shirley Bernstein, Burton Bernstein, Jennie Bernstein and students at Tanglewood, 1952

But mostly, survival. I have always thought of you as the chief survivor—of the welts of passion, the agony of commitment, of a long chain of beautiful work-failures. Never have I seen such glowing failures, all in a row, like falling (but not fallen) angels. You have rushed, singing but orderly, from one failure to another: another, another; always singing. How does one write a commemorative tribute to a survivor?

Dear Marc, they are asking me to finish your uncompleted works. (They say you are dead.) The *Sacco* opera is only half-composed, and full of unresolved choices. Who can guess at how you would have resolved them? Then there's *Idiots First*; that is almost finished. A short scene to be written here and there, ten bars of accompaniment missing here, twelve bars there. It could be done, they tell me. Done? With what notes? Only yours, your own private and mysterious notes. Neither I nor anyone I know has access to your luminous caves where those word-notes are forged. Come back from Martinique, come soon, and make more falling angels. They will look lovely in descending flight, like the sea gulls we used to watch those summers on the Vineyard. Come back, and we'll play mental Jotto in five languages. It's winter here now, and you have that fine cold-weather suit with the six-button vest. Your god-daughter Jamie is twelve years old now; and little Nina is named for your heroine.

Come back. Those unfinished manuscripts of yours stare at me grimly, melodramatically, reminding me of the technique you so often used of ending a scene or a song without a flourish—no compromise, flat, just like that: with an empty bar. Challenge. But so many empty bars make the challenge absurd.

We all send our dearest love. Everyone misses you terribly—Lillian, Morris, Minna, Felicia. I don't think any of them believes you are dead either; we are all waiting for you to write and say you are coming home.

Lenny □

Speech given at
Brandeis Creative Arts Award Dinner
New York City
26 May 1964

ON MOTIVATION

Less than a week ago I was sitting in attendance at the Spring Award Ceremonies of The American Institute of Arts and Letters here in New York.

As you know, this is the season for awards: these warm days, the academic and artistic honors fly about us like spring pollens. Someday soon we ought to get sensible and change the honor season to something nice and chilly, like December; receiving honors as you swelter beneath academic robes and mortarboards is more like torture than honor.

In any case, at that distinguished occasion last week there was a curious moment during one of the citations. A young composer, sitting on my left, but unknown to me, was receiving a grant; and as he rose to receive it, and bask in the glory of his citation—which was very fancy gibberish —I heard, among a welter of extraordinary phrases, this one: "a composer of deeply motivated music." This positively riveted me; and so while the young man was gone to collect his check, I asked the fellow Institute member on my right what she thought "motivated music" might be. She had no idea, and asked the gentleman to *her* right; and so it went down to the end of our row and back to me, with no answers forthcoming, except some snickering witticisms, which I won't go into.

Needless to say, this trivial incident produced a fat intellectual discussion during the postceremonial drink period; and several giants of the Institute, *and* the Academy, like Truman Capote, and Louis Kronenberger, put their heads together over the martini glasses to decide what motivates music or, for that matter, any art at all. The young composer himself rather waspishly said that his motivation was money—which is understandable from a man with a new check in his hand. And there is a certain truth in it: money is a perfectly valid motivation for art, as much as we'd like *not* to think so; but since it's also the chief motivation for selling shoes, or Buicks, or chewing gum, it doesn't quite explain what motivates *art* in particular. The same might be said for the other low-down motivating forces, like success, fame, popularity, adulation, and the rest; they are all, undeniably, motivations for the artist, for all artists; but insofar as these ideals also motivate Senators, Beatles, and fan dancers, one cannot say that they are uniquely motivations for art—that useless, most unsenatorial endeavor called Art.

Of course, our discussion at the Institute inevitably settled for clichés; *communication* and *self-expression* were voted the two *real* motivations of the artist; every creator *is* one because he must express himself and, what's more, must share that expression with mankind. These may be platitudes, and they may also be true, as far as they go. But whether true or not, they do not explain that devil with a pitchfork who goads an artist into doing dangerous, unpopular, and unpredictable works. What about Carl Ruggles, whom we are honoring here tonight? None of the motivations I have named could possibly apply to him: his music never earned him a penny, or formed him a fan club; he has never been able to walk into Maxim's in Paris as the band greeted him with his latest hit tune. As for self-expression, that may well be; but as for communication, his music is rarely, if ever, played. Then with whom is he communicating, to whom expressing himself?

Ah, there's the mystery. And in these days of explaining mysteries, these days when Dr. Kubie can explain the creative process by simply invoking the word *preconscious*—

With Yehudi Menuhin, André Previn, and Mstislav Rostropovich at Wolftrap, 1978

when the duration of our planet can be estimated by the rate of expansion of the universe—please, God, leave us this one mystery, unsolved: why man creates. The minute that one is solved, I fear art will cease to be. And in that artless and unmysterious world, I would also preferably cease to be.

There aren't too many mysteries left, you know; one of these days some superbrain is going to come up with a brilliant revelation of original cause; DNA, or whatever it is, is going to explain heredity; and XYZ will remove the last veil from the chemical wonder of sexual attraction. And then what will we be left with? Man and his mystery—the mindless, useless, glorious pursuit of artistic truth. And all, hopefully, without a shred of motivation.

All right, you say: Carl Ruggles—that's an exception, an old-time rugged individualist. Well, then, consider a really commercial artist—a theatrical producer. Who could be more motivated than a theatrical producer, more corrupted by the need to succeed, to make money, to achieve the most material gain? And yet, here sits Cheryl Crawford: now, just try to explain her incredible record of courageous flops. Why? Motivated by what? That, thank Heaven, is still a glorious mystery; and it is a mystery that enshrouds every good artist I know, rich or poor, successful or not, old or young. They write, they paint, they perform, produce, whatever, because life to them is inconceivable without doing so. And it is for that mad compulsion, that unmotivated persistence, that divine drive—it is for that that we are honoring these seven artists here tonight. I ask you now to join me in paying tribute to them, and through them to all artists everywhere. They may yet save the world.

Leonard Bernstein

The New York Times
Sunday, 24 October 1965

WHAT I THOUGHT . . .

The great benefit of a sabbatical year is not so much that it affords a rest from one's labors as that it provides the glorious luxury of time to meditate—off-schedule, at ease, and without fixed limits. This fact leads people to expect someone who is just emerging from a sabbatical to reappear newly wise—overflowing with insights, reappraisals, and majestic philosophical conclusions. These I do not have handy.

The one conclusion I have reached after a year's mulling is simply the ancient cliché that the certainty of one's knowledge decreases in proportion to thought and experience. The moment you have time to intellectualize your perceptions, established certainties will begin to crumble, and the "other side" of any controversy will beckon appealingly. The inevitable result is that one's liberalism becomes stretched to the point of absurdity. It is a Hamlet-like torture to be truly liberal; everything becomes susceptible to contradictory interpretations; bias is impossible, opinion wobbly, and immortal words are out of the question.

It is in this context that I have been thinking all year about music, especially about the present crisis in composition and its possible consequence in the near future. What has happened to symphonic forms? Are symphonies a thing of the past? What will become of the symphony orchestra? Is tonality dead forever? Is the international community of composers really, deeply ready to accept that death? If so, will the music-loving public concur? Are the new staggering complexities of music vital to it, or do they simply constitute pretty *Papiermusik*?

Having mulled these questions for a year or more, with open-mindedness *ad absurdum*, I naturally cannot provide a single answer. Or, to be more accurate, I can provide far too many answers, all of them possibly true. For each ques-

With his family, ca. 1967

tion there are two answers, roughly corresponding to Yes
and No, and attended by innumerable variations.

For example, does that mean that symphonies can no
longer be created? No; in a loose sense, the word "symphony" can be applied to all kinds of structures. On the
other hand, Yes; in a strict sense, the decline of the symphony can perceivably be dated back to the beginning of
our century, and the last "great" symphony I can think of
is Stravinsky's in 1945.

Then if the symphony as a form is all but over, what will
happen to our orchestras? Will they become museums of
the past, with conductors as curators, who hang up the old
masterpieces with solicitude as to position and lighting?
Yes, inevitably, since our orchestras were created specifically to perform these masterpieces. But also No; there can

conceivably be any number of new forms of composition which could gradually and subtly change the shape and content of our orchestras. No, yes; no, yes; yes, no. What is really true?

If I may be pardoned for a quasi-existential paradox, I suggest that the answer is in the questioning. By experimenting with the problem, by feeling it out, by living with it, we are answered. All our lives are spent in the attempt to resolve conflicts; and we know that resolutions are impossible except by hindsight. We can make temporary decisions (and do, a thousand times a day); but it is only after death that it can be finally perceived whether we ever succeeded in resolving our conflicts. This is patent, since as long as we live we continue the attempt to resolve them. That attempt is the very action of living. So, in the case of the symphony problem, we are attempting to solve it by instituting a two-year Philharmonic survey on the subject of the symphony in the twentieth century. I don't pretend that at the end of two seasons we shall have a pat answer; but we will have answered the questions by having asked them *in music,* by having experienced the survey itself.

I suddenly realize that these remarks are in danger of sounding like sophistry. I hope not; I have never meant anything more solemnly. Let me try an analogy: how should one read a palindrome? The fact that it *is* a palindrome tempts you to read it backward; but don't forget that you have already read it forward: A MAN, A PLAN, A CANAL—PANAMA! The essence of it, the whole point of it, is that it can be read both ways. And not only can, but should, and must, if its meaning is to exist.

Still sophistic? Think of a great novel—*Billy Budd,* for instance. We are presented with two heroes, two stories, really depending on how you read Melville's symbolism. Melville himself remains impartial, and does not cue you on how to read it, so the sought-for resolution turns out to be the tragedy itself. The ending is a sublime catharsis, but it is not a resolution, since the pain of the conflict remains with us, unassuaged. The same goes for *The Brothers Karamazov, King Lear*, Brahms's *Fourth*. A work of art does not answer questions: it provokes them; and its essential meaning is in the tension between their contradictory answers.

With Lukas Foss, 1977

This kind of dialectical thinking is certainly not new; what may be new is applying it to contemporary musical matters, which suffer generally from overopinionatedness. Consider the avant-garde, with its short-lived fads and in-groups, its chic efficiency, its cavalier attitude toward communication with a public. One is tempted to settle for a firm No; but with extra time to think and spend with the scores, one is bowled over by the phenomenon of Boulez, or by the incredible imagination of Lukas Foss. The No turns to Yes overnight; yet both answers have been objectively arrived at. This is not merely a matter of distinguishing talent from the mass of new composers; it is a question of resolving the riddle of the existence of these two geniuses in a specious musical moment. And the riddle is its own answer: their struggle is tomorrow's history book.

Of course I, personally, have an added dialectical problem: as a conductor I am fascinated by, and wide open to, every new sound-image that comes along; but as a composer I am committed to tonality. Here is a conflict indeed; and my attempt to resolve it is, quite literally, my most profound musical experience. And if this sounds far too existential for an old romantic like me, well and good: I am ready to switch and consider the teleological approach, and wrestle with that. Another synthesis to be sought.

Such is the pass to which my sabbatical year has brought me. I have two answers to everything and one answer to nothing. And this lovely absurdity extends finally to writing this very report. And the choice between lies is the question "Which one is true?"—to which there is no single answer.

. . . AND WHAT I DID

In glad compliance with your request,
O New York Times, that I testify
On my late sabbatical (dubious rest!)
And the fruits thereof, I now comply.
But why in verse? I do not know.
This is the way it wants to go,
Spontaneously. It may be rhymed,
Or not; and tetrametric, though
Here and there I may add a foot or so,
Indulge in quatrains, couplets, or
In absolutely blank pentameter—
Anything, only not in prose.
End of apology. Here goes.

Since June of Nineteen Sixty-four
I've been officially free of chore
And duty to the N.Y. Phil.—
Fifteen beautiful months to kill!
But not to waste: there was a plan,
For as long as my sabbatical ran,

Washington, D.C., 1957

To write a new theater piece.
(A theater composer needs release,
And West Side Story *is eight years old!*)
And so a few of us got hold
Of the rights to Wilder's play The Skin of Our Teeth.
This is a play I've often thought was made
For singing; and for dance. It celebrates
The wonder of life, of human survival, told
In pity and terror and mad hilarity.
Six months we labored, June to bleak December.
And bleak was our reward, when Christmas came,
To find ourselves uneasy with our work.
We gave it up, and went our several ways,
Still loving friends; but still there was the pain
Of seeing six months of work go down the drain.

The picture brightens, come New Year:
The next nine months restore some cheer
That vanished when our project died.
I firmly brushed regrets aside,
And started a whole new sabbatical,
Forgetting all projects dramatical,
And living, for once, as a simple man,
Partaking of life, as you never can
With a full Philharmonic season to run.
Now, here was a project that could be done:
Stay home, go out; see friends, see none;
Take walks with the children, study for fun;
Practice the piano; attend the Bonnard
Exhibit; visit your neighborhood bar;
See more of the people in other arts,
Meet your nonmusical counterparts;
Read the new poets; play anagrams, chess;
Complete the crosswords in the British press;
Restudy Opus 132;
Do, in short, what you want to do.

All these I did, but inevitably
One finds that sabbaticals aren't that free;
There are certain commitments that cannot be
Unmet or interrupted—e.g.,
The Young People's Concerts, recording sessions,
and similar nonsabbatic digressions.
These took time, and a certain amount
of adjusting,
                    But kept my baton from rusting.
Meanwhile, there lurked at the back of my mind
The irrational urge (too late!) to find
Another theatrical project, which meant
That hours and days were now to be spent
In reading plays and considering oceans
Of wild ideas and desperate notions.
None took fire, which is just as well,
For I then had the luxury, truth to tell,
Of time to think as a pure musician
And ponder the art of composition.
For hours on end I brooded and mused
On materiae musicae, used and abused;

On aspects of unconventionality,
Over the death in our time of tonality,
Over the fads of Dada and Chance,
The serial strictures, the dearth of romance,
"Perspectives in Music," the new terminology,
Physiomathematomusicology;
Pieces called "Cycles" and "Sines" and "Parameters"—
Titles too beat for these homely tetrameters;
Pieces for nattering, clucking sopranos
With squadrons of vibraphones, fleets of pianos
Played with the forearms, the fists and the palms
—And then I came up with the **Chichester** Psalms.
These psalms are a simple and modest affair,
Tonal and tuneful and somewhat square,
Certain to sicken a stout John Cager
With its tonics and triads in E-flat major.
But there it stands—the result of my pondering,
Two long months of avant-garde wandering—

With Harry Kraut and John McClure at Chichester psalms rehearsal,
Vatican, 1973

My youngest child, old-fashioned and sweet.
And he stands on his own two tonal feet.
Well, that was my major sabbatical act—
At least, the most tangible; but in fact
There were other boons from my newfound leisure
Which brought me (and, I hope, others) pleasure.
In doing research for this résumé
I've looked through my datebook since New Year's Day
To see what I actually did, for fun—
Things I could otherwise not have done.
I cannot go into the bulk of it:
Let suffice one item per month. To wit:
Jan. Conducted Stravinsky's Histoire du Soldat
For a benefit. Staging and all. A ball.
Feb. Flew out to Aspen. Institute Seminar
With skiing on the side. Came back revivified.
Mar. Conducted new Robbins ballet Les Noces.
Stravinsky again. Now, there's a blessed pen.
Apr. Practiced and played and recorded Mozart
G-minor, with Juilliard Quartet. Not to forget.
May. To Denmark. The Sonning Prize. As thanks,
Played Nielsen's Third. A marvel, take my word.
Jun. To Puerto Rico. Conducted before
Casals, musician supreme. A lifelong dream.
Jul. To Chichester, en famille, to hear
My Psalms in the place for which they were written. Smitten.
Aug. To Tanglewood, scene of my happiest youth,
To conduct, on its quarter-centennial, Carmen, Act IV.
Tanglewood! Twenty-five years! So much to remember!
For instance . . .
              . . . and suddenly here it is, September.

Refreshed and rejuvenated, I
Regard the new season with eager eye.
Tanglewood's brought back a breath of my youth:
Stravinsky and Mozart, Beauty and Truth.
Denmark provided a glorious spring.
In Chichester I heard angels sing.
Skiing at Aspen has brought me health.
This whole sabbatical's been like a tonic.
Can't wait to get back to the Philharmonic!

Tel Aviv, 1981

Remarks delivered to music critics
27 April 1965

ON PROGRAM-MAKING

Over the next two seasons we shall embark on a survey of what has happened to the symphonic form during our century. I'd like to take this occasion to amplify that sentence and explain a little of why we are doing this survey. There is a belief held by some—and reinforced by historical thinking—that the symphony, as a form, along with its satellite the concerto, has undergone a great cycle from Mozart to Mahler—a one-hundred-fifty-year-long arc whose apogee is commonly held to be Beethoven. Those who hold this point of view will naturally tend to regard all symphonic expression after Beethoven as part of a decline; and they will certainly regard everything from Mahler on as the ultimate decadence. If we accept this deterministic idea, it follows that the twentieth century is, symphonically speaking, an epigonous age, in which symphonies of one kind or another have indeed been written, some of them even considered masterpieces, but none of them resulting from a vital current or growth. Symphonies would now seem to be sports of a kind, appearing intermittently, and ever more rarely. It also follows that the symphony orchestra, by the same token, would become a kind of museum of the past—if we regard the symphony orchestra as a natural externalization of this symphonic growth over a century and a half. It then follows that conductors would become curators, and the whole institution of symphonic concerts inevitably cut off from the mainstream of contemporary composition.

These are strong ideas, not easily accepted or discarded, and they present philosophical problems which cannot be overlooked. It therefore seems to me natural and important that the New York Philharmonic should, at this mid-century point, cast a reflective look over the whole symphonic progress of our century, and give our thinking public a chance to decide for themselves the validity of this concept. Such a survey cannot be accomplished in one year; even two are not sufficient for a thorough investigation; but I feel that in two seasons our audiences can hear enough of these works so that they can form at least a theoretical idea of what has happened.

The plan for this coming season is that every one of my programs is to include at least one significant example of a twentieth-century symphony or concerto. The one exception to this will be the final week's program of the season, which is to be devoted to Haydn's *Creation*. We shall make no effort to pursue this survey chronologically, by starting in 1900 with Mahler, and working forward; the laws of the "well-balanced" program would forbid that. But we hope this will be a comprehensive survey.

Since Mahler represents the key turning point of our century, we shall devote three whole programs to his last three great symphonies—the *Seventh, Eighth,* and *Ninth.* For the moment we exclude the controversial, unfinished *Tenth.*

The other great turning-point symphonist was, of

course, Sibelius; and since this happens to be his centennial year, we shall celebrate it by playing all seven of his symphonies, fashionable or not, distributed over the whole season.

Besides the works of these two key men who ushered in our century, we shall hear other major European symphonies such as the *Fourth* of Vaughan Williams; the Webern symphony, Opus 21; the Prokofiev *Fifth;* and the Shostakovich *Ninth*—all highly diverse and remarkable works. From American symphonists, we shall perform the *Third Symphony* of Ives, the *Third* of Copland, and the *Third* of Harris, plus two new symphonies: the *Second* of Leo Smit and the *Fifth* of David Diamond.

In the realm of the concerto, we shall be hearing the world premiere of the Chávez *Violin Concerto,* the Stravinsky *Violin Concerto,* the Nielsen *Flute Concerto,* the Rachmaninoff *Third Piano Concerto,* David Diamond's *Piano Concerto*—also a world premiere—and the Bartok *Two-piano Concerto.* The Nielsen work is being played in honor of his centennial year, and the two Diamond works in honor of his fiftieth birthday. There will, of course, be a sprinkling of standard repertoire too: Bach, Haydn, Saint-Saëns, and so on.

Now, all this, of course, occurs on my programs only. It would be pleasant to have our guest conductors join me in this survey, but I don't wish to impose on them a scheme which might limit their freedom of program-making.

In the second year of our survey we hope to make up for the omission of some very significant symphonic names in this coming season—particularly that of Schoenberg, to whom we plan to devote an entire program. Hindemith will also be represented by his *E-flat Symphony,* a remarkable work not heard in New York for eighteen years. There will be more Mahler symphonies—his *Sixth,* and possibly that controversial *Tenth.* I hope also to program symphonies and concerti by such important symphonists as William Schuman, Elliott Carter, Roussel, Honegger, Sessions, and, of course, examples of the newest symphonic trends that turn up between now and then. Whatever those symphonic trends may be—if indeed they exist at all

• *Leonard Bernstein*

—I hope that after this two-year survey our audiences will have as clear a picture of them as we can possibly provide. I also trust that these programs will turn out to be not just a didactic survey, but moving and enjoyable in themselves. □

17 June 1965

CARL NIELSEN

In all the excitement attendant on our performing and recording Nielsen's *Third Symphony* there has been one nagging question hovering in the air: why are we now suddenly discovering this composer, Carl Nielsen of Denmark, one hundred years after his birth and thirty years after his death? If he's *that* good, why hasn't he been championed before this? Well, I think the answers are not so hard to come by. For one thing, his music was never quite nationalistic enough to become the definitive Danish music, alongside *the* Hungarian music of Liszt, or *the* Norwegian music of Grieg. Nor was Nielsen's music *inter*national enough to take its place next to the Beethovens of the world. It's just what it is: an odd mixture of past and future, of tradition and prophecy, sounding now like Brahms, now like Berlioz, and sometimes even like Shostakovich. But what makes it always sound like Nielsen is its total unpredictability.

Then, the other obstacle to Nielsen's recognition has been the shadow of his Finnish neighbor Sibelius, who loomed large enough for both of them in the early years of this century. How could there possibly be *two* great modern Scandinavian composers? Well, there are. And in this year of 1965, when we are celebrating the centennials of *both*

Holding a copy of a new album release

composers, it is time we saw these two men on an equal plane. I think many people are in for pleasant surprises as they get to know Nielsen: his rough charm, his swing, his drive, his rhythmic surprises, his strange power of harmonic and tonal relationships—and especially his constant unpredictability—all these are irresistible. I feel confident that Nielsen's time has come. □

Address given on the presentation
of the Eleanor Roosevelt Humanities Award
20 November 1966

ROOSEVELT AWARD ACCEPTANCE SPEECH

Ambassador Roosevelt, Mr. Justice, distinguished guests, my dear friends:

I wonder how many of you have had the experience of standing in the nation's capital, surrounded by persons of overwhelming stature and distinction, and receiving an honor of this magnitude. How can I possibly tell you what it feels like—the dreamlike buoyancy, the sense of being airborne? It is a glorious feeling; but it carries with it a penalty—the penalty of having to make a speech. It is a price I am willing to pay, and a small price at that. At any rate, a small speech.

Part of this dream-of-glory feeling comes, as I said, from the fact that this is Washington, and part from the brilliance of this assembly. But the feeling is enhanced by the knowledge of the good cause for which we are gathered tonight, and by the presence of so many dear friends and colleagues. Over and above all this, there hovers a halo, a name—the spirit of that woman in whose name this award is given me. I have always revered the name Eleanor Roosevelt, and always shall; and to have my name linked with hers on this medallion is a transcendental experience. You see, I grew up in what might be called the Roosevelt generation—a generation that not only loved and trusted President Roosevelt, but lived in his terms, was molded in his image. I was fourteen years old when he first came to the White House, and I was twenty-six years old when he finally departed it. And all those twelve years, in all that welter of activity and emotion, we always looked to our President, taking strength from his mind, his intelligence, his articulateness, his compassion, his elegance.

With Eleanor Roosevelt and Yehudi Menuhin, 1948

And through it all, moment by moment, behind him and beside him stood Mrs. Roosevelt: those two figures were inextricably merged in my mind; the same intelligence and compassion streamed from them both. Of course the climax of my young life would have been to meet them; I never had that privilege, while the President lived. And then, on that sorrowful twelfth of April, 1945, I cried tears for the first time since I had been a child.

But Mrs. Roosevelt remained, and I did have the privilege and the joy of meeting her. And slowly, as I came to know her better, a miracle occurred: she was my friend. It was then that I was finally able to separate her from the double image I had adored as a college boy; it was then that I began to perceive the marvels of which she as an individual was composed. These marvels have been cited and re-cited for so many years that they are almost clichés now: her goodness, her limitless energy, her clarity of thought, her simplicity, her intuitive rightness, her courtesy, her inexhaustible patience—all virtues that are so easy to put down these days. They are almost forgotten values, those old-fashioned virtues. You'll hear people say, "Yes, she was a real old-fashioned do-gooder." Do-gooder. What a lamentable word! These days to be a do-gooder is to call forth a sneer; but dammit, she *was* a do-gooder, and I will bless her for it all my life! God grant us more do-gooders in this perilous and cynical world of ours. Give us back a few of those old-fashioned virtues: patience, courtesy, moral fearlessness, plainness of living—why, we would sit at dinner in her crowded little apartment and if there should be a last-minute guest, his chair would as likely as not be an end table with a shawl flung over it. Even more to the point, it could just as easily be *her* chair.

But her greatest virtue, and her greatest triumph, was her relation with time, her fiercest enemy—time, the grim enemy we all struggle with, all our lives. I don't know how Mrs. Roosevelt did it, but she did conquer time. She had time for everything and for everyone—unrushed and un-reluctant. I have always tried to emulate this astonishing quality of hers, and I have always failed. How did she do it? She was always there. If there was a mouth to be fed, a thirsty mind to be filled, a captive to be freed, a stranger to be made welcome, a mourner to be comforted—she was there. If there was a banner to be raised, a myth to be exploded, a wrong to be righted, a gulf to be bridged—she was there. And she was all there, without tension or im-patience: she gave herself totally. Can we do less?

Can we *afford* to do less, now that time is running out, now that madness is rampant beneath the cloak of afflu-ence, now that patience and concern and clarity of thought and goodwill are no longer just old-fashioned virtues, but matters of life and death?

Thank you from the bottom of my heart for the Eleanor Roosevelt Award: it binds me to her forever. □

Rockford, Illinois
5 June 1966

"CHARGE TO THE SENIORS"

President Howard, worthy deans and doctors, learned masters, distinguished scholars and guests of Rockford College:

It seems that I have come here today to receive honor, and also to render it. For what I am about to receive I thank you most warmly. And in rendering honor I am also deeply thankful to you: for the one I mean to honor was born and raised right here in Rockford. Her name is Helen Grace Coates, and she is well named, for Helen means "bright," and Grace means what it says. Miss Coates is both bright and gracious, and much more. For more than thirty years she has been a guide, confidante, helper, and inspiration —first, long ago, when I was in my teens, as my piano teacher, and then, for the last twenty-two years, as my indispensable private secretary. In both roles she has enriched and eased my life. As teacher she introduced me to discipline, to the most profound meaning of work, to the control and penetration of musical beauty. She also listened to my problems, musical and nonmusical, gave liberal and sage counsel and comfort. As my secretary and friend and assistant, she is still doing the same. And today she has honored me by accompanying me to Illinois: she is even now sitting among you.

There are two kinds of honorary degrees: those you accept and those you don't. The latter far outnumber the former; one could make a busy career every June out of just college-hopping. This is clearly impossible: there are conflicts of dates; there is very little time in life, after all; and many of these degrees are mutually exclusive. Then why say yes precisely to Rockford College, a thousand miles from home? Because Helen Coates was born here, and I want to pay her homage. But in honoring her I mean to honor all teachers, in all fields and disciplines; I mean to honor teaching itself, man's noblest profession, as well as

With Jennie Tourel

his most underrated and underpaid profession. The best teachers I have had—and I have been lucky enough to have had many good ones—have consistently taught me not only the stored-up illuminations of their minds, but inevitably something about teaching itself. And to whatever extent I am today a teacher, in whatever unorthodox ways, I owe this overwhelming urge to share my ideas with others to those very teachers, Helen Coates among them. I have learned from them to suggest the profound meanings of work to others, and to foster the penetration of beauty.

Now that I have paid my homages, the moment has arrived for me to execute the chief duty of every commencement speaker: to say something brilliant and memorable to the graduating class. This is what is usually called the "Charge to the Seniors," and I must confess I find it a difficult and dangerous enterprise. I charge you, O Seniors —with what? Do I have the right to charge you with anything? Well, perhaps I have; I was also once a senior, somewhere in the murky past; and I am from time to time a teacher. Therefore I am presumably entitled to give advice.

But advice is far too easily given, and too easily ignored. It is largely facile, and cynical, and there is too much of it around. We are awash in a sea of admonitions; we are lucky if we can simply stay afloat. What makes it even more difficult these days is that we are living in a world dominated in so many ways by the young. Extreme youth has now become the most desired goal of man, as if he could mature backward; and we are confronted with the embarrassing spectacle of the middle-aged imitating the teen-aged—dressing like them, dancing like them, being with it, digging it, waiting it out like them. Then how shall the old give advice to the young? Should I not rather say to you, along with my whole generation—Charge me, O Seniors: tell me how not to despair, how to feel immortal again, how not to fear old age and death, how to get high and stay there, how to lose myself ecstatically in the Watusi?

These thoughts have been troubling me ever since I agreed to come here today; and I have meanwhile been moved to reread some of the more famous examples of advice-giving in literature: Machiavelli's advice to his prince, Lord Chesterfield's letters to his son—that sort of thing. And I find them mostly, as I said before, cynical and facile. They aim mainly at success, rather than at virtue; at accomplishment rather than integrity; at a brilliant life rather than a noble or rich one; at how to get away with it, how to get the most out of it; how to get, rather than how to give. And even at this level, of self-improvement for the sake of self-advancement—even at this coldly pragmatic level, they don't seem to make sense anymore. We can no longer accept the totalitarian advice of Machiavelli, any more than we can accept Lord Chesterfield's superficial image of a well-bred young man. Not, at least, if we are serious people, and respond to the great gestures of history. The tremendous idea of democracy has catapulted us light-years ahead of Machiavelli's prince, and if Machiavellianism still shows in our governments, we know it is there to be fought, to be howled down, not submitted to. And psychiatry has, in its way, hurled us equally forward; Lord Chesterfield's son could do with a few dozen sessions on the couch.

But there is one admonitory tract that is still adhered to, still believed in, and taught to our children at face value, and that is Polonius' famous "few precepts" to his son, Laertes. It isn't chic to shrug off Shakespeare, and *Hamlet* is, after all, his greatest play. And so I thought I'd have another look at old Polonius, to see whether he still stands up. If I really must charge you seniors, I could do worse, I thought, than purloin from Polonius. Well, let's see what he has to tell us.

Precept Number One:
Give thy thoughts no tongue,
Nor any unproportion'd thought his act.

Alas, poor Polonius. He simply did not live in this age of communication. Can you imagine him living in our world of television, of political oratory flowing like rivers through our ears, of letters to the editor, of opinion polls, of public interviews, interviews-in-depth, *Life* and *Time* magazines, panel shows, Madison Avenue image-making—can you imagine Polonius now, in all this maelstrom, saying, "Give thy thoughts no tongue"? Why, this is, as no time before, a time of tongues; if he wanted Laertes to be a real smash in Paris, he would have said, "Give every thought thy tongue; and if you have no thoughts, give them tongue anyway." And as for not giving "any unproportion'd thought his act"—well, psychoanalysis has certainly changed that. Today, Polonius would simply be accused of urging his son into a morass of repression and inhibition.

Precept Number Two:
Be thou familiar, but by no means vulgar.

On the face of it, that sounds like valid enough advice; but once we stop to think that by vulgar Polonius must have meant the literal definition—"of the people"—then again we see that time has passed him by. Polonius, the old courtier and decadent aristocrat, would naturally have wanted his son to avoid vulgarity in the democratic sense; today he would have a hard time making that one stick.

And what of *Number Three*:
The friends thou hast, and their adoption tried,
Grapple them to thy soul with hoops of steel;
But do not dull thy palm with entertainment
Of each new-hatch'd, unfledged comrade.

In other words, keep to your circle, the class of friends to which you are accustomed, where you are safe; do not seek out new friends; the stranger is guilty until proved innocent. And certainly not worth your buying him a hot meal. Well, our contemporary culture dictates otherwise; our class delineations become mistier each day, along with national boundaries. Can you imagine Laertes in the Peace Corps, or becoming pals with a folksinger in Washington Square?

On to *Number Four*:
Beware
Of entrance to a quarrel; but being in,
Bear't that the opposed may beware of thee.

I am afraid that a good measure of our Vietnam policy hinges on that piece of advice. No further comment.

Number Five:
Give every man thine ear, but few thy voice;
Take each man's censure, but reserve thy judgement.

Let's take that bit by bit. "Give every man thine ear"! Imagine, in this verbal maelstrom I spoke of before, giving every man your ear! It could result only in confusion, deafness, and insanity. ". . . but few thy voice," says Polonius: again, that's not cut out for democracy. Polonius was not yet aware of the ideal of universal franchise. Our voice is our vote; and not only should we give it, we must give it. "Take each man's censure": Now, that's a real impossibility. What if I took seriously the censure of all the music critics I constantly read? I would be finished. "But reserve thy judgement": well, if I were to follow that precept, I could not be saying these things at this moment, could I? Someday, when *you'll* be asked to charge seniors, you'll see what I mean. And so on to

Precept Number Six:
Costly thy habit as thy purse can buy,
But not express'd in fancy;
Rich, not gaudy;
 Well, we don't have to spend five seconds on that one;
Carnaby Street has changed all that. And it goes on:

For the apparel oft proclaims the man,
 I think that these days it rather proclaims the age—the
age of the nonman, the antihero, to be found in one anti-
novel and nonplay after another. And Polonius even goes
on to say:

And they in France of the best rank and station
Are most select, et cetera
 Of course, as we know, our big fashion center is now
London. Poor Polonius.
 Then follow the famous lines

Neither a borrower nor a lender be, et cetera
 —which again is highly inapplicable to our society,
where everyone, by definition of our economic system, is
either a borrower or a lender. So much for Precept Seven.
 But all this is nothing compared with the grand finale,
the climactic Eighth:

This above all: to thine own self be true,
And it must follow, as the night the day,
Thou canst not then be false to any man.
 Now, anything I would say in disfavor of these beloved
lines would amount to blasphemy. For one thing, they are
such beautiful lines that we believe them for the sheer
music that is in them. But even more, we believe them
because they are true. Of course they are true, and I could
easily get off the hook by simply quoting them and saying
goodbye, and the seniors would be well charged. But in all
good faith, I can't; in the centuries that have elapsed since
Shakespeare wrote those words, we have grown. Yes, I
insist—risking all dangers of being called old-fashioned,
Panglossy, and foolishly hopeful—I insist that man does

grow, does make progress, is infinitely improvable. Otherwise why do we agonize, study, wrangle, make charges to seniors, fret, think, try, fail, try again—live at all? Because we grow. And the thing we know now that Polonius didn't is that the problem is not so much being true to thine own self, as knowing truly what that self is. How much disaster, crime, and horror has resulted from someone's being true to what he thought was his own self! Wasn't Hitler being true to his own self? Wasn't the Church being true to its own self when it burned Jan Huss and excommunicated Martin Luther? Isn't the teen-aged rapist being true to his own self? Aren't our ubiquitous American bigots being true to their own misbegotten ideals? How many lies, how many destructive acts ensue from this fallacy! How many millions of sick people on this earth have only the most distorted, grotesque images of their own true selves, and act according to them! This much we have learned since Polonius' time: it is all too easy to deceive ourselves, to forge a self-image that we may need for our own ego-starved reasons, but an image that is ultimately hollow and destructive. Your job, as each of you a twentieth-century Laertes, on the brink of adult life, is to find your true selves: to build a self that is not conditioned only by birth pangs and adolescence pangs, by environment and conformism, by status needs and power needs, by indulgences and kicks —no; but to develop a self that is illuminated by conscience, answerable to honor, and nurtured by compassion. Oh, how quickly I have seen those qualities recede since I was a senior! Where is that nobility which was once the whole reason for music? Where is the compassion in our new drama and literature? Where is conscience to be found among the fatuous fads that parade as art in our time? And not only in art: you know all the rest. College students know everything.

Here, then, is my charge: go out, seniors, and find honor again, retrieve compassion and conscience, cherish them; and in their light find your own true self. And then, in the clarity of knowing to whom you must be true—only then will it follow, as the night the day, that thou canst not then be false to any man. ☐

Written for High Fidelity *magazine*
in conjunction with the first integral release (CBS)
of Mahler's nine symphonies
April, 1967

MAHLER:
HIS TIME HAS COME

Has come? *Had* come, rather; was there all along, even as each bar of each symphony was being penned in that special psychic fluid of his. If ever there was a composer of his time, it was Mahler—prophetic only in the sense that he already knew what the world would come to know and admit half a century later.

Basically, of course, all of Mahler's music is about Mahler —which means simply that it is about conflict. Think of it: Mahler the creator vs. Mahler the performer; the Jew vs. the Christian; the Believer vs. the Doubter; the Naif vs. the Sophisticate; the provincial Bohemian vs. the Viennese *homme du monde*; the Faustian Philospher vs. the Oriental Mystic; the operatic symphonist who never wrote an opera. But mainly the battle rages between Western Man at the turn of the century and the life of the spirit. Out of this opposition proceeds the endless list of antitheses—the whole roster of Yang and Yin—that inhabit Mahler's music.

For the first time, now, with this issue of all nine symphonies in one monumental unit, we can feel the full impact of Mahler's dualistic vision. (I regret the absence in this album of *Das Lied von der Erde*: not only because it is a supreme masterpiece, but particularly because it stands as a revealing philosophical commentary on all of the nine symphonies—a kind of Talmudic exegesis. I do not, however, regret the omission of the so-called *Tenth Symphony*; I have never found it, in any of its various "completions," worthy of a place in the Mahler *corpus*. It has always seemed to me that the *Ninth* is the ultimate farewell, in a long and arduous series of farewells, and that the *Tenth* was an attempt to say yet again what had already and finally and unsurpassably been said.)

But back to the Yang and the Yin. What was this duple vision of Mahler's? A vision of his world, crumbling in corruption beneath its smug surface; fulsome, hypocritical, prosperous; sure of its terrestrial immortality, yet bereft of its faith in spiritual immortality. The music is almost cruel in its revelations; it is like a camera that has caught Western society in the moment of its incipient decay. But to Mahler's own audiences none of this was apparent: they refused (or were unable) to see themselves mirrored in these grotesque symphonies. They heard only exaggeration, extravagance, bombast, obsessive length—failing to recognize these as symptoms of their own decline and fall. They heard what seemed like the history of German-Austrian music, recapitulated in ironic or distorted terms—and they called it shameful eclecticism. They heard endless, brutal, maniacal marches—but failed to see the imperial insignia, the Swastika (make your own list) on the uniforms of the marchers. They heard mighty chorales, overwhelming brass hymns —but failed to see them tottering at an abyss of tonal deterioration. They heard extended, romantic love songs—but failed to understand that these *Liebesträume* were nightmares, as were those mad, degenerate *Ländler.*

But what makes the duplicity heartbreaking is that all these anxiety-ridden images were set up alongside images of the life of the spirit—Mahler's *anima,* which surrounds, permeates, and floodlights these cruel pictures with the tantalizing radiance of how life *could* be. The intense longing for serenity is inevitably coupled with the sinister doubt that it can be achieved. Obviously, the innate violence of the music, the excesses of sentiment, the arrogance of establishment, the vulgarity of power postures, the disturbing rumble of status-non-quo are all the more agonizing for being linked with memories of innocence, with the aching nostalgia of youthful dreams, with aspirations toward the Empyrean, noble proclamations of redemption, or with the bittersweet tease of some Nirvana or other, just barely out of reach. It is thus a conflict between an intense love of life and a disgust with life, between a fierce longing for *Himmel* and the fear of death.

With John McClure and Clive Davis at Philharmonic Hall, 1967

The dual vision of Mahler's, which tore him apart all his life, is the vision we have finally come to perceive in his music. This is what Mahler meant when he said, "My time will come." It is only after fifty, sixty, seventy years of world holocausts, of the simultaneous advance of democracy with our increasing inability to stop making war, of the simultaneous magnification of national pieties with the intensification of our active resistance to social equality—only after we have experienced all this through the smoking ovens of Auschwitz, the frantically bombed jungles of Vietnam, through Hungary, Suez, the Bay of Pigs, the farce-trial of Sinyavsky and Daniel, the refueling of the Nazi machine, the murder in Dallas, the arrogance of South Africa, the Hiss–Chambers travesty, the Trotskyite purges, Black Power, Red Guards, the Arab encirclement of Israel, the plague of McCarthyism, the Tweedledum armaments race—only after all this can we finally listen to Mahler's music and understand that it foretold all. And that in the foretelling it showered a rain of beauty on this world that has not been equaled since.

The recording of Mahler's *Seventh* is of special satisfaction to me because of the challenge that this symphony represents. It has long been the ugly stepchild of the Mahler symphonies, a sort of puzzle to performers and audiences alike, and never really a success. This is partly due to the extremely different natures of the various movements. Its tremendous, rhetorical first movement and the equally long and riotous fifth movement are like two huge arms that hold the three shorter middle movements cradled between them. And these three inner movements are anything but grandiloquent or rhetorical. They consist of a *Nachtmusik* (which might be translated as *nocturne*), a shadowy *scherzo*, and a second *Nachtmusik* in which the orchestra is cut down to chamber size. And in these three movements you can hear some of the loveliest, most tuneful, lilting, and campy music ever written.

Part of the difficulty of understanding this symphony has always been just this sort of lilting tunefulness. How does that fit in with the grandeur of the outer movements? But the minute we understand that the word *Nachtmusik* does not mean *nocturne* in the usual lyrical sense, but rather *nightmare*—that is, night music of emotion recollected in anxiety instead of tranquillity—then we have the key to all this mixture of rhetoric, camp, and shadows.

The biggest problem has always been the finale, which critics have traditionally considered unworkable. It combines mighty chorale music with other music of such tawdriness that it would seem to belong only to Viennese operetta or café bands. But once we realize that this movement is Mahler's document on the end of the great European tradition, the breakup of the safe, bourgeois nineteenth century, then the piece suddenly makes marvelous sense, and becomes both ironic and exacting, and ultimately heartbreaking.

Now that the world of music has begun to understand the dualistic energy source of Mahler's music, the very key to its meaning, it is easier to understand this phenomenon in specific Mahlerian terms. For the doubleness of the music is the doubleness of the man. Mahler was split right

Vienna Philharmonic rehearsal of Mahler's Seventh, *Vienna, 1974*

down the middle, with the curious result that whatever
quality is perceptible and definable in his music, the dia-
metrically opposite quality is equally so. Of what other
composer can this be said? Can we think of Beethoven as
both rough-hewn and epicene? Is Debussy both subtle and
blatant? Mozart both refined and raw? Stravinsky both objective and maudlin? Unthinkable. But Mahler, uniquely,
is all of these—rough-hewn *and* epicene, subtle *and* blatant,
refined, raw, objective, maudlin, brash, shy, grandiose,
self-annihilating, confident, insecure, adjective, opposite,
adjective, opposite.

The first spontaneous image that springs to my mind at
the mention of the name *Mahler* is of a colossus straddling
the magic dateline *1900.* There he stands, his left foot

(closer to the heart!) firmly planted in the rich, beloved nineteenth century, and his right, rather less firmly, seeking solid ground in the twentieth. Some say he never found this foothold; others (and I agree with them) insist that twentieth-century music could not exist as we know it if that right foot had not landed there with a commanding thud. Whichever assessment is right, the image remains: he straddled. Along with Strauss, Sibelius and, yes, Schoenberg, Mahler sang the last rueful songs of nineteenth-century romanticism. But Strauss's extraordinary gifts went the route of a not very subjective virtuosity; Sibelius and Schoenberg found their own extremely different but personal routes into the new century. Mahler was left straddling; his destiny was to sum up, package, and lay to ultimate rest the fantastic treasure that was German-Austrian music from Bach to Wagner.

It was a terrible and dangerous heritage. Whether he saw himself as the last symphonist in the long line started by Mozart or as the last *Heilige Deutsche Künstler* in the line started by Bach, he was in the same rocky boat. To recapitulate the line, bring it to climax, show it all in one, soldered and smelted together by his own fire—this was a function assigned him by history and destiny, a function that meant years of ridicule, rejection, and bitterness.

But he had no choice, compulsive, manic creature that he was. He took all (all!) the basic elements of German music, including the clichés, and drove them to their ultimate limits. He turned rests into shuddering silences; upbeats into volcanic preparations as for a death-blow. *Luftpausen* became gasps of shock or terrified suspense; accents grew into titanic stresses to be achieved by every conceivable means, both sonic and tonic. *Ritardandi* were stretched into near-motionlessness; *accelerandi* became tornadoes; dynamics were refined and exaggerated to a point of neurasthenic sensibility. Mahler's marches are like heart attacks, his chorales like all Christendom gone mad. The old conventional four-bar phrases are delineated in steel; his most traditional cadences bless like the moment of remission from pain. Mahler is German music multiplied by n.

The result of all this exaggeration is, of course, that neurotic intensity which for so many years was rejected as

Paris, 1975

unendurable, and in which we now find ourselves mirrored. And there are concomitant results: an irony almost too bitter to comprehend; excesses of sentimentality that still make some listeners wince; moments of utter despair —often the despair of not being able to drive all this material even further, into some kind of para-music that might at last cleanse us. But we *are* cleansed, when all is said and done; no person of sensibility can come away from the *Ninth Symphony* without being exhausted and purified. And that is the triumphant result of all this purgatory, justifying all excesses: we do ultimately encounter an apocalyptic radiance, a glimmer of what peace must be like.

So much for the left foot; what of the right, tentatively scratching at the new soil of the twentieth century, testing it for solidity, fertility, roots? Yes, it was found fertile; there were roots there—but they had sprung from the other side.

All of Mahler's testings, experiments, incursions were made in terms of the past. His breaking up of rhythms, his post-Wagnerian stretching of tonality to its very snapping point (but not beyond it!), his probings into a new thinness of texture, into bare linear motion, into transparent chamber-music-like orchestral manipulation—all these adumbrated what was to become twentieth-century common practice; but they all emanated from those nineteenth-century notes he loved so well. Similarly, in his straining after new forms—a two-movement symphony (No. 8); a six-movement symphony (No. 3); symphonies with voices, not only in the finales (No. 3, No. 8, *Das Lied*); movements that are interludes, interruptions; movements deliberately malformed through arbitrary abridgement or obsessive repetition or fragmentation—all these attempts at new formal structures abide in the shadow of Beethoven's *Ninth* and of his last sonatas and string quartets. Even the angular melodic motions, the unexpected intervals, the infinitely wide skips, the search for "endless" melody, the harmonic ambiguities—all of which have deeply influenced many a twentieth-century composer—are nevertheless ultimately traceable back to Beethoven and Wagner.

I think that this is probably why I doubt that I shall ever come to terms with the so-called *Tenth Symphony*. I have never been convinced of those rhythmic experiments in the Scherzo, of the flirtation with atonality. I often wonder what would have happened had Mahler not died so young. Would he have finished that *Tenth Symphony*, more or less as the current "versions" have it? Would he have scrapped it? Were there signs there that he was about to go over the hill, and encamp with Schoenberg? It is one of the more fascinating If's of history. Somehow I think he was unable to live through that crisis, because there was no solution for him; he had to die with that symphony unfinished. After all, this man's destiny was to complete the great German symphonic line and then depart, without its being granted to him to start a new one. This may be clear to us now; but for Mahler, while he lived, his destiny was anything but clear. In his own mind he was at least as much part of the new century as of the old. He was a tormented, divided man, with his eyes on the future and his heart in the past.

And so we come to the final incredible page. And this page, I think, is the closest we have ever come, in any work of art, to experiencing the very act of dying, of giving it all up. The slowness of this page is terrifying: *Adagissimo*, he writes, the slowest possible musical direction; and then *langsam* (slow), *esterbend* (dying-away), *zögernd* (hesitating); and as if all those were not enough to indicate the near stoppage of time, he adds *dusserst langsam* (extremely slow) in the very last bars. It is terrifying, and paralyzing, as the strands of sound disintegrate. We hold on to them, hovering between hope and submission. And one by one, these spidery strands connecting us to life melt away, vanish from our fingers even as we hold them. We cling to them as they dematerialize; we are holding two—then one. One, and suddenly none. For a petrifying moment there is only silence. Then again, a strand, a broken strand, two strands, one . . . none. We are *half in love with easeful death . . . now more than ever seems it rich to die, to cease upon the midnight with no pain . . .* And in ceasing, we lost it all. But in letting go, we have gained everything. (*The lecture concludes with a performance of the Finale of Mahler's* Ninth Symphony.)

But his destiny did permit him to bestow much beauty, and to occupy a unique place in musical history. In this position of Amen-sayer to symphonic music, through exaggeration and distortion, through squeezing the last drops of juice out of that glorious fruit, through his desperate and insistent reexamination and reevaluation of his materials, through pushing tonal music to its uttermost boundaries, Mahler was granted the honor of having the last word, uttering the final sigh, letting fall the last living tear, saying the final goodbye. To what? To life as he knew it and wanted to remember it; to unspoiled nature; to faith in redemption; but also to *music* as he knew it and remembered it; to the unspoiled nature of tonal beauty; to faith in its future—goodbye to all that. The last C-major triad of *Das Lied von der Erde* was for him the last C-major triad of all Faustian history. For him?   □

Speech made at Mount Scopus concert, Israel
9 July 1967

JERUSALEM

My dear friends:

I cannot let this solemn moment pass without a word about Mahler's *Resurrection Symphony*, and why it is so especially meaningful to us today. In all the years I have performed this symphony, the performances I recall with most emotion were those we gave here in Israel nineteen years ago, during the war for Independence. The idea of Resurrection at that time was momentous; after all, this land had literally just been reborn. But still the ancient cycle of threat, destruction, and rebirth goes on; and it is all mirrored in Mahler's music—above all, the expression of simple faith—of belief that good must triumph—*En b'rerah!* [There is no alternative].

With Jennie Tourel and Netanya Devrath at Mt. Scopus, 1967

I am especially moved that this restatement of faith takes place here on this mountain in Jerusalem, a city which is this day united and at peace—a city of new activity, friendliness, and charm—and endless possibilities. This golden city of Jerusalem can become a model for the world—a microcosm of coexistence and interexistence. Is it too much to hope that this growing together of people in peace may radiate out from here to the whole region, farther and farther, eventually covering the world? Why not? This is no ordinary city—this is *Y'rushalayim, raboti bagoyim, sarati bam'dinot* [Jerusalem, great among the nations, prince among the states]. This is the very center of faith: let it spread. Let the walls come down. And then we can say in truth: *"Ki mitziyon tetze Torah, ud'var Adonai mi-Y'rushalayim"* [For the Torah shall go forth from Zion, and the word of the Lord from Jerusalem]. □

A TOTAL EMBRACE

Life without music is unthinkable,
Music without life is academic.
That is why my contact with music is a total embrace.

With Jennie Bernstein

With music

Part Four

THE LAST DECADE TILL NOW

1969–1980

A fictitious review
written by L.B. August, 1969
Unpublished

A BERNSTEIN PREMIERE

L.B., now a boyish 58, began his annual guest period with the New York Philharmonic last night in Philharmonic Hall. Laureate he may be, but he'll get no laurels from this department for last night's exhibition. For what Bernstein has done is to have finally made his bid to join the avant-garde. And a weak bid it is, in the form of his latest composition, which last night received its world premiere at his own hands. It is called, pretentiously enough, *Fanfare for Me, Tape, and Orchestra.*

How can one describe this puny effort without sounding cruel or vindictive? I have nothing against Bernstein the composer, nothing personal, as long as I don't have to listen to his music. But last night I had to, along with almost 3,000 others, and I am not happy. For one thing, Bernstein has no business writing for electronic tape. Tape is simply not his bag; he never has liked or admired or studied electronic music, and he is obviously using it only because it's fashionable. Granted that he knows the orchestra well, and has in the past demonstrated a decent grasp of orchestration; but in this *Fanfare* the orchestra does nothing but tap its instruments, snap its fingers, and occasionally make moaning sounds, for which the orchestral players have no appreciable talent. These noises, combined with the pseudo-concrete sounds issuing from the loudspeakers, succeeded only in revealing Bernstein as an opportunistic lightweight.

But the worst part of the *Fanfare* was certainly the element referred to in the title as "Me." This element was, of course, Lenny himself, who would periodically turn to the audience and talk. Having delivered himself of a few grating sentences (meant, I suppose, to be poetic), he would then turn back to the orchestra and resume conducting.

This happened many times. The sense of what he was saying was hardly clear, but as far as I could make out, he was putting down his own composition, explaining it and at the same time deprecating it. One typical phrase remains in the mind: "Squeak, squawk, squeak and talk, speak and squawk." At the end of the composition, the whole orchestra was cued into a mad improvisation, each musician playing anything he wished, until the whole thing was stopped by a cutoff gesture from the mighty Maestro's arm. There was a shocked silence, and then loud applause, naturally —since Bernstein's audience will applaud anything he does, including deep knee-bends. Alas.

Needless to say, this novelty number was sandwiched in between two warhorses, in the most old-fashioned tradition of program-making. The upper slice of stale bread was the thrice-familiar *Béguins* by Boulez. The lower one was the Bartok *Concerto for Orchestra*. Both these repertoire items were conducted in the familiar Bernstein manner— overstated and underprepared, overstressed and underlined. It was as if the listener's attention were constantly being drawn to climaxes, inner voices, bass lines, details of orchestration. Look, everybody, get this! Did you hear that? Wait till you hear it upside down in the recapitulation: wow! The Maestro might as well have been delivering a lecture simultaneously with the musical performance. Perhaps that is what he is eventually coming to—turning every performance into a Lenny-lecture. Then his happiness will surely be complete. As for our happiness, that is another matter entirely. □

OF TANGLEWOOD, KOUSSEVITZKY, AND HOPE

May I take the liberty of skipping the customary formal salutations to my learned colleagues, honored guests, *et alii*, and address myself directly to you, my young friends who have come here to work and live with music this summer at Tanglewood. Thirty years ago, almost to the day, I was sitting there, almost where you're sitting—a couple of hundred yards from there; this building wasn't up then—but there I was sitting, in a state of wild excitement and anticipation. It was the first day of the first season of the Berkshire Music Center, and I had just miraculously been accepted by its founder and director, Serge Koussevitzky, as one of his conducting students. And Koussevitzky was standing here, so to speak, where I am today. I don't know if I can even begin to give you an idea of what that felt like —what Koussevitzky represented then in the world of music, what radiance emanated from him, what it was like to be in his presence. He was a man possessed by music, by the ideas and ideals of music, and a man whose possessedness came at you like cosmic rays, whether from the podium or in a living room or in a theater like this. You see, in all the years I had lived and grown up in Boston, I had never met Koussevitzky: for me he was that distant, glamorous figure that I saw and heard from the dizzying height of the second balcony in Symphony Hall, and it was only after I had graduated from Harvard and had spent a long winter studying in Philadelphia that I read in the newspaper of the impending opening of this new Music Center at Tanglewood. I rushed up to Boston armed with letters of recommendation from anybody who would give me one, gained entry into the Maestro's study, and—I must confess I was so awestruck, I don't remember a moment of that interview, except his saying at the end of it, "Of course, my dear, I vill except you in my class." Unquote. Faint. Fade-out. Fade-in, and I'm sitting there, where you are, July 8, 1940.

And the great Koussevitzky was standing here talking to us. He was talking about commitment—commitment to art, devotion to music, dedication to one's work. I remember his using the phrase "The Central Line"—I'll never forget that—meaning the line to be followed by the artist at any cost, the line leading to perpetual discovery, a mystical line to truth as it is revealed in the musical art. It was an inspirational kind of speech—by which I mean something other than "inspiring": which it was—immensely inspiring. But besides that, it was an "inspirational" kind of speech, full of phrases that I suppose today would be smiled at as old-fashioned clichés. Does anyone speak of "dedication" anymore, or "commitment"? Does one dare, in 1970, to speak of "values" or of "virtues" such as hard work, faith, mutual understanding, *patience*?

Well, the answer is *yes*; one does dare. Even though it's thirty years later, and I'm not Koussevitzky with his inspirational oratory, and you're not in any mood to listen to it. You've had a bellyful of rhetoric, I know that. So have I. But here I am, standing in his place, bearing the title of Adviser, and as the senior member of this triumvirate, I am called upon to advise you. Advice comes cheap—we all know that. It's too easy to give, and too hard to give sincerely and with clarity, precisely because today is not thirty years ago. Something basic has changed. Let's see if I can make you feel something about the difference between then and now, and then perhaps we can level with each other.

We who were sitting there in 1940 were a generation of hopers. We came out of the Roosevelt decade, the thirties, educated by the Great Depression, the National Recovery effort, which was a great social spasm in our history. We were filled with causes: we had Spain, China, Czechoslovakia, the labor movement, racial equality, antifascism. We were dedicated to social progress and to the end of fascism

With Serge Koussevitzky at Tanglewood, 1948

in all forms. We kids who had spent our college days
marching with strikers, giving one benefit after another for
one cause after another—we kids were committed to the
future. We had hope.

Whereas now all I hear from the youth is tales of despair,

hopelessness. I have spent long hours this last year sitting with university students, in America and abroad, and rapping with them—but mostly listening. And what I hear is a constant refrain of hopelessness. The system is too big, too evil. You can't fight it except by extremist action, and how many of us are extremists? You can't cope with the madness of a divided world—again, after thirty years!—a world divided into two mindless juggernauts who are even now doing battle by proxy in Southeast Asia and in the Middle East. And most of these students cannot identify with either side, so they have no cause; and the result is hopelessness. And that's the main difference between us then and you now.

Perhaps we can see this difference with more clarity in terms of music. In fact, the clarity is startling when you think about it. In the decade surrounding 1940 the key to musical expression was nobility. We still had a form called the symphony, the noble symphony. We had the Shostakovich *Fifth,* for the first time; the Prokofiev *Fifth* for the first time; Copland's *Third*; towering symphonic works by Hindemith, Bartok, Roy Harris, Bill Schuman, and what may have been the last of them all, Stravinsky's great *Symphony in Three Movements.* All this music was heroic music: it spoke of struggle and triumph; it reflected the basic nobility of man. And there stood Serge Koussevitzky, ready and eager to play them all.

Now, today, all that is gone. The symphonic life that we lead—and it is a flourishing one—is no longer fed by the noble symphony, nor is it fed by much of anything else, for that matter. New music has splintered into dozens of movements, groups, and experiments, ranging from the most didactic superserialism to the most frivolous Dada. And in between these extremes some of it is fascinating, some is titillating, some of it is touching and even beautiful, and some merely opportunistic—but one thing it almost never is is *noble*. And this negativism ranges right across the arts into almost all thinking disciplines, so that these university students I see and meet with hardly know where to turn. One after another they tell me, "Well, look, there's nothing to write but protest, there's nothing to sing but satire, there's nothing to feel but irony and despair. So we drown ourselves in decibels of rock, we drop out with dope; we don't know what else to do." Even the most taciturn, the bitterest, bushiest radicals I've met on campus break down after four hours of rapping and beg me to tell them what to do. "We have no leaders," they say; "we have no models, no idols, no heroes. The only heroes we have sometimes are in the pop field, and they change every three minutes. Or a couple of radical leaders that not all of us can accept." One of them said to me, "What do you expect us to feel when we have grown up watching one hero after another being shot down before our eyes—both Kennedys, Malcolm X, Martin Luther King?" I have nothing brilliant to answer to that. I have nothing brilliant or immortal to say to any of you who feels despair. Of course, I can reach back to Serge Koussevitzky and retrieve his sense of commitment, his dedication and patience, and pass them on to you. I can do that, and I do do that; and I wish that were enough—now, thirty years later. But it isn't enough, we know that; something has changed. So I have to tell you something else—maybe not brilliant or immortal, but something very important—about the nature of despair.

I have been reading an extraordinary book which unfortunately exists only in German, called *Das Prinzip Hoffnung* —"The Principle of Hope"—by the contemporary German philosopher Ernst Bloch. That's a coincidence, that name, Ernst Bloch: this Bloch is not the composer of *Schelomo,* but a poetico-historico-psycho-philosopher in the great German tradition of Hegel and Nietzsche and Marx and Freud, and he's very much at the forefront of thinking today among the German-speaking youth. It seems really remarkable that this Bloch, having once fled Germany during the Nazi period and now once again having left East Germany for West Germany, should produce as his major philosophical work a book called "The Principle of Hope." And yet he has, and in it he demonstrates in the most convincing way that this principle is an absolute, in the Platonic sense, and that in a purely scientific sense hope resides in us. He describes an aspect of consciousness that goes beyond Freud, which he calls the "Not-Yet-Conscious"—*Das Noch-Nicht-Bewusste*—which is the psychic representation of the Not-Yet-Become: is that too hard? The Not-Yet-Happened, *das Noch-Nicht-Gewordene*—in other words, that which has not yet happened, but which is sensed in anticipation. And he shows that this Not-Yet-Consciousness is just as integral a part of man's total Consciousness as is the Unconscious or the Subconscious of Freud, and that man does not exist without it. This built-in Anticipation is a *quality* of man—he calls it "Dreaming Ahead," "Dreaming Forward" . . . I don't know how to translate it: *Träumen nach Vorwärts*—and it works like a precognition, sensing what is to come; it colors and shapes our dreams, daydreams, our wish-fulfillment drives. In other words, it's what we ordinary laymen call Hope—only a scientific description of Hope.

Now, the moment we apply this psychological force to living history, we see the trouble beginning. Because the timing of the two doesn't always work out right; you see, a crucial social change, something "Not-Yet-Become" like universal justice, racial equality, the end of war, can seem to be imminent, just within our grasp, and when it doesn't come it causes great frustration. It may skip a generation or more, it may lie dormant for innumerable reasons, and suddenly awaken in its own time. But the youth today cannot wait: their great problem is massive impatience, sensing the changes that must come, and wanting them *now*, as a baby cries to be fed at the instant it senses hunger. And this has always been the problem of youth, the hardest obstacle of youth to overcome; in fact, all of growing up is simply the overcoming of that infantile impatience. That's what we call maturity: the overcoming of impatience; and many of us never reach it—especially today.

How much harder it is to come to terms with impatience today, in an age which is so hectically speeded up, in which you take for granted instant knowing of all world events, problems, and catastrophes, and demand an equally instant remedy. It's an age in which instant gratification is offered by the advertising media—*instant* headache relief, *instant* energy, *instant* tranquilization. It's also an age in

With Serge Koussevitzky at Tanglewood, ca. 1948

which *instant* destruction of the human race is a real possibility we all live with day and night. You grew up in this age: you are the Instant Generation. How can we expect you to be patient?

And there lies the real cause of the famous "generation gap": we grew up before all this instantaneousness and you grew up after it. And the dividing line between us is Hiroshima. To quote the great scientist Albert Szent-Gyorgyi, you've got the atom in you, we just know about it; you were born with it, we just learned about it. That's a marvelous book, by the way, Szent-Gyorgyi's new little book—have you come across it? It's called *The Crazy Ape*, and I wish you'd all read it. It's short and it's in English, unlike Bloch's book, and once you read it you will understand why Hiroshima is the crucial dividing point.

At the moment of Hiroshima the Berkshire Music Center was five years old. Today it's thirty years old. And in that intervening span of twenty-five years resides the new generation—which is you. Of course you are impatient: how could you not be impatient, growing up in a world of instant knowing, with the promise of instant gratification, and the threat of instant overkill?

Not that we're trying to cop out, we oldies. We can't cop out. We prepared you very carefully: we made you the best-educated generation the world has ever known, the most sophisticated, the most politically oriented, the best read, the most informed, best equipped for a democratic society. We saw to that. We taught you to believe, and to expect, that the world could work; that all mouths could be fed—every last Eskimo and Hottentot; and that no man need ever again raise a gunsight at another; that the world is rich and blooming, there is enough for all—enough food and clothing and music and leisure and love. All we have to do is find the simple means of distributing it all, fairly and universally. We taught you all that; we taught you to hope as no one has ever hoped before in history; we developed your sense of the "Not-Yet," your Forward-Dreaming. We developed that to a boiling point.

But there's a catch: because what we taught you was what we had learned *before* Hiroshima. We taught you that

Sergei Alexandrovitch Koussevitzky, 1874–1951

there need never be a war again; but what you learned from us was that there *must* never be a war again, because then the world is finished. We talked and you heard, but between the talking and the hearing, the linguistics had changed. How were we to know that the dropping of a bomb on Hiroshima would make every one of you a stranger to us; that what we had learned and would now pass on to you would automatically undergo a chemical change because of the phenomenon of instantaneousness?

So okay, you say, thanks a lot; we've learned about progress and democracy and international brotherhood and racial equality and the elimination of the class struggle—so okay, thanks very much, where is it? Where are they? Let's have it! Peace, freedom, United Nations, all this stuff you talked about—where are they? You told us there could never be political prisoners again after the defeat of Nazism: so what's new in Greece and Nigeria and Russia—and Chicago, for that matter? What's a United Nations without China in it? What do you mean, International Brotherhood, when national boundaries have never been tighter? What do you mean, Peace, when the whole world is being juggled and inflamed by two Superpowers?

Well, you're right, you're absolutely right. And thank God you're impatient, because—and this is the whole point—because that impatience is a certain signal of hope—yes, hope. You couldn't feel that impatience, that urge for instant dream fulfillment, if you didn't feel hope. Then what is this despair we keep hearing about? The answer is it's not despair—it's impatience, frustration, *fury*: let's go; all right, already; enough talk; enough with political self-seeking, and power grabs, and hate campaigns. Enough with guns, and blood all over our TV sets, all over our consciences. Enough with black-white-red-pinko-Commie-fascist-faggot-hippy hatreds. You're right: *enough.* But the solution is not going to come like instant gratification, like mother's milk, like televised headache relief. It's going to take a lot of doing; and you've got the overwhelming problem of relearning patience—patience, that old-fashioned word which is still as relevant as it ever was. So you see, we are back to Koussevitzky's morality after all, atom or no atom, Hiroshima generation gap or not. Because the need for instant gratification is still the mark of infancy, and the instant remedy can be just as dangerous and foolish as the instant overkill.

Nothing comes instantly except death, and every generation has to learn that anew, including yours. Nobody is going to dream on Sunday of becoming a great oboe player and wake up Monday morning being one, or a great composer, or a world-saving statesman. And social democracy is a hard proposition—it's harder than playing the oboe, believe me. Nobody ever said it was easy; it just *sounds* easy. Good Lord, our own country is not yet two hundred years old. There's still hope for everything; even patriotism —a word that is being defiled every day—even patriotism can be rescued from the flag-wavers and bigots. It's true that we have to work faster and harder if we're going to take our next social step before the overkill stops us dead in our tracks; but if anybody can do it, faster and harder and better, it's you, the best generation in history.

And especially you here today, *artists* of that generation. Because it's the artists of the world, the feelers and the thinkers, who will ultimately save us; who can articulate, educate, defy, insist, sing and shout the big dreams. Only the artists can turn the "Not-Yet" into reality. All right, how do you do it? Like this: Find out what you can do well, uniquely well—that's what studying is for: to find out what you can do particularly well. You. Unique. And then do it for all you're worth. And I don't mean "Doing your own thing," in the hip sense. That's passivity, that's dropping out, that's not doing anything. I'm talking about *doing*, which means—another old-fashioned phrase—serving your community, whether that community is a tiny town or six continents. And there's no time to lose, which makes your position twice as difficult, because you're caught in a paradox. You see, you've got to work fast, but not be in a hurry. You've got to be patient, but not passive. You've got to recognize the hope that exists in you, but not let impatience turn it into despair. Does that sound like double-talk? Well, it is, because the paradox exists. And out of this paradox *you* have to produce the brilliant synthesis. We'll help you as much as we can—that's why we're here—but it is you who must produce it, with your new, atomic minds, your flaming, angry hope, and your secret weapon of art. If there are still any among you who doubt that you possess hope in you, I will now prove you wrong. You surely have hopes that this speech has reached an end; well, congratulations: your hopes are fulfilled. Thank you. □

Reminiscences of a musical friendship
High Fidelity magazine
November, 1970

AARON COPLAND AT 70: AN INTIMATE SKETCH

On November 14, Aaron Copland will be seventy years old. November 14—it's a date seared into my mind. Two of the most important events of my life occurred on that day—the first in 1937, the second in 1943—and so I never forget Aaron's birthday.

In the fall of 1937 I had just begun my junior year at Harvard. Although I had never seen Copland, I had long adored him through his music. He was the composer who would lead American music out of the wilderness, and I pictured him as a cross between Walt Whitman and an Old Testament prophet, bearded and patriarchal. I had dug up and learned as much of his music as I could find; the *Piano Variations* had virtually become my trademark. I was crazy about them then—and I still find them marvelous today— but in those days, I especially enjoyed disrupting parties with the work. It was *the* furthest you could go in avant-garde "noise," and I could be relied upon to empty any room in Boston within three minutes by sitting down at the piano and starting it.

At the time, one of my close friends was a fellow student who went by the name of I. B. Cohen. (He's now known as I. Bernard Cohen, Professor of the History of Science at Harvard, but nobody yet knows what the I. stands for.) He was way beyond me—a graduate student who knew everything about anything—but we did have two things in common: the name Bernstein (his mother's maiden name) and a great crush on Anna Sokolow.

Anna Sokolow was a young and very striking dancer whose recital in Boston I.B. and I had attended. We both promptly fell in love with her. When we learned that her Boston performance was in effect a pre-Broadway tryout for her New York debut, we determined that nothing in the world would stop us from going down to catch that recital.

I.B. acquired tickets through a friend of his, the poet Muriel Rukeyser, and on magical November 14, we came to New York, met Muriel, and went with her to the Guild Theater on Broadway for the recital. Our seats happened to be in the first row of the balcony; I made my way through, followed by Muriel and I.B. Already in his seat on my right was an odd-looking man in his thirties, a pair of glasses resting on his great hooked nose and a mouth filled with teeth flashing a wide grin at Muriel. She leaned across to greet him, then introduced us: "Aaron Copland . . . Leonard Bernstein." I almost fell out of the balcony.

At the end of the recital, Copland announced that it was his birthday, that he was having a few people up to his "loft" (Aaron Copland's famous loft! Where he worked!) and would we care to join him.

It was indeed a loft, above a candy factory on Sixty-third Street, where Lincoln Center now stands. (He worked in the loft, lived down the block at the Empire Hotel, still standing at Sixty-third Street and Broadway.) As was my shameless wont, I gravitated to the piano. Naturally, I began with the Variations. It must have startled everybody that this last-minute guest, whom nobody knew—a provincial college boy from Boston who had been to New York only once or twice before and who was now obviously thrilled to be in a loft! . . . with artists!!—was playing their host's ferocious work. I was so excited to be the center of such a party that I followed the *Variations* with every piece I could remember; I recall, to my shame, that I must have stayed at the piano for hours.

From that time on, Aaron and I were fast friends. He seemed to be terribly taken with the conviction with which I played his music, and even made such extravagant remarks as "I wish I could play it like that." And thereafter, whenever I came to New York I went to Aaron's. I would arrive in the morning and we'd have breakfast at his hotel, then wander around and sometimes go to a concert. And all during those years I would bring him my own music for his criticism. I remember that I was writing a violin sonata during those Harvard days, and a two-piano piece, and a four-hand piece, and a string quartet. I even completed a trio. I would show Aaron the bits and pieces, and he would say, "All that has to go. . . . This is just pure Scriabin. You've got to get that out of your head and start fresh. . . . This is good; these two bars are good. Take these two bars and start from there." And in these sessions he taught me a tremendous amount about taste, style, and consistency in music. I had never really studied composition with anybody before; at Harvard I had taken Advanced Harmony and Fugue with Walter Piston and Orchestration with Edward Burlingame Hill, but those were all theoretical elements of composition. Through his critical analyses of whatever I happened to be working on at the moment, Aaron became the closest thing to a composition teacher I ever had.

We of course played other music than mine at these sessions. We played his. Not while he was composing it, though; Aaron was very jealous of the music he was working on and would never show anything before it reached its reasonably final form. But then would come that glorious day when he would pull something out and we would play it, four hands, from the score. I learned such works as *Billy the Kid* and *An Outdoor Overture*—later, the *Piano Sonata* and *Third Symphony*—that way before they were ever performed publicly, and the scores to *Quiet City*, *Of Mice and Men*, and *Our Town* before Hollywood got

With Aaron Copland

them. *El Salon Mexico* had already been composed—and first performed by Carlos Chávez in Mexico City a few months before I met Aaron—but the published piano transcription was made by me.

During those years, I was also very much concerned about my own future, and I'd bring all my problems to Aaron. He became a surrogate father to me. Even after I developed the close relationship to Koussevitzky that made me his official (according to the press) substitute son, it was always Aaron to whom I would turn with my worries. I was quite a whiner in those days, and I would constantly bewail my plight to him: "When is anybody ever going to play my music?" or, in later years, "Oh, Lord, how does anybody ever get to conduct an orchestra?" He would always giggle first—the infectious giggle is his most common reaction to anything—then, with an attempt at sternness, glower, and command me, "Stop complaining. You are destined for success. Nobody's worried about you. You are the one person worried about you," and I would get very angry and insist upon being worried about.

Then on Sunday, November 14 (again), 1943—his forty-third birthday—I was awakened at nine in the morning by a phone call from the New York Philharmonic, of which I was then the assistant conductor. Bruno Walter was sick, and I would have to conduct the concert, scheduled for national broadcast, at three that afternoon. There was no time for a rehearsal and barely time to shake my hangover. That concert, of course, changed my life. It was a dramatic success, all the more so for me since Aaron's words seemed to come providentially true on his birthday. When the review, incredibly, made the front page of *The New York Times* the following morning, Aaron's response was "Oh, it's only what everybody expected," and I, of course, got twice as furious with him as ever.

I was not, certainly, the only young musician for whom Aaron was a beacon. In America he was The Leader, the one to whom the young always came with their compositions. Every premiere of a new Copland work found the concert hall filled with young composers and musicians. And from all over the world young composers would come

"All the News That's Fit to Print."

The New York Times.

LATE CITY EDITION

Copyright, 1943, by The New York Times Company.

VOL. XCIII..No. 31,341.

NEW YORK, MONDAY, NOVEMBER 15, 1943.

THREE CENTS NEW YORK CITY

LACK MACHINERY DIRECTLY TO RAISE 'WHITE COLLAR' PAY

Federal Officials and Congress Stumped on Adjusting It to 'Little Steel' Formula

SPLIT ON SUBSIDY METHOD

Some Urge Price-Wage Control, While Others Seek WLB Provision for Unorganized

By LOUIS STARK
Special to THE NEW YORK TIMES.

WASHINGTON, Nov. 14—There is no immediate, direct method of adjusting the pay of about 15,000,000 clerical, white collar, unorganized employes to the 15 per cent "Little Steel" formula which applies to organized wage earners, according to Federal officials and legislators who were asked by THE NEW YORK TIMES for their views on the subject.

Some of those questioned, however, thought that an indirect approach could be made through a subsidy bill such as the one now before Congress, which is designed to keep prices of certain commodities from rising. Others, opposing subsidies as inflationary, made different suggestions that warned the they had no "panacea."

William H. Davis, chairman of the War Labor Board, said that his solution would have been similar to that of Bernard Baruch a the halting of wages and prices at the same time.

He told of receiving letters from persons complaining that they had not benefited by the 15 per cent formula, but said that he could not help them if they had no union to speak for them. Their only recourse, he said, were to "go out and get another job" or "tell the boss about it."

If "the boss" made a voluntary application for a wage adjustment it might be approved, he explained, but if he refused to act, the employes could do nothing because he could not apply to the board as an individual.

Price Ceilings as Protection

Chester Bowles, director of the Office of Price Administration, said that for the 15,000,000 whose pay envelopes had not appreciably increased and who normally live on a close budget, "each increase in the cost of living brings a lower standard of living."

"They have had no one to plead their cause in contrast with the cases presented by organized farmers and workers," he said.

There is only one way to protect this group and all other American citizens from a higher cost of living and that is to stop prices from rising. That is what price ceilings are for.

"Citizens can help hold prices against wartime pressures by watching for ceiling prices when they shop and by refusing to pay more than the maximum legal prices."

Frances Perkins, Secretary of Labor, felt that the subsidy bill was the practical approach to the problem.

"It is vitally necessary to hold the line on living costs and the white-collar people who have not had their living wage increases can be helped if the subsidy program is adopted by Congress," she said.

Senator Robert F. Wagner of New York agreed that the subsidy method was the proper approach to alleviate the situation.

Byrd Stresses Wage-Price Plan

On the other hand, Senator Harry F. Byrd of Virginia, who scored the Baruch plan, declared that "wages and prices should have been stabilized at the beginning of the war."

"I am opposed to subsidies as a means of paying the farmer for his labor and other costs," he said.

"I don't know what the answer is. The WLB puts a lot of red tape in the way when employers want to raise wages. They have to fill out forms and then it takes months to get them approved.

"I know of a printing machine manufacturer who took so long to fill merit raises approved that his social employes left.

"To show you how organized employes benefit in wages, I found the War Department approved wages for truck drivers which on a basis of eight hours a day seven days a week would give them an annual income of $5,200, or the same period concrete mixer would get $7,200."

Senator Bennett C. Clark, Democrat of Missouri, said that if the bill a solution we would "about all

Continued on Page Twenty-four

Cardinal Proposed To Head the Reich

By Cable to THE NEW YORK TIMES
STOCKHOLM, Sweden, Nov. 14—A plan for one of Germany's Roman Catholic cardinals to be chosen to head the post-Hitler régime until the Reich found a democratic balance has been advanced in anti-Nazi circles at Berlin, according to advices received here today.

The proponents of this idea argue that the Allies would not approve of military rule or a monarchy, but that a stable government would be needed at once until democratically chosen leaders appeared.

Public support of a Catholic prelate as Reich Chancellor would be assured, they believe, from the fact that a recent survey showed 50 per cent of all Germans were now Roman Catholics, although before the war Catholics numbered only a third of the population.

LA GUARDIA GRANTS CURRAN TIME ON AIR

Offer for Next Sunday Follows Reading of Letter From Fly Calling Talk 'Accusatory'

Acting on the advice of James L. Fly, chairman of the Federal Communications Commission, Mayor La Guardia announced yesterday that Thomas J. Curran, chairman of the New York Republican County Committee, would receive time during the Mayor's broadcast from City Hall next Sunday to reply to Mr. La Guardia's recent charge that the Republican party was responsible for the election of Thomas J. Aurelio to the Supreme Court. The Mayor's charge was made during the weekly broadcast from City Hall on Nov. 7 over WNYC, the municipal radio station. Mr. Curran said that he would take advantage of the invitation to reply to much of the Mayor's statements as he would be unable to cover in a radio talk that he will make at 10:30 o'clock tonight over radio station WHN.

After the Mayor's broadcast of Nov. 7, Mr. Curran demanded time on yesterday's program from City Hall. The Mayor wrote to Mr. Fly for advice, enclosing copies of his own talk, of Mr. Curran's demand and of statements issued by Mr. Curran before and after the Nov. 7 broadcast. Mr. Fly's reply was on the Mayor's desk Saturday morning, but was given by the Mayor to an Associated Press reporter for safekeeping, to be returned unopened when yesterday's broadcast started.

"Political" Issue Sidestepped

In his letter Mr. Fly sidesteps the question of whether the Mayor's talk was "political." It was "accusatory," he wrote, and made serious charges and sought to place serious blame on the Republican organization. The Republican County Committee, he said, was entitled to express the views and the public to hear them.

"The time and facilities extended to the Republican organization," he declared, "should be no less desirable or effective than that enjoyed by you."

"It is surely necessary to hold the line on living costs and the white-collar people who have not had their living wage increases can be helped if the subsidy program is adopted by Congress," she said.

Mayor La Guardia did not touch upon the Curran matter yesterday until he was well along in his weekly talk. Then to the controversy and of his appeal to Mr. Fly for advice, after which he read excerpts from the letter. "Mr. Fly has replied," the Mayor said, "and he read excerpts from the national income."

Continued on Page Fourteen

Young Aide Leads Philharmonic, Steps In When Bruno Walter Is Ill

A nation-wide radio audience and several thousand persons in Carnegie Hall were treated to a dramatic musical event yesterday afternoon when the 25-year-old assistant conductor of the New York Philharmonic-Symphony Orchestra, Leonard Bernstein, substituted on two hours notice for Bruno Walter, who has become ill, and led the orchestra through its entire program.

Enthusiastic applause greeted the performance of the youthful musician, who went through the ordeal with no signs of strain or nervousness. Artur Rodzinski, the orchestra's permanent conductor and musical director, who arrived at intermission time after motoring from his home in stockbridge, Mass., declared the young man had "proformal tone." adding that "we wish to give him every opportunity in the future."

Mr. Bernstein received hearty applause at the end of the first Schumann overture, but was recalled four times when he concluded the Rozza variations. The audience

Continued on Page Forty

poet at the beginning of the current season was notified of Mr. Walter's illness in the morning by Bruno Zirato, assistant manager. Mr. Walter, who was said to be suffering from a stomach disorder, was to have been the guest conductor for the afternoon performance, broadcast over the Columbia network.

The young conductor a native of Lawrence, Mass. and a Harvard graduate, had no opportunity for rehearsal before opening the program with Schumann's Overture to "Manfred." The program also included Rozza's "Theme, Variations and Finale", Strauss' "Don Quixote" and Wagner's Prelude to Die Meistersinger."

Mr. Bernstein received hearty applause at the end of the first Schumann overture, but was recalled four times when he concluded the Rozza variations. The audience

---

$2,500,000,000 COST SET FOR WAR RELIEF IN TENTATIVE PLANS

U. S. to Pay $1,000,000,000 of $1,500,000,000 and United Kingdom $625,000,000

QUOTA SYSTEM PROPOSED

Seen as Gaining Support From Congress—Our Share to Be Less Than Hoover Spent

By RUSSELL B. PORTER
Special to THE NEW YORK TIMES.

ATLANTIC CITY, N. J., Nov. 14—The Council of the United Nations Relief and Rehabilitation Administration (UNRRA) is working on a plan whereby the costs of the entire post-war relief and rehabilitation program, for which funds will have to be raised, may be kept down to $2,500,000,000, it was learned today.

Through a flexible formula whereby quotas are to be assigned to the non-invaded countries, it has been estimated that the United States share of the bill-may run between $1,000,000,000 and $1,500,000,000 and that of the United Kingdom about $625,000,000. Being an invaded nation, Russia is not to pay anything for the relief of other peoples, according to the program, but she is expected to pay for the relief goods she herself receives.

This became known after an informal meeting in the Claridge Hotel by a group of advisers of Director General Herbert H. Lehman of UNRRA. Dr. Harry D. White, special assistant to Secretary of the Treasury Henry Morgenthau Jr., attended the meeting.

Seen Aid to Congress Action

Although those at the meeting declined to talk, it was disclosed in other quarters that the plan has been designed to solve the relief problem in such a way as to smooth its way through Congress. The first appropriation to be asked for is expected to be not more than $500,000,000 and possibly much less.

It was pointed out that the total cost of the entire world relief plan in this country, if this plan prevails would be only 40 to 60 per cent of the $2,500,000,000 that the United States spent on foreign relief after the last war through Herbert Hoover and the American Relief Administration, which he headed. The United States would pay from 40 to 60 per cent of total monetary cost of relief this time against about 35 per cent for the British, but it was pointed out that contribution from the Dominions would increase the amount for the British Empire or Commonwealth of Nations.

Several Quota Suggestions

A subcommittee headed by Dean Acheson, Assistant Secretary of State, United States member of the Council, and chairman of the present session, is to discuss the plan and make recommendations which will come before the Council as a whole later on. If the Council accepts the plan, it will assign quotas in the "community chest" manner, but it has no power to make assessments against any nation. The UNRRA agreement gives the Congress or legislative body of every country the right to accept or reject the quota assigned to it.

Several possible formulas have been suggested for determining the quota of each nation. One, which Mr. Lehman is said to favor, would take 1 per cent of the national income. This would carry

Continued on Page Eight

BERLIN REPORTS RUSSIAN BREAK-THROUGH BY 30 DIVISIONS WITHIN THE DNIEPER BEND; BITTER FIGHTING CHECKS ALLIES IN ITALY

ATESSA IS CAPTURED

Victory by Eighth Army Is Sole Advance of Day on All Fronts

COUNTER-BLOWS BEATEN

Americans and Britons of Fifth Army Smash Germans— Air Action Increases

By MILTON BRACKER
By Wireless to THE NEW YORK TIMES
ALGIERS, Nov. 14—There was a good deal of fighting on the Italian front yesterday but little progress was made.

The British Eighth Army ground forward three miles to capture Atessa and also sent patrols across the Sangro River for the usual exploratory work. But the advance of Lieut. Gen. Mark W. Clark's Fifth Army were strictly limited. German artillery and aviation demonstrated increased power.

In one of the day's sharpest clashes the American units of the Fifth Army smashed back elements of two German battalions northwest of Montaquila. In the Mignano area, German guns cracked in a series of short, sharp counterblows, but the Allies had no great trouble in battering them down.

In the air, light bombers and fighters concentrated on points within twenty-five miles of Isernia. Altogether, as many as sixty German fighters were seen over the battlefront, the greatest strength that the Germans have chosen to send up in many days. Nine enemy fighters were shot down in savage combats.

Evacuations Seen Near

From the Eighth Army positions at Riccero, great columns of smoke were seen rising in the vicinity of Aifedena and Rocca Cinquemiglia, suggesting preparation to abandon these central points. This would not involve any appreciable loss on the Carpinano-Sangro line from Pescara to Rome. This information as always shows its determination to keep his ground. He is safe for the time being but that does not mean that he will be safe indefinitely.

Continued on Page Seven

ENEMY INSTALLATIONS AFIRE ON BOUGAINVILLE

Smoke rises from Japanese posts on Torokina Point after an attack by dive bombers before our marines were sent ashore. Landing barges and a transport are seen in the foreground.
Associated Press Wirephoto

BADOGLIO TO RESIGN AFTER ROME FALLS

Premier Pledges Action When Capital Has Been Freed— King Retains Throne

By HERBERT L. MATTHEWS
By Wireless to THE NEW YORK TIMES
AT PREMIER BADOGLIO'S HEADQUARTERS, in Italy, Nov. 13 (Delayed)— Premier Pietro Badoglio announced today that he would resign after Rome had been liberated by the Allies and that he was acting only to help his King in this difficult time.

Premier Badoglio has four years of subject of the King's abdication was: "At the age of 17 swore loyalty to the King, and I will continue to keep faith as long as I live."

Actually, there was never any question or any possibility of the King's abdication, despite respect to the current. There is a powerful demand for it in all political circles, but the King himself has always shown his determination to keep his throne. He is safe for the time being but that does not mean that he will be safe indefinitely.

Continued on Page Seven

Allies Deal Record Air Blow To New Guinea Madang Area

By The Associated Press
ALLIED HEADQUARTERS IN THE SOUTHWEST PACIFIC, Monday, Nov. 15—Liberator and Mitchell bombers, following up a strafing raid by fighter planes, plastered Madang and nearby Alexishafen with 223 tons of bombs Saturday morning in the heaviest aerial assault yet thrown against the Japanese on New Guinea.

P-40 and P-39 fighters swept the air strips at Alexishafen shortly after dawn, at the expense of one enemy plane, to enable 30 medium-aircraft opposition. Then came waves of Liberators at medium height, followed by Mitchells at tree-top height, to give the enemy a thorough going over.

Towering fires were started in fuel and supply dumps at Alexishafen, where four Japanese planes were destroyed on the ground, and the entire target area was covered with a heavy pall of smoke as bombers left. Gen. MacArthur's communiqué said.

A strong force of P-47s and P-40 was on hand as a protective cover, but not a Japanese plane was in the air.

Since earlier attacks on the Wewak and Madang air strips kept the Japanese from aerial interference with the Australians progress up the Markham and down the Ramu valleys, it was presumed that a giant assault such as this was intended to hamper the enemy's aerial supply of troops in forward areas.

The only heavier attack on bomb tonnage was the Oct. 12 raid on Rabaul, New Britain, which received 350 tons of explosives. The previous record tonnage on New Guinea was the 221 tons dropped on Battleburg last Oct. 21.

There was no new word of the ground situation at Empress Augusta Bay, the Bougainville beachhead secured by marines on Nov. 1 and reported by General MacArthur Saturday as having been extended.

A Catalina bomber that aimed

Continued on Page Seven

NAZI CHUTISTS WIN LEROS STRONGHOLD

Enemy Seizes Narrow Waist of Island, Separating Two British Defense Bodies

By C. L. SULZBERGER
By Wireless to THE NEW YORK TIMES
CAIRO, Egypt, Nov. 14—Fierce fighting continued today on the island of Leros between the British defenders and the German invasion force, with the British managing to drive the Nazis back on the range of hills on the northeastern peninsula of the island. The Germans enlarged their beachhead however.

Today's communiqué said:

"Heavy fighting continues on Leros, where the enemy has further reinforced his troops. In the northern sector our forces made local gains. In the central sector the enemy has somewhat inspissated his position but is being continued by our troops."

Already it would appear that the British forces have been cut from each other by the German thrust across the narrow neck of the island, just west of the town of Leros. One part of the town of Leros with a German bridgehead on Point Bianca has been enlarged.

Thus, the town of Leros appears on the map to be threatened on two sides, while the defenders north and south of the neck bisecting the island at present are cut off from

Continued on Page Seven

BIG RETREAT LOOMS

Nazis Report Breaches From Zaporozhe to Krivoi Rog Sector

ZHITOMIR GAINS WIDENED

50 Villages Seized in 3-Pronged Push Toward Berdichev— Kerch Battle Unabated

By The Associated Press
LONDON, Monday, Nov. 15—Berlin announced early today that nearly 500,000 Russian troops had broken through the German Dnieper River bend defenses in a new assault aimed at closing a gigantic trap on the huge Axis forces in the south. The Russian communiqué was silent on that point, but it did reveal that the northern Ukrainian Red Army had driven, to within sixteen miles southeast of Korosten in a drive that scooped up fifty more villages.

The gains announced by the Russian communiqué and midnight supplement, coupled with the Soviet monitor, revealed that Gen. Nikolai F. Vatutin's armies were only twenty-one miles north of Berdichev, after having captured Pryazhev, six miles north of Zhitomir.

Korosten is the upper anchor of the last German north-south rail line short of the old Polish border and Berdichev is only sixty miles from the vital Lwow-Odessa line over which men and armament used to flow to the Germans facing disaster in lower Russia.

The Berlin broadcast, possibly preparing the home and front for a grand-scale retreat in the south, said forty Red Army rifle divisions and numerous tank formations had snapped German lines between Zaporozhe and the area north and northwest of Krivoi Rog "at heavy cost" and that a big battle was continuing through the night.

Moscow's Silence Customary

Moscow's silence is customary at the unfolding of each new offensive, and the late German bulletins bore out previous German propaganda claims that a Nazi retreat to avoid encirclement in the south might be impending, if not under way.

The northern prong of General Vatutin's forces captured Chepowichi, a rail station on the Kiev-Warsaw line only sixteen miles southeast of Korosten.

The central units pushed on westward from captured Zhitomir toward Novgorad-Volynski, near the Polish border, and also turned southward toward Berdichev.

The southern group battering toward Romania cuts still off opposition at Fastov, thirty-five miles southwest of Kiev, but beat off Germans at Fastovetz, just southeast of there.

In liberating Chepovi hi and other towns and villages, the Russians said their troops had killed 1,600 Germans, captured thirty 1,900 prisoners, and freed 4,000 civilians being herded westward for "slave labor in Germany."

In the storming and capture of two enemy strong points near Kerch in the eastern Crimea, the bulletin said, the Russians killed 840 Germans. It reported that 1,620 more had died in the Pripet Marshes south of Parichsk, where seven more villages were seized by units outflanking Gomel.

Russian Forces Closing

Hundreds of thousands of German soldiers are anchored in the Dnieper bend along the southern battlefront. Three Russian armies moving against them form the southern pincers of the trap that General Vatutin's forces are creating in the northwest with their striking pincers of the trap that have closed Moscow to within ten miles from Kiev to Zhitomir in a week of hard fighting about the enemy.

The capture of Zhitomir set the Russians toward the Polish and Rumanian borders moved about which the same speed that had carried the Russians eighty-odd miles from Kiev to Zhitomir in a week. Thrust toward Moscow to include General Vatutin "Lightning." In the Crimea, where the Germans

Continued on Page Two

War News Summarized

MONDAY, NOVEMBER 15, 1943

A German broadcast, as yet unconfirmed by the Soviet Government, announced that thirty Russian divisions had broken in the Dnieper Bend. Meanwhile other Russian armies, fanning out from Zhitomir, Ukraine rail junction, captured fifty more places and reached points sixteen miles from Berdichev, the latter only sixty miles from the Odessa-Lwow railroad, the principal artery for Germans in southern Russia. [1:8. map. P. 2.]

There was an official Washington comment on the statement by Soviet Ambassador to Mexico that Russia would claim the Polish territory occupied under the Soviet-German pact of 1939. [3:8.]

The British Eighth Army captured Atessa, in a three-mile push on the Adriatic end of the battle line in Italy, while General Clark's forces stopped enemy counter-attacks northwest of Montaquila. In air duels over the central and western fronts, the German planes were shot down. [1:4. map. P. 7.]

Seventy-two-year-old Premier Badoglio, who arranged the Italian armistice and declared war on Germany, announced that he would resign when Rome was liberated. He pledged his loyalty to King Victor Emmanuel, whose abdication is urged in some circles. [1:6-7.]

In the Aegean Sea battle, the Germans extended their beachhead on Leros Island, threatened

the town of Leros from two sides and split the north-south British forces. The vital naval base is still in British hands. [1:7. map. P. 8.]

In the Balkans the Partisans captured the Slavonian railroad junctions at Virovitica, where 500 Germans were captured, and Koprivnica, where 400 more Nazi soldiers surrendered. [8:1.]

British Mosquito bombers attacked Berlin in another "mosquito" assault and pounded other targets in western Germany. Last night marked the third anniversary of the N.z. raids of Coventry, where 60,000 buildings were hit. [10:5.]

The Germans were greatly alarmed in Jutland, Denmark, possible Allied invasion point, where they threatened to proclaim martial law to check widespread sabotage. [11:1.]

As a gesture of sympathy toward the Lebanese, whom Government leaders have been imprisoned by the French, Egyptians youth rioted and broke windows in the French Delegate headquarters in Cairo. The Egyptian Premier said he would ask the United Nations to aid in bringing about the release of the prisoners in Lebanon. [10:2.]

Allied bombers dropped 223 tons of explosives on Alexishafen and Madang, New Guinea, in a record attack there. [1:6-7.]

American submarines sank seven more Japanese vessels and damaged two others, bringing the total number of Japanese ships sunk or damaged by our submarines to 496. [1:6-7.]

Japanese Plane Transport Sunk As Our Submarines Bag 7 Ships

Special to THE NEW YORK TIMES
WASHINGTON, Nov. 14—One of the war are now 348, with thirty-tinuing their assault against the six probably sunk and 114 others life-lines of Japan's mainland the damaged, or a total of 496 vessels shrinking empire. American submarines have sunk seven additional enemy vessels including a plane transport, and damaged two others, the Navy Department reported today.

The Navy's communiqué did not explain the term plane transport, but it was believed that this vessel was a large freight ship carrying short-range Japanese fighting planes to the battle front in the southwest Pacific.

Besides the plane transport, the ships listed today as sunk were one large freighter, a medium-cargo large freighter, a medium-sized cargo vessel, a small freighter, and an oiler.

One large freighter and one medium freighter were damaged.

A single sunk or damaged by our submarines since the start ties of the war are now 348, with thirty-six probably sunk and 114 others damaged, or a total of 496 vessels.

The plane transport sunk as reported today as which we had far her identified by the Navy and toward there was a question as to exactly what sort of ship was meant by that term, a spokesman carefully explained that it was not an aircraft carrier or a combat aircraft tender.

It might be either a regular merchant ship which had loaded with planes or a seaplane carrier. The Japanese have used float planes extensively both in the North and South Pacific. They are short-range craft and to haul them about over the ocean the Japanese had special merchant-type ships equipped with cranes and catapults and presumably with supply and repair facilities.

Continued on Page Two

to study with him at Tanglewood. (Aaron and I used to spend our summers there; we opened the first Tanglewood season together in 1940—he as administrative head of the school, I as a student.)

But then, after the war, the Schoenberg syndrome took hold and was heartily embraced by the young, who gradually stopped flocking to Aaron. The effect on him—and therefore on American music—was heartbreaking. He is, after all, one of the most important composers of our century. I am not thinking historically now, but musically. In fact, he became an impetus to subsequent American music only because his own music *is* so important. It contains a rare combination of spontaneity and care: his creative material is purely instinctive and his crafting of it extremely professional. Unlike much of the past decade's transient works, Aaron's music has always contained the basic values of art, not the least of which is communicativeness.

As these virtues became unfashionable, so did Aaron's music. One of the sadnesses I recall in recent years occurred at the premiere of his *Inscape*, when he said to me, "Do you realize there isn't one young composer here, there isn't one young musician who seems to be at all interested in this piece—a brand-new piece I've labored over?" The truth is that when the musical winds blew past him, he tried to catch up—with twelve-tone music, just as it too was becoming old-fashioned to the young.

When he started writing twelve-tone, I figured that it was inevitable—everybody has to fool with serialism. God knows I spent my whole sabbatical in 1964 in a desperate attempt at it; I've actually thrown away more twelve-tone pieces and bits of pieces than I have written otherwise. But still I asked him, "Of all people, why you—you who are so instinctive, so spontaneous? Why are you bothering with tone rows and with the rules of retrograde and inversion, and all that?" And he answered me, "Because I need more chords. I've run out of chords."* And that lasted for four

* This reminds me that Paul Simon (of Garfunkel fame) told me the summer before last that when he met Bob Dylan for the first time, Dylan's first sentence was "Hey, have you got any new chords? *I've run out of chords.*"

more pieces and then he didn't write any more. How sad for him. How awful for us.

Of course, as Aaron himself pointed out when I complained to him about his forsaking composition for the stage (He's become quite an excellent conductor, by the way, and has always been a marvelous lecturer), how many composers have lived into their late sixties still writing? We know the obvious example of Verdi, who at sixty thought he was through as an operatic composer, struggling halfheartedly with a *King Lear*, only to emerge after a fifteen-year hiatus, in his mid-seventies, with his two masterpieces *Otello* and *Falstaff*. Perhaps, we can hope, this will happen to Aaron. All it will take, it seems to me, is another musical turn—this time to a rediscovery of the basic simplicities of art, in which Copland will once more be looked to as a leader, will once again feel wanted as a composer.

Happy Birthday, Aaron. We miss your music. □

Written to the music critic of
Die Neue Freie Presse, *Vienna*
20 April 1970

A LETTER TO FRANZ ENDLER: BEETHOVEN'S *NINTH*

Dear Endler:

These notes are written just after having had the extraordinary experience of conducting two different performances of the *Ninth Symphony* within six days of each other: one with the Vienna Philharmonic, in Vienna, and the other with the Boston Symphony, in Boston. I have always been aware of the extreme range of interpretive differences in performances of any work by Beethoven, but never so acutely as in this case, with a work so mysterious, complicated, elusive, with so unorthodox an orchestration, and with two great orchestras of such differing natures within so short a time. And in this year, when we are all more than ever Beethoven-conscious, it becomes more apparent than ever that Beethoven, of all composers, is the most "interpretable." The reason would seem to be the complexity of his symphonic thought, but not at all; I now realize it is precisely the opposite—it is the utter simplicity of his thought. It is a simplicity so basic, so believed-in, so elemental that it necessarily invites interpretation, in the same way that the simplest, most basic statements always have. (Let there be light; *Cogito ergo sum*; All is vanity; Blessed are the meek; Existence precedes Essence; God is One; God is Three; God is dead.)

In the case of Beethoven's *Ninth*, it is not a matter of reverting, in performance, to one or another extreme of conception, but rather a matter of emphasis, leaning *toward* one extreme or the other. For the sake of clarity, let me try briefly to articulate these extremes. The one is a highly literal, faithful, rhythmically and dynamically accurate reading of the score, free of orchestrational changes or additions, without gratuitous pauses or retardations or *rubati*, faithful even to the highly controversial (sometimes even impossible) metronomic markings, and with no dynamic adjustments in the cause of orchestral balance. Let us call this Approach Alpha. The other, Approach Omega, would be a highly romanticized conception, based on extramusical ideas such as Formless Chaos (the opening bars), Germinal One-cell Creation (the first motive), culminating in The Development of Man in Full Reason and Spirit, complete with *fermate, rubati,* dynamic exaggerations and/or changes, vacillating *tempi*, poetical meanderings, and personal, subjective indulgences. Somewhere between Alpha and Omega lie all the performances of the *Ninth* we have ever heard; but I have rarely heard two performances from any one conductor that tended so divergently toward the two alphabetical extremes as these two I heard myself conduct.

eonard Bernstein

NEUNTE SYMPHONIE

mit Schlußchor über Schillers Ode an die Freude

L. van Beethoven, Op. 125

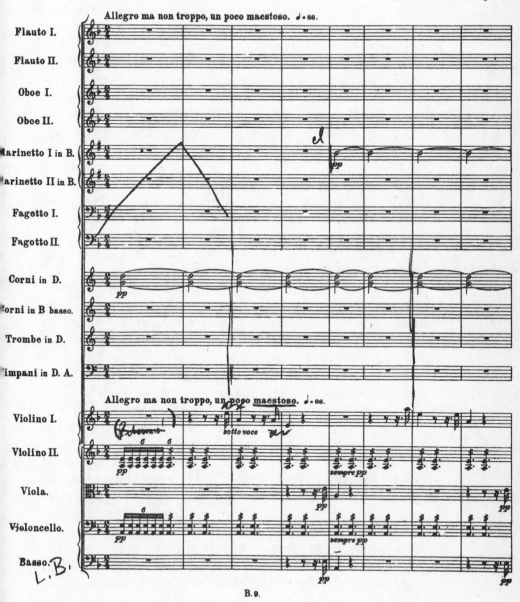

For example, the first sixteen bars. Should the opening sextuplets in the second violins and celli *sound* like sextuplets, rhythmically agitated, electrifying even in their *pianissimo,* or should they emerge as an indistinct tremolo ("Formless Chaos") with rhythmic vitality, and be absorbed into the pedal notes of the horns? Should the first note of the two-note motive, the thirty-second note, be treated literally as a thirty-second note, or be made to coincide with the sixth note of the sextuplet? Should the progressive entrances of new pedal tones (clarinet, oboe, flutes) be heard as entrances, or somehow mysteriously just be there, as new overtones of the horn fifths? Should the *crescendo* be as gradual as possible, given the very brief duration in which it must occur, or should it erupt like some subterranean upheaval? Should the *fortissimo,* when it does arrive, hit us in strict time, with no preparatory enlargement for the anacrusis, or should it crash in on us like a wave which we see coming, and which has its suspenseful moment of maximum height and threat before it descends in all its elemental strength? Should . . .

And many more are the questions that arise in those first twenty seconds of the music. But none of them can really be answered in Alpha/Omega terms except by a conductor who is out to prove something about himself rather than about Beethoven. I shall certainly not try to answer them here. I can say, only in the most general terms, that the Vienna performance leaned more in the Omega direction, almost like a Mahlerian adumbration—more *sostenuto,* perhaps more romantic. The Boston performance favored clarity, immediacy of attack, what some might call a more classic approach. And yet it was I, with no premeditation or cause, who performed them both.

A number of reasons could be given for this. One is a vast difference in the acoustical qualities of the two halls, the Konzerthaus and Symphony Hall. Another is particular orchestral tradition. Another might be the personal qualities of the solo players—clarinet, or concertmaster. Another, the actual make of instruments—the American trumpet, for instance, versus the German. But all these are exterior conditionings: these are forces that impinge on the

Conducting Mahler's Third Symphony in Vienna, 1972

conductor, who to some extent must take his cue from them, allowing the ambiance to be formed by them, since in both cases the orchestra is not "his" orchestra.

But I admit that that is all undue conductorial modesty. The truth is that in both cases the performances essentially came from the podium, based on my relationship with that mighty score, *as of that moment*. Although there had been only four days between the last Vienna performance and the first Boston rehearsal, I had again gone through a crucial reexamination of the score in those four days, as I had in the days preceding the Vienna rehearsals, and as I have always done before any performance of a major score, no matter how often I have previously conducted it. And each time there is a difference, even if it is only a difference between Mu and Nu. And with Beethoven, the difference tends to be greater than with any other composer. It can go from Gamma to Phi, from Kappa to Rho.

Why should this be? Why is Beethoven eternally rediscoverable? I could probably explain it, or try to, in ten thousand more words. But perhaps one example will point the way.

In one of these performances of the *Ninth* (I won't say which) I discovered a new element in Beethoven's music. Imagine—a new element in Beethoven's music! Is it possible? Hasn't everything been said that can be said about Beethoven? And yet it happened: I discovered that Beethoven's music has *charm*. What? Charm in Beethoven? Of all qualities, this would be the least expected. Charm, from that fierce face, that lion's head, that stunted, pockmarked body? And yet there it was to be found, buried under layers of severity, austerity, uncompromising insistence, passionate hammering, demonic ruthlessness, earth-free mysticism—all those clichés. There, underneath, lay charm. Underneath? But charm is an outward attribute, exteriorized, isn't it? Not Beethoven's charm. His is not of the shy sort, never coquettish, not rococo, not Mozartian, not sophisticated. His is the charm of utter naiveté: the pure simplicity of his childlike belief. What is more deeply charming than childlike belief? It is total, overwhelming. To play Bee-

B. 9.

thoven's music is to give oneself over completely to the child-spirit which lived in that grim, awkward, violent man. It is to be seduced by a ravishing innocence. Without that utter submission it is impossible to play the Adagio of the *Ninth*. Or, for that matter, the Scherzo. Or, Heaven knows, the first movement. And the Finale? Most of all! It is simply unplayable unless we go all the way with him, in total, prepubescent faith, in that certainty of immortality which only children (and geniuses) really possess—to go all the way with him as he cries out *"Brüder!" "Tochter!" "Freude!" "Millionen!" "Gott!"* But especially *"Brüder!"* That above all is his child-inspired cry. We must believe it in order to play it. That is why we of this cynical world are still charmed by that quaint, old-fashioned notion of all men together as children of God—when we hear it articulated by Beethoven. It is the irresistible charm of Beethoven's belief that makes the idea and the music imperishable.

And I firmly believe that it is the performer's relation to that belief which determines his performance. It is one's ability to identify with Beethoven the charming child, the innocent spirit of Grace, that enables one to re-create the music. To the extent of that identification, all those sextuplets, thirty-second notes, *crescendi, fortissimi*, and everything else simply fall into place, naturally and inevitably.

And this is the answer to my riddle of the Boston and Vienna performances. What was the ratio of hope to despair that I felt in Boston or in Vienna? How long were my arms in one city or the other—long enough to embrace my brothers, the orchestra; or only the cello section; or everyone including the chorus? How childlike was I capable of letting myself become? How trusting? How willing to suspend disbelief? How desperate about Vietnam, Israel, the Soviet Union, a newly lost friend? How hopeful for new music, for Kreisky, for the black American, for peace? *Brüder!* ☐

Written for London Symphony concert
and television broadcast
6 April 1972

HOMAGE TO STRAVINSKY

One year ago today the world said its final goodbye to Igor Stravinsky, the last great father-figure of Western music. In the course of his long and abundantly creative life, Stravinsky produced a highly personal body of work, which seems, paradoxically enough, to sum up and embrace all of music itself—from primitive folk art to highly sophisticated serialism, from rarefied church music to outspoken jazz. His embrace is even more specific: there is an essence of Bach in his music, and of Mozart, and of Tchaikovsky, and of many others—but through some private alchemy, some secret magic, he absorbed all these essences, metamorphosed them, and gave them all back to us shiny-new, original, inimitable.

His textures go from the richest to the leanest; his spirit was both devout and irreverent; his music is at once tender and spiky, emotional but antiromantic; it can be popular and esoteric, nationalistic or intercontinental. In this sense he was probably the most universal composer who ever lived. Tonight we are paying homage to that universality by playing three Stravinsky masterpieces, three works that suggest the extraordinary range of his art.

We begin with *The Rite of Spring*, that volcanic work which established him as a world figure. It was written in the years just preceding the First World War when Stravinsky was a leader of the avant-garde in Paris, along with Serge Diaghilev and his circle, artists like Pablo Picasso and Jean Cocteau. The opening night of *The Rite of Spring* at the Théâtre des Champs-Élysées was one of the most famous scandals of all time, a scandal which resulted in creating a public image of Stravinsky as a revolutionary, iconoclast, *enfant terrible*, and author of a work that would forever change music, and in the minds of some, possibly destroy it. And this fear existed even among certain serious musicians as well as the fashionable public at the Russian Ballet that memorable evening.

Today, sixty years later, we hear the work very differently: we perceive Stravinsky the magician already deep in his alchemy, turning the past into the future. We hear how basically *traditional The Rite of Spring* is, how deep are its roots in tonality, in triadic harmony, in Russian nationalism, and even in specific composers such as Scriabin, Rimsky-Korsakov, Debussy, and Ravel. But from these roots there emerged a miraculous new creation of such originality and power that still today it shocks and overwhelms us.

By the mid-twenties it had become clear that Stravinsky had not destroyed music; in fact, he had become an international leader of new musical thought. His watchword was now *neoclassicism*, which meant simply that his borrowings from the past had become a conscious and deliberate element of his creative process. The old alchemy was not in full swing; and it is this aspect of his art that we celebrate next in our program of homage, by playing the *Capriccio* for piano and orchestra—a model of his neoclassic style, with its echoes of Bach and Mozart.

But there are elements less classic than Mozart and Bach in the score of *Capriccio*: especially the ballet style of Tchaikovsky. And other elements less classic still, like a certain French salon atmosphere recalling Chaminade or Offenbach. All these, together with a hint of jazz rhythms, combine to make a piece of delicious artificiality, an essay in wit —and wittiness was something he possessed in quantity, along with an existential sense of the absurd.

The *Symphony of Psalms,* which will be our closing work tonight, brings us the devotional Stravinsky, the true believer. This choral symphony is undeniably the greatest musical celebration of the religious spirit to have been written in our century. It is his Song of Songs, in which the simple, the complex, and the monumental combine to create a serene Godliness. And yet even here Stravinsky is still "stealing," as he puts it, from Russian Orthodox church music, from Bach, from plainchant—and as always, from

With Igor Stravinsky in New York, 1962

himself. But again this genius-alchemist makes every note he writes unmistakably his own. From that brusque opening chord to the utterly pure final chord, not one bar could have been composed by anybody else.

For another four decades after the *Symphony of Psalms*, Stravinsky went on constantly stealing, and constantly surprising his audiences by what he chose to steal, including the biggest surprise of all: Schoenberg's serialism. The range of his musical embrace was so vast that he not only borrowed *from* everyone but also composed *for* everyone: there is Stravinsky for the uninitiated, for the connoisseur, and for everyone in between. In this way he captured the imagination of the whole world. Honors were heaped upon him as upon no other composer of this age—from the Kremlin to the Vatican, from heads of government to Texas cowboys.

It seems fitting that we open tonight's program with *The Rite of Spring*. Igor Stravinsky was born in the spring and died in the spring. In a sense, he lived his whole life in a springtime of creativity. All his music is springlike, newly budding, rooted in the familiar past, yet fresh and sharp, with that stinging, paradoxical combination of the inevitable and the unexpected. And so this spring evening we celebrate Stravinsky as we celebrate spring itself, like an eternal renewal. We all join, musicians and music-lovers of whatever tastes or persuasions—we all join in homage to our departed musical father. □

At Harvard University, 1973

*Sung and played at a benefit concert
of the Israel Philharmonic Orchestra
Ramat Gan, Israel
1972*

THE ISRAEL PHILHARMONIC BLUES

*I woke up this morning
    with an awful ache in my head—
I woke up this morning
    with an awful ache in my head—
When I came to rehearsal, I wished I had
    stayed in bed.*

*The flutist was late; the harpist was sick;
The timpanist had lost his timpani stick.
Oh, Tizmoret,* Tizmoret!
    Oy, is das a Tizmoret!
I just adore it, but I got those Tizmoret Blues!*

*Everyone was late after Hafsaka,†
While Surovicz was screaming B'vakasha‡—
Oh, Tizmoret, Tizmoret!
    Oy, is das a Tizmoret!
I just adore it, but I got those Tizmoret Blues!*

*Ginzburg schläft, mitten drinnen,
Und Segal patchket auf sein Tambourinen—
Oh, Tizmoret, Tizmoret!
    Oy, is das a Tizmoret!
I just adore it, but I got those Tizmoret Blues!*

(PIANO INTERLUDE)

* Orchestra
† Intermission
‡ Please!

It's a great Tizmoret, but the tempo is hard to take:
It's a great Tizmoret, but the tempo is hard to take:
We give so many concerts we just can't stay awake.
With specials and extras, and Ain-Harod,
Dunkel ist das Leben, ist der Tod:
Oh, Tizmoret, Tizmoret!
     Oy, is das a Tizmoret!
I just adore it, but I got those Tizmoret Blues!

Preface for Charles Schwartz's book
on George Gershwin
19 April 1973

ON GERSHWIN

All cultural disciplines are subject to the tyranny of fashion. Suddenly, it's all about Hume or Diderot or *The Post Royal* grammarians; suddenly Thomas Mann is out and Macaulay is in; Coleridge is down five and a half points . . .

The world of music is not exempt from this epochal whimsicality. In fact, it tends to be more fickle and volatile than even the brave new world of linguistics. I remember vividly causing a sensation as a Harvard undergraduate by announcing that I loved the music of Tchaikovsky. It was considered an outrageous heresy; Tchaikovsky was located one pigeonhole beneath Contempt at the time, as was Verdi. The fashion dictated pre-Beethoven and post-Wagner. Today, half a lifetime later, Verdi is musicologized as solemnly as is Monteverdi; Hindemith is unfashionable, Ravel grossly underrated. Alas, the musical marketplace.

One of the most egregious victims of this musical *haute couture* in our century has been George Gershwin. He is not only unfashionable and underrated; he is hardly ever even discussed. The name just doesn't come up. The Higher

Criticism does not permit that name to enter the category of Significant Composers. Of course, Gershwin's songs have become part of our language, or the vernacular, if you will, and they are hummed and whistled by people who don't know who wrote them, and don't care, and who would react with disdain to the name of the author if they did know. (That should be rephrased: they would happily accept the name of the song composer; the disdain would be directed toward the Composer of Works.) All of this is sad, because Gershwin was certainly one of the true, authentic geniuses American music has produced. Time and history may even show him to be the truest and most authentic of his time and place.

It is sad, and yet understandable. Gershwin was, after all, a songwriter—in his nature, his origin, his experience, and his craft. He came from the wrong side of the tracks; grew up in the ambiance of Tin Pan Alley, song-plugging, and musical near-illiteracy. His short life was one steady push to cross the tracks, both musically and socially—an effort guided and sustained by ambition, a profound learning capacity, and an enormous reservoir of sensibilities. This book will trace that track-crossing, from songs to shows, from shows to real theater pieces (works) such as *Of Thee I Sing*, from structurally weak concert pieces like the *Rhapsody in Blue* through the *Concerto in F* to the final amalgamation we see in *Porgy*. All these works are easily demolished by the Higher Criticism: The *Rhapsody*, for example, is a model of structural inefficiency. It is episodic, loosely strung together by rather artificial transitions, modulatory devices, and secondhand cadenzas. But what's important is not what's wrong with the *Rhapsody*, but what's right with it. And what's right is that each of those inefficiently connected episodes is in itself melodically inspired, harmonically truthful, rhythmically authentic. Again we call upon that word; it was no less a master of form and structure than Arnold Schoenberg who recognized the "authenticity" of Gershwin's music.

Gershwin's tragedy was not that he failed to cross the tracks, but rather that he did, and once there, in his new habitat, was deprived of the chance to plunge his roots firmly into the new soil. He was given only a little more than a decade to develop the fruits of this transplantation, and died, shockingly and maddeningly, in his thirties, a few years older than Mozart was when he died. These two names may be felt to be an uncomfortable pairing, but they make a fascinating comparison. Both men were "naturals," each evolving a body of music that sprang like a phenomenon of nature from his soil, fertile and flourishing. But Mozart had no tracks to cross; his was one great continuing harvest from childhood to death. Gershwin, on the contrary, had to plow, sow, reap, and thresh anew, over and over again. By the time of *Porgy* we sense an incipient Master. We can only speculate on what degree of mastery he might have attained if he had lived. The tragedy of his death-in-the-prime is a great one; but we only compound the tragedy if we persist in the Higher Criticism, and ignore the radiant fact that Gershwin was, and remains, one of the greatest voices that have ever rung out in the history of American urban culture. ☐

Adapted from the eulogy
9 December 1973

JENNIE TOUREL: 1910–1973

It took me a long time to discover the values of a funeral ceremony: I had always abhorred and avoided them as pomposities—*pompes funèbres*—and as a poor way to say goodbye, a needlessly public way of paying one's private last respects.

And then, on one especially personal occasion, I suddenly discovered what everyone else had apparently known all along: that funerals are for the living; that they cause us to come together in a way we otherwise never do, to lean on one another, to feel the communality of emotions, to cry together, and—yes—to rejoice together, to

With Jennie Tourel

rejoice in the one who has caused this coming together. The one in our case this day is a Great One, one who gave us constant cause for rejoicing over the years, and does again today.

In using that badly abused word "great" I am not speaking in the obvious sense of Great Lady, or Grande Dame, or even of Great Artist—all of which, of course, are classifications to which Jennie Tourel eminently belongs. Those are all evident to anyone who knew her or her art, whether in intimacy or only from the heights of the second balcony. The greatness of Jennie that fills me today, and fills this room to bursting, is the abundancy of Jennie.

Over the three decades in which it was my delight to know her, I learned to know a multiplicity of Jennies, an abundance of languages and rhythms and styles, of complexities and childlike simplicities. There was an abundance, too, in her capacity for friendship, in her generosity to colleagues and students. She was also abundantly critical of those same colleagues and students, and at the same time more vulnerable than any of them.

Most remarkable of all was that in any one of these aspects—colleague, hostess, teacher, émigrée, patriot, friend, *femme du monde*—in any of these she was totally involved and utterly convincing. Her multiplicity was matched only by her authenticity. I used to marvel at this, and wonder how it was possible; from where did she take the inner energy to be all these things—not to play the roles, but to be them? They were all convincing because they were all true; and she had that special energy. It was possible; but she paid a heavy price: ultimately, her most intimate companion was loneliness.

The paradox of Jennie: so richly endowed; surrounded by loving friends, gallant admirers, and adoring fans. Yet she was never free of the always shocking awareness of isolation—except in those few thousand minutes of her life when she was transported by the bliss of communication through her art. That communication was her credo: the maximum penetration to human sensibilities; yet an hour later she was isolated. She lived her life on the assumption that "no man is an island"; but she also knew, and so often told me she knew, that every man is an island.

In her wonderfully engaging anti-intellectual way, she echoed the Wittgensteinish idea that the limits of the individual do not describe his outline: they describe that of the universe surrounding him. She knew that birth and death are lonely acts, painfully private and incapable of being shared. But she was determined that every moment in between would be shared to the greatest possible degree.

The paradox of Jennie: the incurable romantic, yet just enough the existentialist to recognize the universality of isolation. The Russian fatalist, yet just pragmatic enough to face destiny—even, sometimes, to try to cheat it. She trembled in her mortality, like all of us; and yet had long ago accepted the concept of Death. And out of all these paradoxes came her sensitive, charming perception of the Absurd; and out of that perception came her extraordinary humor, which saved her time after time from the horrors of loneliness, and endeared her to everyone who knew her.

I have been asked to speak here on behalf of her many friends, her associates, and especially of the New York Philharmonic, with which she had so long and enriching an association. But I find I can speak only as one who loved her deeply and knew her, perhaps, a little better than most. Am I trying to say too much in a few words? Can we judge whether she had a happy or an unhappy life?

The Hassidic rabbis tell a beautiful parable of the Four Supreme Holinesses: that on all of earth the holiest spot is the Holy of Holies in the Temple at Jerusalem, *Kodesh Hakadoshim*; that among all earthly tongues the holiest word is the Name of God, *Shem Adonai*; that of all the days of the year the holiest is the Day of Atonement, *Shabbat Shabbatot*; and that of all God's creatures the holiest is the High Priest, *Kohen Hagadol*. At a certain hour, on a certain day of the year, all these four holinesses met together. This took place on the Day of Atonement, at the hour when the High Priest entered the Holy of Holies and there revealed the Divine Name. . . .

What was Jennie's life? Wherever she stood to sing, that stage was the Holy of Holies. And when she opened her mouth in praise of music, she was a High Priestess, and each phrase was the Name of God; and that moment was the Sabbath of Sabbaths.

Was Jennie Tourel unhappy? The Greeks said that you could never tell if a human being was happy until he had died. Well, now we know: Jennie sang God's Name up to the last possible moment. □

Comments made during an intermission conversation
with the young musicians of the World Orchestra
who played in the concert at Tanglewood
honoring the 100th anniversary of Serge Koussevitzky's birth
July, 1974

FOR S.A.K.

Serge Koussevitzky, whose hundredth birthday we celebrate July 26, was an extraordinary man, because he was not just a conductor. There are many conductors in the world; many fine conductors; even some great conductors. But Koussevitzky was more: he was a great spirit. Incredible man, beautiful to look at, beautiful inside, and a natural musician.

He was not primarily an intellectual conductor. I had the lucky experience of studying with two masters: one was Koussevitzky and the other Fritz Reiner. They seemed to me exact opposites.

Reiner was an intellectual conductor who demanded certain standards of knowledge that were absolutely basic, minimal—and these minimal standards were maximal, I can tell you. He was very analytical, precise, and taught a stick technique that was very *genau*—very exact.

That is not the way Koussevitzky taught at all, and so the summers when I came to Tanglewood, more than thirty years ago—I began in 1940—I had a whole other kind of teacher in Koussevitzky, who taught in an inspirational way. It wasn't a stick technique—in fact, I didn't use a stick in those days; I conducted bare-handed—but he taught the essence of the music and the spirit of the music.

It was all spirit, all love, relationships, and humanity; and I recalled that, of course, very personally and profoundly last Sunday when I conducted the *Fifth* Tchaikovsky. It was like a signature of Koussevitzky; it was like his theme song—one of his national anthems, one might say; and I felt his presence very strongly on the stage. Many people said it reminded them of *his* performances of the Tchaikovsky, which is very flattering, but the main thing

With Koussevitzky after performing The Age of Anxiety *at Tanglewood, 1949*

to me was that I felt his presence in the orchestra, and those members of the Boston Symphony Orchestra who did play with him relived an experience of that great spirit.

The greatness of this spirit not only caused memorable performances of music to happen, but caused this place to come into existence, the Berkshire Music Center, which he had always dreamed of establishing in order to bring together the most talented musicians of all kinds, from all over this country and abroad, to work together, and to work in a highly intense way.

I remember, in 1940 and 1941, when I was your age, I don't think we ever slept. It was so exciting: we were working all the time, or playing all the time, because it became the same thing; playing music and playing with each other, making love, making music was all one thing, and it was constant, and of constant intensity. And over it all was the spirit of Koussevitzky, who held it all together and made it all so important. Everything that we did—every note, every phrase, the way we walked—was influenced by Koussevitzky because his charisma, if one can use that overused word, was so strong that his presence here at a rehearsal, for example—if I was rehearsing the student orchestra, he would be sitting there—would make it supremely important that everything you did be as good as possible.

How can I say it? Koussevitzky gave a sense of "gala" to everything. Every time he walked out on the stage to conduct, it was a gala performance. It was like *the* performance of the century, no matter what it was—a Mozart symphony, the *Ninth* Beethoven, or the *Missa Solemnis*, or a modern piece. He was a great advancer of modern music, especially Stravinsky, Prokofiev, Hindemith, Bartok, and the Americans, Copland, Piston, Harris, and Schuman.

He was a pioneer and adventurer, and the most instinctive musician I think I have ever met. Everything he did was completely natural in music—even if you didn't agree with it; even though sometimes it was exaggerated. And maybe some of the things I did last Sunday in the Tchaikovsky *Fifth* were exaggerated, because I was remembering his *ritardandi*, which were, maybe, bigger than they should be

Koussevitzky recording Beethoven for RCA; L.B. singing bass, Tanglewood, 1950

in the *Hochschule*, and the *accelerandi* that weren't in the score that he would put in, and so on. But it all came from such a spontaneous source that it was always convincing. And I don't think there's any way of replacing him.

That's my heritage from Koussevitzky: the spontaneity of musical instinct, and that you have to trust it. Of course, you have to have knowledge, you have to have taste, you have to have background, you should know languages, you should know the literature of the various periods in which the music that we play came forth; but above all that, the main thing that counts is the natural instinct that comes from the spirit. ☐

Written for the
Schwann Catalog
25 June 1975

AARON AND MOSES:
COPLAND AT 75

I have known Aaron Copland for half of his lifetime, and loved him all those years. I have known his music for even longer than that, and have loved it with equal constancy. But critics and colleagues have been writing about the-man-and-his-music for even longer, for half a century, in depth and out of it. And so, at this seventy-fifth milestone, I find myself shying away from the requisite Tribute; such panegyrics are streaming in by the dozens. We are about to be saturated with Coplandiana regarding the Lincoln-esque, the homespun, charming, plainspoken, youthful, kindly, humorous, energetic, affectionate Aaron. We shall be hearing enough, and more, about his giggle, his Socratic pedagogy, his solitary discipline, his dedication to the young.

One curious birthday thought springs to mind; let me ponder it. It has occurred to me that Aaron is well named. Like his Biblical namesake, he has functioned as the High Priest of American music, the gentle but forceful leader and taste-maker, adored by his disparate tribes for his flexibil-ity, facility, and immensely appealing articulateness. And yet this is a superficial portrait—this benign bestower of the Golden Calf. For within this pleasant and reassuring persona called Aaron lives the mysterious anima of the brother Moses, the stern and stammering lawgiver. It is as though the amiable, cultivated Aaron provided the public voice for the harsh and resolute prophet that rages within. And it is this inner voice which ultimately informs the whole Copland musical corpus, uniting all its flexibility and "eclecticism" into a significant and lasting whole. Those critics who speculate, not quite sympathetically, on how

With Aaron Copland and Serge Koussevitzky at Tanglewood, ca. 1948

the same composer could have written the pop-toned *Music for the Theatre* and the thornily severe *Connotations* should listen more carefully. They will find in both works, and in all others between, that unmistakably consistent Mosaic voice, attenuated, adorned, or mollified to varying degrees according to the changing visibility of the Aaronic vestments, of the gleaming, opulent priestly breastplate.

One of the most fascinating studies of Copland's music is the reconciling of that opulence with the much-discussed directness and "plainness" of the Copland image. For me the reconciliation took place easily, and long ago. As a student, back in the mid-thirties, I heard my first Copland piece, a recording of his *Piano Variations*. In my instant, overwhelmed reaction to this harsh and dissonant music I automatically envisaged the composer as patriarch, perhaps bearded like Whitman, certainly Mosaic. Some time later I met the patriarch, cleanly shaven, broadly smiling, a young thirty-seven. In fact, the occasion of our meeting coincided with his birthday; there was a party in his studio, all charm and gaiety, and I "entertained" by playing those rather *un*-charming *Piano Variations*. There it all came together, and so it has remained. Our relationship has been long and joyous, but at its core those *Variations* have been ceaselessly hammering. Similarly with his music: from *Billy the Kid* to *Inscape*, from *El Salon Mexico* to the *Nonet*, those *Variations* are the key. There is always the prophetic statement, the reflective meditation, that curiously tender hesitancy; there are those angular leaps, those *scherzando* spasms. Moses in Aaron's garb. I love all this music, in all its degrees of severity and charm. And I love the man, in all those same degrees.

It is futile to say, May he live forever! Of course he will. □

Speech given in Philadelphia
27 February 1975

MEMORIES OF THE CURTIS INSTITUTE

Well, here we are, safe and moderately sound, we old boys and girls of the fifty-year-old Curtis Institute. It is a warm and affectionate occasion, and I am delighted and honored to have been asked to participate in it in this oratorical way. It gives me a chance to praise Curtis publicly, to celebrate

Fritz Reiner

it, and to thank it for all it gave me and so many others: its great teachers; its caring and considerate administration; its scholarship—both musical and financial; and its much-needed monetary loans, which I hope I have repaid with multiple compound interest. When I think back to the two years I spent here in Philadelphia, my immediate memory is of a deeply moving experience, full of hard work, intense relationships, and fascinating new frontiers to cross. Even though I arrived having just graduated from Harvard, where I had, of course, majored in music, I found Curtis a whole new musical world. For one thing, I had never entertained the notion of being a conductor; that was a brand-new idea which had just that summer been instilled in my brain by Dimitri Mitropoulos, and it turned out fortuitously that Fritz Reiner was at that very moment about to hold auditions for a conducting class. So audition I did, and accepted I was, and suddenly I was studying conducting with the great and fanatically severe Fritz Reiner. Then there was the great Vengerova, also fanatically severe; never had I had a piano teacher so demanding and tyrannical as my dear Isabella Afanasiovna Vengerova. That too was new for me. For another thing, my Harvard curriculum had not included the study of species counterpoint—that was considered old hat in Cambridge—and so here was the remarkable and gentle Dr. Richard Stoehr to teach it to me. Nor had I ever studied good old-fashioned solfège, and now here was the lovable and gifted Renée Longy to teach it to me—or Mme. Miquelle, as she was called in those days—who also worked magic in her score-reading classes. So all in all it was a major new experience—not to mention the proximity of the Philadelphia Orchestra, or the totally new experience of drinking Philadelphia water.

I could, of course, end my remarks right here, on this panegyrical note of *Hosannas* and *Laudas* and *Gratias*, and everybody would be happy as a clam. That is the customary and conventional way of addressing reunions and anniversaries—all paeans and laudations—but I'm not feeling very conventional these days. The more I dig into my memory of those two Curtis years, the more of a mixed bag I find it to be. Let me see if I can give you even a small idea of what that experience was really like—and forgive me if I reminisce and ramble a bit.

I arrived at Curtis in September 1939, after four college years filled with noble causes and a sense of history hurtling forward. How many of you can remember those years—the *tone* of those years? The big subject was fascism; and our great enterprise was antifascism. Only recall Spain, a goner; China, Ethiopia, Czechoslovakia, Austria. There were refugees all around us, and great ones: Thomas Mann, Hindemith, Einstein, Schoenberg. There was constant excitement in the air, the excitement of a huge and glorious struggle. At Harvard we had all-night bull sessions; we marched, we demonstrated; I played the piano for strikers, for Spain, for blacks, for one cause after another. And none of this seemed to conflict with my studies, whether musical or literary or philosophical; it all blended together in an interdisciplinary way, under the bright Keatsian formula "Beauty is truth, truth beauty; that is all/Ye know on earth, and all ye need to know." I was aflame with this equation; I felt myself a young artist *and* a young citizen, endlessly eager for more and more knowledge.

But by the time I came to Curtis I was also confused and depressed. There were so many sticky problems to be figured out, so many contradictions. There was the infamous nonaggression pact between Germany and Russia. Whose side should one be on? Certainly not Hitler's. And yet, there was poor Shostakovich being denounced by his government for his beautiful *Fifth Symphony*. Where were truth and beauty now? What truth? Whose beauty? And most depressing of all, Hitler had just invaded Poland, that very September, with the devastating results you all know.

It's very hard for me to give you an accurate picture of that particular combination of excitement and depression that I was experiencing as I entered Curtis. But the great poet Wystan Auden does give the picture with magnificent clarity in his poem called "September 1, 1939." Let me read you just two stanzas from it. The opening stanza:

> *I sit in one of the dives*
> *On Fifty-Second Street*
> *Uncertain and afraid*
> *As the clever hopes expire*
> *Of a low dishonest decade;*
> *Waves of anger and fear*
> *Circulate over the bright*
> *And darkened lands of the earth,*
> *Obsessing our private lives;*
> *The unmentionable odour of death*
> *Offends the September night.*

And now I skip to the final stanza:

> *Defenceless under the night*
> *Our world in stupor lies;*

Yet, dotted everywhere,
Ironic points of light
Flash out wherever the Just
Exchange their messages:
May I, composed like them
Of Eros and of dust,
Beleaguered by the same
Negation and despair,
Show an affirmative flame.

There you have it—a picture of the inner me walking into the Curtis Institute of Music; and it was like walking into an alien land. The school at that time was a fairly accurate reflection of the isolationist attitude that gripped so large a part of our country. The motto was: Avoid entanglements. Curtis was an island of musical enterprise; there seemed to be no one with whom I could share my Auden-esque feelings, at least not among the students. Those first few months were lonely and agonizing.

In short, to continue this candid confession, I was not a smash hit with the student body. As you can imagine, they regarded me as a Harvard smart aleck, an intellectual big shot, a snob, and a show-off. I know this to be true because they later told me so. Well, maybe they had a point; but the fact remains that I was the only university type around, and we may all have overreacted. After all, not one of them had gone to college; some were still in short pants; others had entered the school in short pants years before, and were still totally immersed in hammering out the Étude in thirds faster than the nearest competitor; or perhaps it was a Paganini Caprice, or a Puccini aria. In any case, interdisciplinary it was not. Philosophy, history, aesthetics—all irrelevant. The school seemed to me like a virtuoso factory, turning out identical virtuosi like sausages. I exaggerate, of course; but that's how it *seemed* to me in September, 1939.

Now, no one was more aware of this state of affairs than the good people who ran this conservatory: the distinguished Mrs. Bok, a true lady of culture, and her associates, especially Dr. Reiner and our beloved Rudy Serkin, both of them very literate refugees. Something had to be done, and something *was* done; they engaged as the new director Randall Thompson, a composer, an intellectual, and—good Lord!—a Harvard man. He was engaged to change this school from a conservatory into a true school based on the axiom that there *is* truth beyond virtuosity. We came in together, that fall of '39, he as director and I as a student; and two years later we departed together, I as a graduate, and he, rumor had it, fired. It just hadn't worked out. But oh, how he tried: he brought lecturers to Casimir Hall; he initiated new courses of an interdisciplinary nature; he tried to create a scholarly, questing atmosphere. I studied orchestration with him, and we became instant and fast friends. We discovered that we shared a freaky love for British crossword puzzles, and spent much too large a part of our orchestration sessions doing the ones in the London *Times*.

In fact, my only real friends, those first few months, were faculty members—and some members of the staff, like the sweet Jane Hill—but above all Mme. Miquelle, whose apartment was always open to me, and who cooked for me her original French concoction which she called Fried Soup. But among the students, no friends. On the contrary, I had enemies, official enemies. There was actually a secret anti-Bernstein club, composed of students some of whom later became my closest friends—Julian Lutz, Leo Luskin, Lynn Wainwright: their names are engraved on my brain. Not too many, perhaps half a dozen, who believed, beyond the gripe that I was a Harvard snob, that I was also a fake, especially in my ability to sight-read orchestral scores. They were convinced that I had secretly prepared them and then passed them off as sight reading. Alas. The word spread; the tension mounted.

Then came the astounding climax. A colleague of mine in Reiner's class went out and bought a gun, plus bullets with my name on them. This highly disturbed young man, who shall remain nameless, was having terrible trouble memorizing his scores for the merciless Reiner—who, as you may know, could stop you at any point in the music and paralyze you with the question "What is the second clarinet playing in this bar?" Well, all this became too much for my colleague, who decided that I was Reiner's favorite, that he was being discriminated against, and that he would therefore clear up the whole situation by shooting not only me, but Reiner *and* Randall Thompson as well. But he made the fatal mistake of announcing his intentions to Randall, laying his gun on the table, *literally*. Randall cleverly soothed him, called the police, and had the poor boy carted away, back to his hometown.

This climactic event somehow changed my whole situation. Foes became friends, overwhelmed with sympathy; Lutz and Luskin rushed to me to confess about their secret society; and suddenly everybody believed that I really could sight-read scores at the piano. What bliss. But with this change something much more important happened. As I got to know these newfound friends, I found to my surprise that they were indeed very much interested in the world at large, in philosophical and political concepts. And musically, many of them did care a great deal about more than virtuosity; they cared about style and period, about scholarship, about the composer in society, about *interdisciplinary* thought.

And with this revelation came another eye-opener: I realized that Harvard had been just as bad in its extreme academic way as Curtis had seemed to me in its conservatory way. The Harvard music department had been all theory and intellectualizing, to the total detriment of practical music-making or teaching. There was no way you could learn to play an instrument or to sing; that was beneath collegiate contempt. Why, you could spend hours wandering through the Music Building and never hear a note of actual music. Indeed, I realized, Harvard was capable of producing as many musical deadbeats as was Curtis— maybe more. Obviously, each school was an extreme example of its type, and the obvious solution for the future was for each to move in a direction toward the other. There had to be practical music-making at Harvard (and now there is), and there had to be far broader horizons at Curtis (and now there are). It all works out in the end: truth and beauty still form a valid equation.

So that's how I found out that yes, in some way I had

Tel Aviv, 1981

326 • Leonard Bernstein

been a bit of a snob, a university show-off. And for the rest of my stay at Curtis everything was different: We formed groups for discussion, for playing new music. We even played for noble causes. My faith was restored: an artist could after all be a responsible member of society, even a political one. And in 1941, the year I left Curtis, our country went to war against fascism and helped to destroy it, we hope.

But why have I burdened you with this historical polemic? What does it have to do with Keats's dictum about truth and beauty? I'll tell you. All this that I have been describing took place more than thirty years ago. Only think what has come to pass since then. The unspeakable Holocaust. The Atom Bomb. Victory. A Cold War. New independent nations. The U.N. The State of Israel. A Korean War. The McCarthy years. Juvenile gangs. The Kennedy years. The Beatles. The unbearable spate of assassinations. The Youth Cult. The civil rights movement. Vietnam. Peace demonstrations. Subcultures. Long hair and jeans. Watergate. In all of this there has been an increasingly sophisticated mishandling of truth. It gets harder and harder to sift lies, harder to know what is true. Is Arab oil buying up the world? Is higher education still genuine, or merely self-interested? Is our morality crumbling along with the economy? Is human greed remediable? Does our avant-garde produce true art, and therefore beautiful art? Should mysticism replace scientific rationalism? Is God dead? Is survival more important than honor? Are these all academic questions, good for bull sessions and TV talk shows, or can we artists really be involved in trying to answer them? Yes, I say, we are involved. I know I am involved; I could never make music if I were not.

By now I have reached a fairly old age, and I'm not too much wiser than I was thirty years ago. I may know more facts, but I have forgotten many more than I ever knew. But one thing I still know: beauty is truth, and truth beauty. That is still a great equation, at least as important as $E = MC^2$. It is still the only way that I as an artist know how to begin to answer those questions. But our sense of truth must be interdisciplinary, and our sense of beauty must be expansive, even eclectic. Our horizons can never be broad enough. We must be able to embrace the intuitive *and* the rational, the theoretical *and* the practical: in other words, Harvard *and* Curtis.

I still hear people asking: What have we artists to do with oil and economy, survival and honor? The answer is *Everything*. Our truth, if it is heartfelt, and the beauty we produce out of it, may perhaps be the only real guidelines left, the only clear beacons, the only source for renewal of vitality in the various cultures of our world. Where economists squabble, we can be clear. Where politicians play diplomatic games, we can move hearts and minds. Where the greedy grab, we can give. Our pens, voices, paintbrushes, pas de deux; our words; our C-sharps and B-flats can shoot up far higher than any oil well, can break down self-interest, can reinforce us against moral deterioration. Perhaps, after all, it is only the artist who can reconcile the mystic with the rational, and who can continue to reveal the presence of God in the minds of men. □

L.B. as Liberty, New York City, 1949

Speech given at Battery Park, New York City
4 July 1976

THE DECLARATION
OF INDEPENDENCE

For as long as I can remember, I have been reading to myself this extraordinary document called the Declaration of Independence on every Fourth of July—each year marveling anew at its precision of rhetoric, its visionary hopes, its solemn legal diction, its stubborn adherence to facts, and its barely contained rage. It has been a fruitful annual exercise. I don't know how many of you also read it once a year; if not, it is my prideful honor to do it for you, in this very special year.

Abraham Lincoln said that we cannot escape history, and he said it in a historical moment far darker than ours. But we today are living a moment from which we will escape only at our utmost peril. It is the moment of rededicating ourselves to the concept of freedom—that blazing idea for which our forefathers pledged to one another their lives, their fortunes, and their sacred honor. We can do no less than to renew that pledge, as we repeat their majestic utterance:

"When, in the course of human events . . ." ☐

ON STILLNESS

Stillness is our most intense mode of action. It is in our moments of deep quiet that is born every idea, emotion, and drive which we eventually honor with the name of action. Our most emotionally active life is lived in our dreams, and our cells renew themselves most industriously in sleep. We reach highest in meditation, and farthest in prayer. In stillness every human being is great; he is free from the experience of hostility; he is a poet, and most like an angel. □

May, 1977

MEMORIES OF MAESTRO DE SABATA

The first word that rises in my mind as I call up memories of Victor de Sabata is *generosity*. It seemed to me to inform and characterize all his actions: his abundant love for music and for the colleagues with whom he produced it; the abundance of his passions and of his patience; his profound gratitude for his own gifts; his kindness to young performers like me; his devotion to his public, whether in Milan or Pittsburgh—all of it generous, generous. It was also in the music he composed: the spirit of *abbondanza*.

• *Leonard Bernstein*

It was because of his sudden illness in 1953 that I was called upon to open the Scala season with Cherubini's *Medea*, Callas and all. There were only six days for me to learn an unknown score; to make cuts and repairs; to meet and cope with Callas—which turned out to be pure joy; to make a difficult debut alla Scala—and all with severe bronchitis. In all this, Maestro de Sabata was intensely helpful

With Maria Callas, Milan, 1953

and encouraging; he gave me the extra measure of courage that I needed. And two years later, when I returned to conduct a new production of *Sonnambula,* he virtually saved my life. "Too slow! Too slow!" I can still hear him chiding. "Bellini was Sicilian; and Sicilian blood runs hot! Run with it! Run!" Who knows what a boring disaster I might have made without that affectionate warning!

There was much other good counsel besides; and of course he was equally generous with his praise. And this abundance of spirit flowed through all his conducting; one has only to listen to his old recording of *Tosca* with Callas. I still believe it to be the greatest recording of an Italian opera I have ever heard. I have only to listen to it—any dozen bars of it—and the spirit of de Sabata is in the room with me. □

Testimony before the House Subcommittee on
Select Education regarding
a bill calling for a White House Conference on the Arts
New York City, 17 December 1977

ON EDUCATION

What I have to say at this aesthetic testimonial is of utmost urgency to me, and, I believe, to our nation. So many words have flowed over the years about the arts in America, the artist and his place in society, the built-in distrust of the arts for which America has long been famous—an aversion based on a long-standing Puritan concept of the artist as somehow unmanly. Congress roared with laughter in the thirties when bills for government support of the artist were introduced. A red-blooded American boy plays baseball, not the violin, and he certainly does not perform pirouettes. As for a red-blooded American girl, she was better off playing with dolls or sewing kits than with cameras or sculptures. In those days of Depression and fascism and antifascism, the arts seemed particularly pointless to our Congress; and it was only the WPA which saved the day and, ironically enough, gave the biggest boost to our artistic life in its entire history up to that point.

Today, almost half a century later, all that has changed. The arts are everywhere, booming and blooming. Anyone with any claim to being civilized *has* to have seen certain plays, heard certain concerts, at least sampled the opera, and contributed his quota of requisite *bravos* at the ballet. There are arts councils everywhere; grants flow in all directions, on federal, state and municipal levels; and there is, of course, this very meeting here today. But, I am sad to say, we are still an uncultured nation, and no amount of granting or funding is ever going to change that, unless— but I anticipate. A White House conference? Of course. Money for artists? Naturally. I have fought all my life for it. Government subsidies? Again, I raise my voice in a loud Amen, as I have always done. But we are still victims of our

At Harvard University, 1973

334 • Leonard Bernstein

ancient attitudes, regarding the arts as a light diversion, an evening out, a curious office building, a comforting blanket of background music, an occasional BBC play about Richard the Third on the educational TV channels—whatever superficially entertaining hour it may be; and we will always retain these attitudes until we become not only an art-producing people, but an art-consuming people; and that means a people *prepared* to receive the aesthetic product; and *that* means an *educated* people. Only a society prepared by education can ever be a truly cultured society. It is a simple case of supply and demand. Let me try to explain what I mean.

The word "education" is a turn-off; we all know that, to our sorrow. But that is only because education has been a forced activity, reluctantly endured because there is no alternative if we wish to succeed in our careers and at our cocktail parties. We tend to tolerate education, in the Victorian manner; to suffer it gladly for our own selfish interests, rather than to embrace it because we have been infused as children with the joy of learning. It is to this joy of learning that I propose the White House conference should address itself—not at the expense of encouraging the arts with financial aid, but in addition to it. In fact, I believe that this urgent need to take hold of and develop the innate curiosity and immense learning capacity which all children share must take precedence over all other considerations.

Let me focus down on the art of music—not only because it is my special field, but because it is the most natural, inborn aesthetic human experience, the most abstract and exalted of the arts. I note with pleasure that on page six of this Joint Resolution 600, the final paragraph lists music first among the arts. I quote: "The term 'arts' includes, but is not limited to, music (instrumental and vocal), dance, drama . . ." and then follows the long list of the other creative and performing arts. Bravo; *but*, though Music may lead the Muses, she is actually the stepchild, in terms of a public prepared for the musical experience. How many Americans can read music? How many Americans are even minimally capable of following the course of a Brahms symphony, to say nothing of a Mozart sonata, or even the fine points of a Gershwin tune? I would guess a fraction of one percent. Music desperately needs a prepared public, joyfully educated ears. After all, everyone learns to read words, to dance the Hustle, to act in school plays, to have some visual appreciation of graphic forms, to understand a poem by Keats or Robert Frost. But almost nobody is taught to read music, or to comprehend its basic principles. Music is an orphan; and will always be that orphan until we get a grip on a methodology of musical education of the young.

I propose that the reading and understanding of music be taught to our children from the very beginning of their school life; that they learn to participate with enthusiasm in the study of music from kindergarten through high school. No child is tone-deaf; every child has the natural ability and desire to assimilate musical ideas and comprehend their combinations into musical forms. Every child can be taught to read music as he or she is taught to read words; and there is no reason why both kinds of reading cannot be taught simultaneously. It is only a matter of presenting this material in a way that does not turn the student off; and I am deeply convinced that with time, intelligent funding, and proper assistance, one can find the ways in which this enormous project can be implemented on a national scale. I, for one, am willing to pledge my energy and time to this end. Children must receive musical instruction as naturally as food, and with as much pleasure as they derive from a ball game. And this must happen from the beginning of their school lives. Only then will we produce a generation of Americans prepared to receive the larger musical experience, and to have the passion to probe ever more deeply. Then we will have our true musical public, an alive, receptive, truly critical public which will demand the best that our artists can supply. That is what I mean by the simple law of demand and supply.

I addressed this problem, long ago, in an article entitled "The Muzak Muse: An Imaginary Conversation with George Washington," to be found in my book *The Infinite Variety of Music*. I respectfully ask that this article be entered into the record.

At the White House, 1964

We *can* become a cultured nation; we have only to learn
how first to apply our energies and public dollars in the
right places. Let us be proud of America, and of our limitless resources and potential. And our children will be
proud of us.   □

Introduction for honors accorded Aaron Copland
Kennedy Center, Washington, D.C.
2 December 1979

COPLAND AT 79

Last month Aaron Copland celebrated his seventy-ninth birthday, out of which evolved a plethora of toasts, lunches, speeches, tributes, and honors, of which tonight's honor is certainly the grandest. But if all this happens when he is only seventy-nine, what volcanoes will erupt when he hits eighty, a year from now? I can't begin to imagine; but whatever monster celebrations, fireworks, and Hallelujahs take place, they will never suffice to honor in proper degree this great gentleman of American music. Never have we had a composer of his superb lyric and symphonic quality who has been personally so admired, respected, and—let's say it—loved by so many people as Aaron. I speak not only of the music, but also of the man. Ask anyone who knows him: What is Aaron like? And he or she will surely respond by describing the Copland grin, the Copland giggle, the Copland wit and warmth, the width of his embrace. He has always had time for everyone—especially the young; that is the mark of a great man: time for people. And his unmistakable sharp "judge-nose," as he once described it, has always been sniffing out new talent, in whatever hamlet or continent it might be hiding in, to encourage with praise, to nurture with criticism, and to help on its way to public exposure. And yet he is the most moderate, balanced, objective, sane and nonmelodramatic man I have ever known. When he exaggerates, it's to make us laugh; when he understates, it's to point up an irony. Everything else is plain truth—"plain" is one of his favorite words—and truth is the very essence of the man.

All of these qualities—the generosity, the wit, the quirkiness, the compassion and tenderness and plainness—all these inhabit his music with a mirrorlike truth. But there are other reflections in the music too, which reflect aspects

done

With Aaron Copland, 1952

of the man he never allows us to see. The music can have an extraordinary grandeur, an exquisite delicacy, a prophetic severity, a ferocious rage, a sharp bite, a prickly snap, a mystical suspension, a wounding stab, an agonized howl—none of which corresponds with the Aaron we loving friends know; it comes from some deep, mysterious place he never reveals to us except in his music. I have known Aaron intimately for forty-two years, and I have only once seen him in a state of anger. Once. And I recall a luncheon date we had during which he was uncharacteristically quiet, mentioning only that he had a headache. I learned much later that day that his father had died on the previous night. And once—again only once—have I seen him weep: when, at a Bette Davis movie that caused me to ooh and aah and marvel and groan, "No No No!" at the unbearable climax—I am always very vocal during Bette Davis movies—he turned to me, his cheeks awash with tears, and sobbed, "Can't you shut up?"

Now, usually men of such restraint and moderation, who also harbor such tumultuous inner passions and rages, are sick men, psychotics who are prone to unpredictable and irrational explosions. Not so Aaron. The unpredictability is all in the music, which is why that music is so constantly fresh and surprising, as is the music of Beethoven. The man himself is sanity itself—and that is why the first moment I met him, on his thirty-seventh birthday, I trusted him instantly, and relied completely on his judgment as gospel, and have done so ever since. It is my honor to present him to you: my first friend in New York, my master, my idol, my sage, my shrink, the closest thing to a composition teacher I have ever had, my guide, my counselor, my elder brother, my beloved friend, Aaron Copland. ☐

Keynote Speech
American Symphony Orchestra League
18 June 1980

THE FUTURE OF THE SYMPHONY ORCHESTRA

My dear friends:

I greet you most warmly, but with curiously mixed feelings. On the one hand, I am very pleased to see you all, and to touch base with so large and significant a segment of our American musical life. I am also flattered to have been asked to make this so-called Keynote Address—whatever that may mean these days when keynotes become increasingly hard to come by. On the other hand, I cannot help asking the question Why me? I am somewhat puzzled that in this of all years—this special, precious 1980 which I have reserved exclusively for composing, in which I am not lifting a baton—that in this very year I should have

been selected to address the problems of the Symphony Orchestra. Ladies and gentlemen, you see before you a nonconductor—which I must emphatically point out does *not* mean a body through which no electricity can pass. On the contrary. But it does mean that my mind is not continuously occupied with the issues that concern *this* body. A strange thing happens when a conductor transmogrifies himself into a composer—at least, to me. There is a drastic change of persona; the public figure becomes a very private person. There are very few if any public appearances—this being one of the few; there is a lot of solitude, and deep inner searching. First there is a transitional period in which one tries to clear the mind of everybody else's notes—Beethoven's, Mahler's, Stravinsky's, Druckman's—all those notes one has been studying and conducting and hearing day in, day out; then follows the period of agony and ecstasy, searching for and finding one's *own* notes. This is what I have been doing; I hardly ever go out, socially or professionally; I have attended very few concerts; I have become a reclusive introvert. It is, in short, a very odd time for me to be making this speech.

Now, having made all my disclaimers, I hope I can talk with you freely. In the course of this period of reflection and reading and rereading, I have come across that remarkable speech made by my esteemed friend and colleague Gunther Schuller at last year's opening exercises of the Berkshire Music Center. I am sure you are all more than familiar with that Tanglewood address, and with Mr. Schuller's follow-up piece in *High Fidelity* magazine; they have both caused an enormous amount of excitement and controversy in the American orchestral world, which is practically synonymous with the occupants of this room. I should say at once that I place myself firmly in his camp: with very few exceptions, every point he has made is true, all too true, as I know from long personal experience.

The early years of my musical activity coincided roughly with the last years of the great tyrants of the podium: Koussevitzky, Reiner, Rodzinski, Toscanini, Stokowski, Szell— those great names that forged, by supreme authority and will, the great American orchestras. I have also lived to witness the apathy and joylessness of which Schuller speaks, and which seems to inhabit so many of those same super-symphony-orchestras today. Of course, back in those Glorious Bad Old Days—or should I say those Grisly Good Old Days?—life was not by any means all joyfulness in the orchestral ranks. There were moans, groans, and mutterings; there were laser beams of resentment aimed at the podium, even semiaudible wisecracks, or ill-concealed infractions of discipline, all related to prolonged rehearsal time and authoritarianism.

But none of this was the result of *apathy*; on the contrary, it had a vehement force behind it; there was a cause being fought for, a valid cause. It *is* true that in those days orchestral musicians were grossly overworked and underpaid, and had few, if any, guarantees of permanence or economic stability. But such was the dedication and charisma of those glorious tyrants of the baton that music triumphed over all. Came the performance, and the ill feelings vanished magically, to be replaced by a radiant glow of pride —pride in the knowledge that perfection was the goal, the perfect serving of the *composer*, not the conductor, and that they, the players, were with each new performance coming closer than ever to that goal, through bone-hard work and the consecrated guidance of their maestro.

Even as I say these words, the memories rush back to me with a new vividness. I can see my beloved master Koussevitzky, a high priest at his altar, raging through an endless rehearsal, indefatigable. I can hear him now: "I vill not stop to vork until it vill not be more beautiful!" "Ve vill play again hundred times until it vill not be in tune!" "*Kinder*, you most *soffer, soffer* for die musical art!"—and suffer they did; but to what glorious ends! And I see Fritz Reiner, my other great teacher, with his impeccable ear and fearsome eye, suddenly stopping a rehearsal to nail the fourth desk of violas and make them play a passage by themselves— two trembling figures suddenly made to audition before their colleagues. And not infrequently such a scene culminated in that terrifying monosyllable, "*Out!*" And in those days, "out" could mean *out for good*. But what performances there were; what Mozart, Bartok, what *Rosenkavaliers* came out of that *soffering!* Everybody suffered— including Reiner himself, who, we are told, was on at least one occasion physically attacked in the stage-door alley by some of his players. What feverish days they were! When in 1943 I became Artur Rodzinski's assistant at the New York Philharmonic, I was appalled to find that his first official act in office was to proclaim twenty-five arbitrary dismissals. Those were the days. I need not prolong the tale with mention of other revered friends and mentors such as Toscanini, who was not above hurling epithets like "Shoemaker!" at a given musician, or George Szell—but, as I say, not to prolong the tale. Suffice it to say that all that is over, ancient history. The artists who make up our present-day symphony orchestras are recognized as artists, respected and rewarded accordingly. They now have a voice in the choosing of a new maestro, in the conditions of a

tour, even in the replacement of retiring colleagues. Then why the apathy, the joylessness of which Gunther Schuller speaks? The explanations have been given most eloquently by Gunther himself, and there is no need for me to repeat them here. But there is something to be added, a kind of historical or philosophical underpinning to this whole dilemma, which may help to clarify some of our problems— not necessarily to solve them, but perhaps to illuminate them.

Let's ask ourselves: Whence cometh this remarkable phenomenon, this *monstre sacré* known as the Symphony Orchestra? Was it born full-blown, like Minerva from the head of Jupiter? Not at all; it grew and developed concomitantly with the growth and development of a musical form called the *symphony*, a tonal and dualistic conception which, along with its allied forms of concerto, symphonic poem, and the rest, traversed a fantastic arc from Mozart to Mahler. This is a piece of deterministic history, if you will, visible to us on an imaginative graph as discernibly as feudalism or the Holy Roman Empire—nascence, ascent, apogee, decline. And as the symphony grew in scope, size, and complexity through Haydn, Beethoven, Brahms, Bruckner, *et alii*, so did the orchestra for which it was written; each new demand by a composer evoked a complementary advance from the orchestra, eventually evolving into the orchestra of Mahler and Ravel—which is to say, the standard one-hundred-piece orchestra that graced the beginning of this century. The truth is that our present-day symphony orchestra is not basically different in concept or composition from that of 1910, say, in spite of the tripling or quintupling of wind instruments, or the addition or invention of the plethora of percussion instruments which sometimes these days seem to be invading the whole stage. Theoretically, one could say that the symphony, as a form, reached its ultimate possibilities with Mahler—certainly, Mahler thought so!—but in fact we know that major symphonic works of real significance continued to be written for another thirty-five years. There are those who consider these latter-day symphonies epigonic, and history may one day prove them right; but one cannot simply dismiss such symphonic masterpieces as have come from Sibelius, Shostakovich, Prokofiev, Hindemith, Schoenberg, Copland, Stravinsky, Schuman, Bartok. And there it seems to end, with an astonishing abruptness. Curious, isn't it, that the last really great symphony, in the broad classical sense of the term, was Stravinsky's *Symphony in Three Movements*, date 1945, exactly coincident with the end of World War Two? It is as though that apocalyptic bomb had demolished not only Hiroshima but, as a side effect, the whole tonal symphonic concept as well.

And so for the last thirty-five years we have had no real symphonic history. If you think that's too strong a statement, only consider those who make it *seventy* years, back to Mahler, or even those who are convinced that the symphony really began to decline with Schubert. All right; let's settle for thirty-five years; but in any case, where does that leave the symphony orchestra now? Obsolete? A doomed dinosaur? If the symphony orchestra grew hand-in-glove with the symphonic form itself, has it not declined correspondingly? The answer is *no* to all of the above. In fact, it is precisely in these last thirty-five years that symphony orchestras have had their heyday, have burgeoned and flourished as never before. How do we account for this striking paradox?

In two ways. First—and this brings up a sore point: be-

Conducting Verdi's Requiem *at St. Paul's Cathedral, London, 1970*

346 · Leonard Bernstein

cause I have spoken to these matters frequently in the past, I have just as frequently been misquoted as saying that the symphony orchestra is dead. It infuriates me to read that misinterpretation. In fact, orchestras have never been more alive and kicking; what I *have* said is that they have become in part kind of museums—*in part*, mind you; remember I said there were *two* ways to account for the paradox. But yes, museums; glorious, living treasuries of art. And what, may I ask, is wrong with a museum—especially one in which we are dealing not with paintings and statues but with live bodies, great performing artists, breathing and re-creating our priceless symphonic heritage, with a director who is no mere curator, but a veritable high priest in this sanctuary? Of *course* this symphonic *Gestalt* is a museum, and we should be proud and grateful for it.

But that is only part one of the answer. Part two involves the very important fact that when the symphonic form disappeared thirty-five, or seventy, years ago—take your pick —it was not by any means the end of musical creativity for the orchestra; quite the contrary. The last thirty-five years have seen a creative ferment unprecedented in musical history; composers have struck out in any number of directions, producing a wealth of new works. Not symphonies, maybe, but so what? Where is it written that what we have come to call symphonies must constitute the exclusive repertoire of the symphonic orchestra? We have extraordinary new works from Carter and Berio and Crumb, Boulez, Stockhausen, Foss, Rorem, Corigliano—Schuller himself. And these works do make new demands on our standard orchestra of seventy strings and thirty winds and a handful of percussionists. There are new ways of grouping those one-hundred-odd instruments, new divisions and dispositions, multiple small orchestras. There are new electronic instruments, and the introduction of prerecorded tapes. There are new instrumental techniques, like multiphonic wind sounds, or caressing the tam-tam. Some of these are minor variations or adornments of the standard Mahler orchestra, but others are of major significance. Most important of all, these composers are compelling orchestral musicians to hear in new ways, especially in nontonal music;

With Van Cliburn

to listen much more attentively to one another—for example, in aleatory music; and to be adventurous in much the same way as Beethoven compelled the Haydn orchestra to venture into new territory, or as Debussy did with the orchestra of César Franck. In other words, the so-called "symphony orchestra" has developed an added function, distinct from its identity as a museum, and that is to provide the fertile soil in which new kinds of orchestral music can be cultivated. And here is where the problems begin to come clear: this rich new area seems to demand different schedules, different approaches, even, at times, different personnel from those serving at the altar of Brahms. And so the trouble begins. Can any one orchestral organization encompass both these functions and still maintain its Koussevitzkian goal of perfection, to say nothing of mere competence?

There are those who say no. Why not two museums? they argue. After all, we have our Metropolitan Museum

With André Watts and John McClure

and our Museum of Modern Art, the Met and the MOMA, different strokes for different folks. Boston and Philadelphia have their Fine Arts Museums, and also their Institutes of Contemporary Art. Why should the musical museum be different? Why not have twofold orchestras, double maestros, double subscription series? Bad ideas, all. Because an orchestral artist is a living being, a musician incorporating all the music that has preceded him, and all the music informing his daily life. He is not a painting on a wall, nor is an orchestra an exhibition—even a Picasso Exhibition. A musical artist is a consecrated part of the world he inhabits; if he is fenced off, he will stagnate. So will the orchestra. So will the public. So will art.

Then where, you ask, is the time and energy to come from that will permit all this to happen without killing our artists with overwork, or driving them mad with stylistic somersaults? Ah, that is where you come in, my friends: it is your imagination; your new inventive ideas; your flexibility, cooperation, and goodwill that can save the situation.

I realize that I am speaking to a highly diverse and composite group representing all aspects of the American symphonic worlds: conductors, managers, agents, composers, union officials, orchestral players, board members—all, I am sure, devoted music-lovers, and, I assume, all gathered here at this great conference precisely to determine how to save the situation. I assume further that you are all highly educated and sophisticated in your particular disciplines—*which may be the whole trouble.* Socrates would say to you: Experts, learn from one another; this is the moment to *begin* your education—an interdisciplinary education. And you can begin right now, here in New York. Use this week as a springboard, and then go on learning and understanding one another more and more deeply. It can no longer be Us against Them; it must be only Us. There is no Them—not if music is to survive the crisis.

I, alas, am not Socrates, nor even much of an expert on the national orchestral scene. But I *have* had long and varied experience both here and abroad, and perhaps I can drop a few hints to some of you Us-and-Thems.

To the conductors I would say: Develop a keener understanding of your responsibilities to your art, in the most universal sense; to your colleagues within the orchestra; and to your specific community. Do not neglect American music; it is the lifestream of your repertoire, the constant refresher and rejuvenator of our musical life. Don't travel so much; and if you do, take your orchestra with you. There is much you can learn from them.

To the orchestral players I would plead: Cherish your love for music; don't ever let orchestral politics cause you to forget your joyful reason for having joined an orchestra in the first place; guard your standards of excellence, which mean much more than fluency or technique. Don't say to your maestro, "Just tell us if you want it louder or softer." That way lies perdition, that fearful hell where everything becomes louder and softer and little else. And a word of warning: Don't get too involved in management unless you want to incur its financial responsibilities as well. Which I'm sure you don't. Besides, the more active a part you play

Israel, 1947

in management, the more inevitably you are going to find yourselves in conflict with your very own unions. Learn from the management, as well as from your maestro.

And to management I would say many things, more than this occasion will permit. But one strong hint: Remember the American conductor. He is out there, in quantity and quality, gifted, brilliant, catholic in taste, and spoiling for action. America has developed world-class orchestras; we all know that—some of the finest on earth, each with its distinctive sound. But is that our true goal? Isn't it rather to have these same fine orchestras each capable of producing the distinctive sound not of itself, but of the *composer* being played? And this goal is more attainable in America than anywhere else; it can be one of the glories of our melting pot. But it is finally attainable only with an American conductor who has comprehensive and international roots, not merely roots in the *Conservatoire* or the *Hochschule*.

And a note to personal managers: You too are servants of music; serve it with all your powers, rather than seeking to derive power from it.

To union officials, only one little but loaded hint: Remember that a symphonic concert is not a gig. Enough said.

And what shall I say to trustees and board members? Again, *learn*. Learn from all the others to whom I've already spoken. Educate yourselves to understand them, especially us musicians. It's not easy; we musicians are a peculiar folk; but we are not irrational, and we are full of love. Get your heads together *with* ours, and *invent*: find new ways of giving concerts, of derigidifying the common practice; invent new and imaginative divisions of labor; keep chamber music always in mind, however small or large. Educate yourselves in ways to educate in turn those for whom you are responsible, especially the musical public. What ever happened to Young People's Concerts? And why have orchestral telecasts surrendered their educational components to mere glamorous camera work? You must remedy that. Of course you must also find money; but you do that very well, and need no hints from me in that department.

My friends, all of you together: Interdisciplinary education can do wonders. Understanding and flexibility can do wonders. Yes, even money can do wonders. But the *energy*, the energy to put all these wonders into action—where does *it* come from? It will come from where it has always come from: it will come from the love of music, the sheer aesthetic delight in this most mysterious and rewarding of all the arts; from the sporting sense, the instinct for continuity, and the joyful and total dedication of our selves to the art we have sworn to serve. I ask you all now to swear that oath again with me: "I vill not stop to vork until it vill not be more beautiful!"

Godspeed, and thank you. □

Originally published in French
in a collection of remembrances
following the death of Nadia Boulanger, 1979

"NI COMMENCEMENT NI FIN . . ."

The last visit I had with Nadia was on her last birthday. I don't think she knew it was her birthday, since she was in coma. But Nature seemed to know it, providing for the occasion an unforgettably radiant September Sunday, with the intense blue of the cloudless sky competing in saturation with the rich greens of the Fontainebleau gardens. The air trembled.

Everything conspired to urge me on to Fontainebleau that day: my one free afternoon in a three-week working visit to Paris; the exhilarating weather; and the certain knowledge that it would be my last time with her. On the other hand, there were some strong contraindicative warnings from her closest friends and guardians: Mademoiselle would be disturbed and exhausted by a visit; she could not speak, and in any event, would not recognize me. *Tant pis:* I paid my visit, as if compelled.

I was ushered into her bedchamber by the angelic and anxiety-ridden Mlle. Dieudonné, who, with forefinger to lips, and seconded by an attending nurse, whispered a sharp order: *Ten minutes only.* As it turned out, the visit lasted closer to one hour.

Nadia was beautifully dressed and groomed, as if for the coffin. Her crucifix gleamed at her throat; her eyes and mouth were closed; her whole face seemed closed in coma. I knelt by the bed in silent communion. Suddenly there was the shock of her voice, deep and strong as always (how? her lips did not seem to move; how?): *"Qui est là?"* I could not respond for shock. The Dieudonné forefinger whipped to the lips. Finally I dared speak: "Lenny. Léonard . . ." Silence. Did she hear, did she know? *"Chèr*

With Nadia Boulanger in New York, 1962

Lenny . . ." She *knew*; a miracle. Encouraging signal from Dieudonné. I persevered: "My dear friend, how do you feel?" Pause. Then that *basso profundo* (through unmoving lips!): *"Tellement forte."* I drew a deep breath. *"Vous voulez dire . . . intérieurement?"* *". . . Oui. Mais le corps—"* *"Je comprends bien,"* I said hastily, to shorten her efforts. *"Je pars. Vous devez être très fatiguée."* *"Pas de fatigue. Non. Point. . . ."* A protracted pause, and I realized she had drifted back into sleep.

Signals from the astonished attending ladies suggested my departure, but I was held there, unable to rise from my knees. I knew there was more to come, and in a few minutes it did come: *"Ne partez pas."* Not a plea, but a command. I searched my mind anxiously for the right thing to say, knowing that anything would be wrong. Then I heard myself asking: *"Vous entendez la musique dans la tête?"* Instant reply: *"Tout le temps. Tout le temps."* This so encouraged me that I continued, as if in quotidian conversation: *"Et qu'est-ce que vous entendez, ce moment-ci?"* I thought of her preferred loves. *"Mozart? Monteverdi? Bach, Stravinsky, Ravel?"* Long pause. *"Une musique . . .* [very long pause] *. . . ni commencement ni fin . . ."*

She was already there, on the other side.

most of these composers, conductors etc. to hear music in their heads "all the time"

Address given
30 May 1980

COMMENCEMENT SPEECH AT JOHNS HOPKINS UNIVERSITY

President Muller, worthy Deans, learned faculty, reverend clergy:

I thank you most sincerely for this honor. In accepting it, I am reminded of the words of your first president, Daniel Gilman, who said, at the dedication of the Medical School, that a university "misses its aim if it produces learned pedants, or simple artisans or cunning sophists, or pretentious practitioners. . . . Its purpose is not so much to impart knowledge as to whet the appetite. . . ."

I should like to take off from there, and, with your permission, speak now directly to the graduating body itself.

My dear young friends:

The notes for these upcoming remarks were made on a Sunday morning a week or so ago—a cold, rainy Sunday morning. I had just put aside the Sunday *New York Times*—or rather, the little of it I could read without ruining my breakfast—and was staring alternately at the gray outdoors and the blank page before me, trying to digest the unrelentingly hopeless reports I had been reading of this, our world; then trying to find something in them that could be the basis for this commencement address; then trying to forget them entirely, so that my mind might be free to invent something hopeful to say to this happy band of departing graduates. No such luck, to quote my mother. I tell you all this only in case what I do say should, by chance, reflect the chill of that gray morning, and of its newspaper.

Now, you and I know that the good, gray lady, pessimism, however elegant she may be, has no business intruding upon a commencement speech, however *in*elegant it may be. I am here to deliver a Charge to the Graduates, *Mandatum Alumnibus*, and send them charging into their future with banners raised. Hail, optimism; be with us, Leibnitz! No such luck.

And so, that Sunday morning, I began to make these notes, putting myself into your place. What do those seniors and graduate students want to hear from me? That you are brilliantly educated; the world is yours, go forth and take it? You are far too sophisticated for such bromides. Or do you await a high moral tone, inciting your acquired idealism to triumph over your native materialism? No, this is not to be a sermon, said I that Sunday morning, nor shall I come as a preacher. But perhaps I might come as an artist, the musician I am, to share with you something of what goes on in an artist's head and heart when confronted with what we blithely call reality.

Two World Wars ago, the great Irish poet Yeats observed a reality remarkably like our own. "Things fall apart; the centre cannot hold," he intoned in that brief but shattering poem called "The Second Coming." "The blood-dimmed tide is loosed, and everywhere / The ceremony of innocence is drowned;"—and then come the two lines that make one's flesh crawl, because they sound as though they were written yesterday:

> *The best lack all conviction, while the worst*
> *Are full of passionate intensity.*

Most uncomfortably familiar. And how did Yeats respond to this chilling picture he himself had drawn? Like all artists, he responded with a vision, an equally chilling vision of a pitiless redemption; I'm sure you all remember that image of the rough beast slouching toward Bethlehem to be born. Who can forget it? And that image, that vision, alarms and alerts us today at least as strongly as it did its readers sixty years ago. But at the same time this poem comforts us and strengthens our faith by its very existence, by its perfect beauty, its aesthetic *Inhalt*. Like all great art, it tells us that we have guardians out there— artists, the prophets among us, scanning horizons we cannot see. Yeats looked beyond reality, and beheld an enduring fantasy.

Every artist copes with reality by means of his fantasy. Fantasy, better known as imagination, is his greatest treasure, his basic equipment for life. And since his work *is* his life, his fantasy is constantly in play. He dreams life. Psychologists tell us that a child's imagination reaches its peak at the age of six or seven, then is gradually inhibited, diminished to conform with the attitudes of his elders— that is, reality. Alas. Perhaps what distinguishes artists from regular folks is that for whatever reasons, their imaginative drive is less inhibited; they have retained in adulthood more of that five-year-old's fantasy than others have. This is not to say that an artist is the childlike madman the old romantic traditions have made him out to be; he *is* usually capable of brushing his teeth, keeping track of his love life, or counting his change in a taxicab. When I speak of his *fantasy* I am not suggesting a constant state of abstraction, but rather the continuous imaginative powers that inform his creative acts as well as his reactions to the world around him. And out of that creativity and those imaginative reactions come not idle dreams, but truths—all those abiding truth-formations and constellations that nourish us, from Dante to Joyce, from Bach to the Beatles, from Praxiteles to Picasso. À propos Picasso, last week I visited that staggering Picasso retrospective at the Museum of Modern Art in New York, and I was overwhelmed by the display of sheer imagination, of fantasy; of the sense of *play*, the joyful switching of styles, the constant freedom to think new, take chances—to have *fun*, in the deepest sense of the word. It is a great lesson, not only in art, but in living, because it is such a stimulus and exhortation for every one of us who views it to refresh our thinking and our attitudes, to cultivate our fantasy.

Which brings me to the salient point: The gift of imagination is by no means an exclusive property of the artist; it is a gift we all share; to some degree or other all of us, all of you, are endowed with the powers of fantasy. The dullest of dullards among us has the gift of dreams at night—visions and yearnings and hopes. Everyone can also *think*; it is the quality of thought that makes the difference—not just the quality of logical thinking, but of *imaginative* thinking. And our greatest thinkers, those who have radically changed our world, have always arrived at their truths by dreaming them; they are first fantasized, and only then subjected to proof. This is certainly true of Plato and Kant, of Moses and Buddha, of Pythagoras and Copernicus and, yes, Marx and Freud and, more recently, Albert Einstein, who always insisted that imagination is more important than knowledge. How often he spoke of having dreamed his Unified Field Theory and his Principle of Relativity—intuiting them, and then, high on the inspiration, plunging into the *per*spiration of working them out to be provable, and therefore true.

But what is *true*? Is Newtonian physics any less *true* for having been superseded by Einsteinian physics? No more than Wittgenstein has knocked Plato out of your philosophy courses. The notion that the earth is flat was never a *truth*; it was merely a notion. That the earth is round *is* a proven truth which may one day be modified by some new concept of roundness, but the truth will remain, modified or not. Truths are forever; that's why they are so hard to come by. Plato promulgated absolute truths; Einstein relative ones. Both were right. Both conceived their visions in high fantasy. And even Hegel, that stern dialectician, said that truth is a Bacchanalian revel, where not a member is sober. Well said, old Georg Wilhelm Friedrich; we hear you loud and clear. To search for truth, one has to be drunk with imagination.

Now, what has all this to do with you, or with the grim realities we face each day? It has everything to do with you, because you are the generation of hope. We are counting on you—on your imagination—to find new truths: true answers, not merely stopgaps, to the abounding stalemates that surround us. But why *us*, you ask? Why are you laying this very heavy number on our generation? I'll try to tell you why.

The generation that preceded yours has been a pretty passive one, and no wonder. It was the first generation in all history to be born into a nuclear world, the first people ever to have had to accept the bomb as an axiom of life. There it is; the world is qualitatively changed; behold the Hiroshima generation. You can understand how this can have caused a profound passivity, a turning-inward to self-interest, a philosophy of Take as much as you can while there's still time. And, of course, this so-called "me" generation was strongly reinforced in its passivistic philosophy by the extraordinary takeover of television; it was the first generation to be reared on and chained to the TV tube, with all its promise of instant gratification, both in the commercials—*instant* relief, *instant* gorgeous hair, *instant* everything—and in the very phenomenon of having that gratification at your fingertips in the form of instant and varied entertainment. And add to those a third element, the enormously increased indulgence in dope, and you have a perfect recipe for passivity. The result, in large measure, has been dropping out in one way or another, or else the mad rush to be fitted for that three-piece suit, as soon as possible, and then an overriding concern with *making it*, in the most cynically materialistic way. I don't have to tell you that neither of these consequences has produced much in the way of imaginative thinking.

But your generation is different. Oh, really? you say. We also live in a bomb-ridden world; we've also got our

TV, our dope, our instant gratifications. Why, some of us have already been measured for a three-piece suit. Ah, but you *are* different, because you have perspective—a priceless asset; you have decades of distance from your predecessors on whom all these influences descended suddenly, together, and without warning. You are the first generation since Hiroshima that can look back and say, No—not for me. You have witnessed the laid-back thinking of your predecessors; you have grown up with Vietnam, Watergate, and all the other cautionary lessons of your two decades. Thus you are, can be, a new and separate generation, with fresh minds, ready for new thinking—for *imaginative* thinking—*if* you allow yourselves to cultivate your fantasy.

What I am asking of you, and what you must ask yourselves, is this: Are you ready to free your minds from the constraints of narrow, conventional thinking, the rigorous dictates of a received logical positivism? Are you willing to resist being numbed into passivity by settling for the *status quo*? More specifically, do you have the imaginative strength to liberate yourselves from the Cold War ambiance in which the eighties have already begun— along with all its accompanying paraphernalia of ever- proliferating borders, barriers, walls, passports, racial and subnational fragmentation and refragmentation? Far too many people have begun to speak of the "Third World War" as if it were not only conceivable but a natural inevitability. I tell you it is not conceivable, not natural, not inevitable, and all the pseudo-professional talk about rates of possible survival after nuclear attack in cities A and B or areas X and Y is dangerous and foolish talk. Survival of what, how, to what end? The height of absurdity is reached in the word *overkill*—a subject much discussed in high places. What on earth can be the point in solemn negotiations to reduce the percentage of overkill from, say 89 to 84? or from 2 to 1, for that matter? *One* percent overkill is enough to extinguish the planet. And the more this useless talk goes on, the more we witness a steady proliferation of nuclear arms. The mind boggles.

What do we do with our minds when they boggle? We quickly put them to strenuous imaginative work. Mind- boggling time is the perfect moment for fantasy to take over; it's the only way to resolve a stalemate. And so I ask you again: Are you ready to dare to free your minds from the constraints we, your elders, have imposed on you? Will you accept, as artists do, that the life of the spirit precedes and controls the life of exterior action; that the richer and more creative the life of the spirit, the healthier and more productive our society must necessarily be?

If you are ready to accept all that—and I am not saying that it's easy to do—then I must ask if you are ready to admit the ensuing corollaries, starting bravely with the toughest one of all: that war is obsolete. Our nuclear folly has rendered it obsolete, so that it now appears to be something like a bad old habit, a ritualistic, quasi-tribalistic obeisance to the arrogance of excessive nationalism, face-saving, bigotry, xenophobia, and above all, greed. Do you not find something reprehensible, even obscene, about the endless and useless stock-piling of nuclear missiles? Isn't there something radically wrong with nation-states' squandering the major portion of their wealth on military strength at the expense of schools, hospitals, libraries, vital research in medicine and energy—to say nothing of preserving the sheer livability of our planetary environment? Why are we behaving in this suicidal fashion?

Obviously I cannot supply the kind of authoritative answers you would receive from a man of politics, economics, of sociology. Those are not my disciplines. I am an artist, and my answer must necessarily be that we do not permit our imagination to bloom. The fantasies we do act out are still the old tribalistic ones arising out of greed, lust for power and superiority. We need desperately to cultivate new fantasies, ones that can be enacted to make this earth of ours a safe, sound, and morally well-functioning world, instead of a disparate collection of societies limping along from crisis to crisis, and ultimately to self-destruction. We are told again and again that there is food enough on this planet to supply the human race twenty times over; that there is enough water to irrigate every desert. The world is rich, nature is bountiful, we have everything we need. Why is it, then, so hard to arrive at a minimal standard below which no human being is allowed to sink? Again, we need imagination, fantasy—*new* fantasies, with the passion and courage to carry them out. Only think: if all our imaginative resources currently employed in inventing new power games and bigger and better weaponry were reoriented toward disarmament, what miracles we could achieve, what new truths, what undiscovered realms of beauty!

Impossible, you say? Inconceivable to disarm without inviting annihilation? Okay. Let's invent a fantasy together, right now—and I mean a *fantastic* fantasy. Let's pretend that any one of us here has become President of the United States—a very imaginative President, who has suddenly taken a firm decision to disarm, completely and unilaterally. I see alarm on your faces: This crazed artist is proposing sheer madness. It can't be done: A President is not a dictator; this is a democracy. Congress would never permit it, the people would howl with wounded national pride, our allies would scream betrayal. It can't be done. But of course it can't be done if everybody starts by saying it can't be done. Let's push our imagination; remember, we're only fantasizing. Let's dare to be simplistic. All right, someone would stand up in Congress and demand that the President be impeached, declared certifiable, and locked away in a loony bin. Others would agree. But suppose—just suppose—that one or two Senators or Congressmen got the point, and recognized this mad idea as perhaps the most courageous single action in all history. And suppose that those few members of Congress happened to be hypnotically powerful orators. It just might become contagious—keep pushing that imagination button!—it just *might* get through to the people, who instead of howling might well stand up tall and proud to be participating in this unprecedented act of strength and heroism. There might even be those who would feel it to be the noblest of sacrifices—far nobler, surely, than sacrificing one's children on the field of Armageddon. And this pride and joyful courage would spread—keep pushing that button!—so that even our allies might applaud us. There is the barest possibility that it just might work.

All right; now what? Now is when we *really* have to push, let fantasy lead us where it will. What is your first thought? Naturally, that the Soviet Union would come plowing in and take us over. But would they really? What would they do with us; why would they want to assume responsibility and administration of so huge, complex, and problematical a society as ours? And in English, yet! Besides, who are the Soviet Union—its leaders, its army, or its people? The only reason for the army to fight is that their leaders would have commanded them to do so; but how can they fight when there is no enemy? The hypothetical enemy has been magically whisked away, and replaced by two hundred-odd million smiling, strong, peaceful Americans. Now keep the fantasy going: the Russian *people* certainly don't want war; they have suffered far too much; and it is more likely that they would displace their warlike leaders, and transform their Union of Socialist Republics into a truly democratic union. And—keep going, keep going!—think of the example that would have been set for the whole world; think of the relief at no longer having to bluster and saber-rattle and save face; think of the vast new wealth now available to make life rich, beautiful, clean, sexy, thoughtful, inventive, healthful, fun! And there would be so many new things to do, to invent, to build, to try, to sell, to buy.

Well, maybe it won't work. But something in all that fantasy trip must have struck you as—well, just possible. And if one little seed or syllable of an idea may have entered one little ear in this vast assembly, where it can grow among the fertile neurons of one imaginative brain, then I could pray for no more. And at the very least you must admit that nothing I have fantasized, lunatic-artist though I may be, is actually inconceivable. After all, we did imagine it together, from beginning to end; which is a hell of a lot better than trying to imagine Armageddon, the extinction of mankind—which for *this* artist, at least, is indeed inconceivable. And this artist challenges you to pursue the fantasy, *all* your fantasies, while there is still time.

Now look what I've done: everything I said I wouldn't do. I have indeed given a Charge to this graduating body, in spite of all my good intentions; I have told you to go forth and take the world; I may even have sermonized. Forgive me: I was carried away by hope—hope in the wake of pessimism. And that hope is you, my dear young friends. May God bless you.

CLASSIFIED LIST OF COMPOSITIONS
(In Alphabetical Order)
Compiled by Jack Gottlieb

ORCHESTRAL WORKS

The Age of Anxiety (Symphony No. 2) (1949)
For Piano and Orchestra, after W. H. Auden
"For Serge Koussevitzky, in Tribute"
Commissioned by the Koussevitzky Foundation
First Performance: 8 April 1949, Symphony Hall, Boston, MA; Leonard
    Bernstein, piano, BSO, Serge Koussevitzky, conductor

Arias and Barcarolles (1988)
Orchestral version, for Mezzo-soprano, Baritone, Strings and Percus-
    sion
Orchestrated with the assistance of Bright Sheng; second orchestration
    by Bruce Coughlin
First Performance: 22 September 1989, Tilles Center, Long Island Uni-
    versity, NY; Susan Graham, Kurt Ollmann, the New York Chamber
    Symphony of the 92nd Street Y, Gerard Schwartz, conductor

Chichester Psalms (1965)
For Mixed Chorus, Boy Soloist and Orchestra, in three movements
"With Gratitude, to Dr. Cyril Solomon"
Commissioned by the Very Rev. Walter Hussey, Dean of Chichester
    Cathedral
First Performance: 15 July 1965, Philharmonic Hall, NYC; John Bogart,
    the Camerata Singers (Abraham Kaplan, dir.), NYP, Leonard Bern-
    stein, conductor

Concerto for Orchestra (Jubilee Games) (1986–89)
For Baritone and Orchestra
"Dedicated to the Israel Philharmonic Orchestra on Its 50th Year"
First Performance: 24 April 1989, Frederic Mann Auditorium, Tel Aviv;
    IPO, Leonard Bernstein, conductor

Divertimento for Orchestra (1980)
"With Affection to the Boston Symphony Orchestra in Celebration of
    Its First Centenary"
Commissioned by the BSO

First Performance: 25 September 1980, Symphony Hall, Boston, MA; BSO, Seiji Ozawa, conductor

Dybbuk (1974)
Originally entitled *Dybbuk Variations,* from the ballet by Leonard Bernstein and Jerome Robbins
First Performance: 16 August 1974, Auckland, New Zealand; NYP, Leonard Bernstein, conductor

Dybbuk, Suite No. 1 (1974)
For Tenor, Bass-baritone and Orchestra
First U.S. Performance: 3 April 1975, Avery Fisher Hall, NYC; Paul Sperry, Bruce Fifer, NYP, Leonard Bernstein, conductor

Dybbuk, Suite No. 2 (Eight Dances) (1974)
First Performance: 17 April 1975, Avery Fisher Hall, NYC; NYP, Leonard Bernstein, conductor

Facsimile (1946)
Choreographic Essay for Orchestra
"For Jerome Robbins"
Commissioned by Ballet Theater
First Performance: 5 March 1947, Vassar College, Poughkeepsie, NY; Rochester Philharmonic Orchestra, Leonard Bernstein, conductor

Fancy Free (1944)
Ballet
"For Adolph Green"
First Performance: 18 April 1944, Metropolitan Opera House, NYC; Ballet Theater Orchestra, Leonard Bernstein, conductor

Fanfare for the Inauguration of John F. Kennedy (1961)
Orchestration by Sid Ramin
First Performance: 19 January 1961, Inaugural Gala, National Armory, Washington, D.C.; Nelson Riddle, conductor

Fanfare for the 25th Anniversary of The High School of Music and Art, New York City (1961)
First Performance: 24 March 1961, NYC; students at the school, Alexander Richter, conductor

Fanfare from Dance Suite (1989)
Movement I of *Dance Suite,* scored for Winds, Brass and Percussion
First Performance: 14 January 1990, American Ballet Theater, Metropolitan Opera House, NYC; Empire Brass Quintet

Halil (1981)
Nocturne for Solo Flute with Piccolo, Alto Flute, Percussion, Harp and Strings
"To the Spirit of Yadin and to His Fallen Brothers"
First Performance: 27 May 1981, Frederic Mann Auditorium, Tel Aviv; Jean-Pierre Rampal (flute), IPO, Leonard Bernstein, conductor

Jeremiah (Symphony No. 1) (1942)
For Mezzo-soprano and Orchestra
"For My Father"
First Performance: 28 January 1944, Syria Mosque, Pittsburgh, PA;
    Jennie Tourel, PSO, Leonard Bernstein, conductor
New York Music Critics Circle Award, 1944

Kaddish (Symphony No. 3) (1963)
For Mixed Chorus, Boys' Choir, Speaker, Soprano and Orchestra
"To the Beloved Memory of John F. Kennedy"
Commissioned by the Koussevitzky Foundation and the BSO
First Performance: 10 December 1963, Tel Aviv; Hannah Rovina
    (speaker), Jennie Tourel, choirs under the direction of Abraham
    Kaplan, IPO, Leonard Bernstein, conductor

A Musical Toast (1980)
"Fondly Dedicated to the Memory of Andre Kostelanetz"
First Performance: 11 October 1980, Avery Fisher Hall, NYC; NYP,
    Zubin Mehta, conductor

Opening Prayer (from *Concerto for Orchestra*) (1986)
For Baritone and Orchestra
Written for the inaugural of the newly refurbished Carnegie Hall
First Performance: 15 December 1986, Carnegie Hall, NYC; Kurt Oll-
    mann, NYP, Leonard Bernstein, conductor

Orchestra Suite from *A Quiet Place* (posthumous, 1991)
Arranged by Sid Ramin and Michael Tilson Thomas with Michael
    Barrett
First Performance: 19 September 1991, The Barbican, London; LSO,
    Michael Tilson Thomas, conductor

Overture to *Candide* (1956)
For Symphony Orchestra
First Performance: 26 January 1957, Carnegie Hall, NYC; NYP, Leonard
    Bernstein, conductor
Transcription for 2 pianos/4 hands by Charlie Harmon

Prelude, Fugue and Riffs (1949)
For Solo Clarinet and Jazz Ensemble
"To Benny Goodman"
Commissioned by Woody Herman
First Performance: 16 October 1955, *Omnibus* broadcast: *The World of
    Jazz*, CBS-TV; studio band, Leonard Bernstein, conductor

Presto Barbaro (1965)
From *Symphonic Suite* from *On the Waterfront*

Reenah (1947)
Hebrew Folk Song for Chamber Orchestra
Score in preparation

Serenade (after Plato's *Symposium*) (1954)
For Solo Violin, Strings, Harp and Percussion
"To the Beloved Memory of Serge and Natalie Koussevitzky"

Commissioned by the Koussevitzky Foundation
First Performance: 12 September 1954, Teatro La Fenice, Venice; Isaac Stern (violin), IPO, Leonard Bernstein, conductor

Slava! (1977)
A Political Overture for Orchestra
"For Mstislav Rostropovich"
First Performance: 11 October 1977, Kennedy Center, Washington, D.C.; NSO, Mstislav Rostropovich, conductor

Songfest (1977)
A Cycle of American Poems for Soprano, Mezzo-soprano, Alto, Tenor, Baritone, Bass and Orchestra
"For My Mother"
First Performance (complete work): 11 October 1977, Kennedy Center, Washington, D.C.; NSO, Leonard Bernstein, conductor

Symphonic Dances from *West Side Story* (1960)
"To Sid Ramin, in Friendship"
Orchestrated with the assistance of Sid Ramin and Irwin Kostal
First Performance: 13 February 1961, Carnegie Hall, NYC; NYP, Lukas Foss, conductor
Transcription for 2 pianos and percussion by Charlie Harmon

Symphonic Suite from *On the Waterfront* (1955)
"For My Son Alexander"
First Performance: 11 August 1955, Tanglewood, MA; BSO, Leonard Bernstein, conductor
Transcription for concert band by Guy Duker (1988)

Three Dance Episodes from *On the Town* (1945)
I. The Great Lover ("To Sono Osato") II. Lonely Town: Pas de Deux ("To Betty Comden") III. Times Square: 1944 ("To Nancy Walker")
First Performance: 13 February 1946, Civic Auditorium, San Francisco, CA; San Francisco Symphony Orchestra, Leonard Bernstein, conductor

Three Dance Variations from *Fancy Free* (1944)
Galop/Waltz/Danzon
First Performance: 21 January 1946; NYCS, Leonard Bernstein, conductor

Three Meditations from *Mass* (1977)
For Violoncello and Orchestra
"For Mstislav Rostropovich"
First Performance: 11 October 1977, Kennedy Center, Washington, D.C.; Mstislav Rostropovich (cello), NSO, Leonard Bernstein, conductor

Two Meditations from *Mass* (1971)
For Orchestra
First Performance: 31 October 1971; Austin Symphony Orchestra, Maurice Peress, conductor

THEATER WORKS

Candide (1956)
Comic Operetta in Two Acts
Original Version (not available for performance)
Book: Lillian Hellman (after Voltaire)
Lyrics: Richard Wilbur, John La Touche, Dorothy Parker, Lillian Hellman and Leonard Bernstein
Orchestrations: Leonard Bernstein and Hershy Kay
First Performance: 29 October 1956, Colonial Theater, Boston, MA; Tyrone Guthrie (dir.), Samuel Krachmalnick, conductor

Chelsea Version (1973)
Book: Hugh Wheeler (after Voltaire)
Lyrics: Richard Wilbur, John La Touche, Stephen Sondheim and Leonard Bernstein
Orchestration (13 players): Hershy Kay
First Performance: 20 December 1973, Chelsea Theater, Brooklyn; Patricia Birch (choreo.), Harold Prince (dir.), John Mauceri, conductor
First Performance (Broadway): 5 March 1974, Broadway Theater, NYC

New York City Opera House Version (1982)
Book: Hugh Wheeler (after Voltaire)
Lyrics: Richard Wilbur, Stephen Sondheim, John La Touche and Leonard Bernstein
Orchestrations: Leonard Bernstein, Hershy Kay and John Mauceri
First Performance: 13 October 1982, NYC Opera; Patricia Birch (choreo.), Harold Prince (dir.), John Mauceri, conductor

Scottish Opera Version (1988)
Revised Opera House Version
First Performance: 17 May 1988, Theatre Royal Glasgow; Anthony Van Laast (choreo.), Jonathan Miller, John Wells (dirs.), John Mauceri, conductor

The Lark (1955)
Incidental music for the play by Jean Anouilh, adapted by Lillian Hellman
For Mixed Chorus and Countertenor (or Septet), A Cappella with Percussion
First Performance: 28 October 1955, Plymouth Theater, Boston, MA

The Madwoman of Central Park West (1979)
An Original Musical Comedy
Book: Phyllis Newman and Arthur Laurents
Including two songs by Leonard Bernstein: *Up, Up, Up* (lyrics: Comden & Green) and *My New Friends* (lyrics: Bernstein)
Orchestrations: John Clifton and Kirk Nurock
First Performance: 6 April 1979, Studio Arena Theater, Buffalo, NY; Arthur Laurents (dir.), Herbert Kaplan, conductor

Mass (1971)
A Theatre Piece for Singers, Players and Dancers

Text: Catholic liturgy (Latin); additional text: Stephen Schwartz and Leonard Bernstein (English)
Orchestrations: Jonathan Tunick, Hershy Kay and Leonard Bernstein
Composed for the opening of the John F. Kennedy Center for the Performing Arts, Washington, D.C.
First Performance: 8 September 1971, Kennedy Center, Washington, DC; Alvin Ailey (choreo.), Gordon Davidson (dir.) Maurice Peress, conductor

Chamber Version
Orchestration: Sid Ramin
First Performance: 26 December 1972, Mark Taper Forum, Los Angeles, CA; Gordon Davidson (dir.), Maurice Peress, music dir., assisted by Earl Rivers

On the Town (1944)
Musical Comedy
Book and lyrics: Betty Comden and Adolph Green (on an idea by Jerome Robbins)
Additional lyrics: Leonard Bernstein
Orchestration: Leonard Bernstein, Hershy Kay, Don Walker, Elliot Jacoby and Ted Royal
First Performance: 13 December 1944, Colonial Theater, Boston, MA; Jerome Robbins (choreo.), George Abbott (dir.), Max Goberman, conductor

Peter Pan (1950)
Incidental music for the play by J. M. Barrie
Lyrics: Leonard Bernstein
Orchestration: Hershy Kay
First Performance: 24 April 1950, Imperial Theater, NYC; John Burrell and Wendy Toye (dirs.), Ben Steinberg, conductor; additional incidental music by Trude Rittman

A Quiet Place (1983)
Opera in Three Acts
Libretto: Stephen Wadsworth and Leonard Bernstein
Commissioned by Houston Grand Opera, Kennedy Center and Teatro Alla Scala
Revised version (incorporating *Trouble in Tahiti*) (1984)
"To the Memory of F.M.B. and N.S.Z."
First Performance: 19 June 1984, Teatro Alla Scala, Milan; Stephen Wadsworth (dir.), John Mauceri, conductor

1600 Pennsylvania Avenue (1976)
A Musical Play about the Problems of Housekeeping
Book and lyrics: Alan Jay Lerner
Orchestration: Sid Ramin and Hershy Kay
First Performance: 24 February 1976, Forrest Theatre, Philadelphia, PA; George Faison and Gilbert Moses (choreo. & dir.), Roland Gagnon, conductor

Trouble in Tahiti (1951)
One-Act Opera in Seven Scenes

Libretto: Leonard Bernstein
"For Marc Blitzstein"
Incorporated into *A Quiet Place*
First Performance: 12 June 1952, Brandeis University, MA; Elliot Silver-
stein (dir.), Leonard Bernstein, conductor

West Side Story (1957)
Musical based on a conception of Jerome Robbins
Book: Arthur Laurents
Lyrics: Stephen Sondheim
Orchestrations: Sid Ramin, Irwin Kostal and Leonard Bernstein
"To Felicia, with Love"
First Performance: 19 August 1957, National Theater, Washington, DC;
Jerome Robbins (choreo. & dir.), Max Goberman, conductor
Best Musical 1960 (London)
Academy Award, Best Picture, and 10 additional Oscars (1961)

Wonderful Town
Musical Comedy
Book: Joseph Fields and Jerome Chodorov
Lyrics: Betty Comden and Adolph Green
Orchestrations: Don Walker; Lehman Engel (vocal arr.)
First Performance: 19 January 1953, Shubert Theater, New Haven, CT;
Donald Saddler (choreo.), George Abbott (dir.), Lehman Engel,
conductor

FILM SCORE

On the Waterfront (1954)
Released: 28 July 1954, Columbia Pictures
Elia Kazan, director; Sam Spiegel, producer; Morris Stoloff, conductor
Academy Award, Best Picture, and Academy Award Nominee, Best
Score (1955); *downbeat* Annual Music Award (1954)

SONGS (OTHER THAN THEATER)

Afterthought (1945)
For Voice and Piano
Lyrics: Leonard Bernstein
"In Memoriam, H.J.R."
First Performance: 24 October 1948, Town Hall, NYC; Nell Tangeman
and Robert Cornman

Arias and Barcarolles (1988)
Texts: by Leonard Bernstein, except No. 3, *Little Smary* by Jennie
Bernstein, and No. 6, *Oif Mayn Khas'neh* by Yankev-Yitskhok Segal
I. Prelude II. Love Duet ("for Jave") III. Little Smary ("for S.A.B.") IV.
The Love of My Life ("to S.W.Z., for K.O.") V. Greeting ("for J.G.")
VI. *Oif Mayn Khas'neh* (At My Wedding) ("for M.T.T.") VII. Mr. and
Mrs. Webb Say Goodnight ("for Mino and Lezbo") VIII. Nachspiel
("in memoriam . . .")
First Performance: in a version for four singers (SABB), 9 May 1988,
private benefit concert for *Young Concert Artists, Inc.*, Equitable Center
Auditorium, NYC; Louise Edeiken, Joyce Castle, John Brandstetter,

Mordechai Kaston; Leonard Bernstein and Michael Tilson Thomas at the piano.
World premiere of the version for two pianos: 28 April 1989, Museum of Art, Tel Aviv. Amalia Ishak and Raphael Frieder; Irit Rub-Levy and Ariel Cohen at the piano. First U.S. Performance of the Version for Vocal Duet: 7 September 1989, Merkin Concert Hall, NYC; Judy Kaye, William Sharp; Michael Barrett and Stephen Blier at the piano.

Dream With Me (1944)

I Hate Music (1943)
A Cycle of Five Kid Songs for Soprano and Piano
Words: Leonard Bernstein
''For Edys''
First Performance: 24 August 1943, Public Library, Lenox, MA; Jennie Tourel and Leonard Bernstein

La Bonne Cuisine (1947)
Four Recipes for Voice and Piano
Words: *La Bonne Cuisine Française* by Emile Dutoit (French); English version: Leonard Bernstein
''For Jennie Tourel, the Only Begetter of These Songs''
First Performance: 10 October 1948, Town Hall, NYC; Marion Bell and Edwin MacArthur

Lamentation (1943)
Finale of *Jeremiah* Symphony

My Twelve-Tone Melody (1988)
Words: Leonard Bernstein
First Performance: Irving Berlin's 100th Birthday, 11 May 1988, Carnegie Hall, NYC; Leonard Bernstein singing at the piano

On the Waterfront (1954)
Lyrics: John La Touche

Piccola Serenata (1979)
Vocalise by Leonard Bernstein
''For Karl Boehm on His 85th Birthday''
First Performance: 27 August 1979, Salzburg, G.D.R.; Christa Ludwig and James Levine

Psalm 148 (1935)
For Voice and Organ
Words adapted by Leonard Bernstein

Sean Song (1986)
For Voice and Violin, Viola, Cello, Harp, Piano or similar Japanese instrument
Lyrics: Yoko Ono and Sean Lennon
Written at the request of Kazuko Inoue
First Performance: 3 August 1988, Riverside Church, NYC

Silhouette (Galilee) (1951)
Words: Leonard Bernstein

"For Jennie Tourel, on Her Birthday in Israel"
First Performance: 13 February 1955, National Gallery of Art, Washington, D.C.; Katherine Hanse and Evelyn Swarthout

So Pretty (1968)
Lyrics: Betty Comden and Adolph Green
First Performance: 21 January 1968, Philharmonic Hall, NYC; Barbra Streisand and Leonard Bernstein

Two Love Songs (1949)
On Poems by Rainer Maria Rilke
Translation: Jessie Lemont
"For Jennie"
First Performance: No. 1: 13 March 1949, Town Hall, NYC; No. 2: 13 March 1963, Philharmonic Hall, NYC; Jennie Tourel and Alan Rogers

Vayomer Elohim ("Let There Be Light") (1989)
Text: Genesis 1:3 (Hebrew)
Score in preparation

Yevarechecha *(from Opening Prayer)* (1986)
For Voice and Orchestra; Transcribed for Organ
Text: Three-Fold Benediction (Hebrew) from the Bible: Numbers 6:24–26
Score in preparation

CHORAL WORKS (WITH KEYBOARD)

The Firstborn (1958)
Incidental music for the play by Christopher Fry
Text: Christopher Fry and Leonard Bernstein
First Performance: 29 April 1958, Coronet Theater, NYC
Score in preparation

Hashkiveinu (1945)
For Cantorial Solo (tenor), SATB Choir and Organ
Words from Friday Evening Service (Hebrew)
First Performance: 11 May 1945, Park Avenue Synagogue, NYC; Cantor David Putterman, Max Helfman, conductor

"if you can't eat you got to" (1973, 1977)
Text: e e cummings
Written for the Krocodillos (male glee club) at Harvard
First Performance: 1973, Signet Society, Cambridge, MA

Kaddish (from *Kaddish No. III***)**
Canon in Five Parts for Boys' Choir

Missa Brevis (1988)
Based on music from *The Lark*
"For Bob Shaw"
First Performance (first version): 21 April 1988, Atlanta, GA; Atlanta Symphony Orchestra and Chorus, Robert Shaw, conductor

Simchu Na (1947)
Setting by Leonard Bernstein for SATB Choir and Orchestra
Music and Lyrics: Matityahu Weiner
Score in preparation

Warm-up (1970)
Round for Mixed Chorus
Words (bell, scat sounds): Leonard Bernstein
"For Abraham Kaplan and His Singers"
First Performance: 7 December 1969, Philharmonic Hall, NYC; Camerata Singers, Abraham Kaplan, conductor

Yigdal (1950)
Round for Chorus and Piano
Words from Sabbath Evening Service (Hebrew)
Written for United Synagogue Commission on Jewish Education

CHAMBER MUSIC

Brass Music (1948)
I. Rondo for Lifey (trumpet and piano) II. Elegy for Mippy I (horn and piano) III. Elegy for Mippy II (trombone solo) IV. Waltz for Mippy III (tuba and piano) V. Fanfare for Bima (brass quartet)
"For My Brother Burtie"
Commissioned by the Juilliard Musical Foundation
First Performance (complete): 8 April 1959, Carnegie Hall, NYC; NYP members

Dance Suite
For Brass Quintet and Optional Percussion
I. *Dancisca* (for Antony) II. *Waltz* (for Agnes) III. *Bi-Tango* (for Misha) IV. *Two-Step* (for Mr. B.) V. *M T V* (for Jerry)
First Performance: 14 January 1990, American Ballet Theater, Metropolitan Opera House, NYC; Empire Brass Quintet

Halil
For Flute, Percussion and Piano

Red, White and Blues (1984)
For Trumpet and Piano
Song from *1600 Pennsylvania Avenue*, transcribed by Peter Wastall

Shivaree (1969)
A Fanfare for Double Brass Ensemble and Percussion
Commissioned by and dedicated to the Metropolitan Museum of Art, NYC, in honor of its centenary

Serenade (1954)
For Violin and Piano

Sonata for Clarinet and Piano (1941–42)
Orchestration by Sid Ramin
"For David Oppenheim"

First Performance: 21 April 1942, Institute of Modern Art, Boston, MA; David Glazer and Leonard Bernstein

Three Meditations from *Mass* (1971)
For Cello and Piano
First Performance: 28 March 1972, Institute of International Education, NYC; Stephen Kates and Leonard Bernstein

PIANO WORKS

The Age of Anxiety
For 2 Pianos/4 Hands

Bridal Suite (1960)
In Two Parts with Three Encores; for Piano/4 Hands
"For Adolph and Phyllis"
Score in preparation

Five Anniversaries (1949–51)
I. For Elizabeth Rudolf II. For Lukas Foss III. For Elizabeth B. Ehrman IV. For Sandy Gellhorn V. For Susanna Kyle

Four Anniversaries (1948)
I. For Felicia Montealegre II. For Johnny Mehegan III. For David Diamond IV. For Helen Coates
First Performance: 1 October 1948, Cleveland, OH; Eudice Podis

Four Sabras (ca. 1950)
Score in preparation

Moby Diptych (1981)
"For Tony (Kuerti) Who Insists with Grace"
Proceeds to Greenpeace Foundation
Became Nos. I and II in *Thirteen Anniversaries*

Seven Anniversaries (1943)
I. For Aaron Copland II. For My Sister, Shirley III. In Memoriam: Alfred Eisner IV. For Paul Bowles V. In Memoriam: Natalie Koussevitzky VI. For Serge Koussevitzky VII. For William Schuman
First Performance: 14 May 1944, Opera House, Boston, MA; Leonard Bernstein

Thirteen Anniversaries (1988)
I. For Shirley Gabis Rhoads Perle II. In Memoriam: William Kapell III. For Stephen Sondheim IV. For Craig Urquhart V. For Leo Smit VI. For Nina Bernstein VII. For Helen Coates VIII. In Memoriam: Goddard Lieberson IX. For Jessica Fleischmann X. In Memoriam: Constance Hope XI. For Claudio Arrau XII. For Aaron Stern XIII. In Memoriam: Ellen Goetz

Touches (1981)
Chorale, Eight Variations and Coda

For the Sixth Van Cliburn International Piano Competition, Fort Worth, TX
First Performance: 28–30 May 1981, by competitors

MISCELLANEOUS

El Salon México by Aaron Copland (1941)
Arrangements for One and Two Pianos by Leonard Bernstein
First Performance: 18 November 1941, Copley Plaza Hotel, Boston, MA; Leonard Bernstein

Haiku Souvenirs (1978)
Five Songs for Voice and Piano
Music: Jack Gottlieb; Words: Leonard Bernstein
First Performance: 22 November 1969, Elmont Jewish Center, Elmont, NY; Joyce Glaser and Jack Gottlieb

JUVENILIA

Piano Sonata (1938)
"For Heinrich Gebhard"
First Performance: 1938, Boston, MA; Leonard Bernstein

Piano Trio (1937)
For Violin, Cello and Piano
First Performance: Harvard University, Boston, MA; Madison Trio: Mildred Spiegel, Dorothy Rosenberg, Sarah Kruskall

Sonata for Violin and Piano (1940)
First Performance: Cambridge, MA; Raphael Silverman (Hillyer) (violin), Leonard Bernstein

Also, numerous occasional songs and piano pieces written as anniversary, memorial and other tributes for friends, family and colleagues

CHRONOLOGICAL LIST OF COMPOSITIONS

[WW = Work Withdrawn]

Year	Work
1935	Psalm 148
1937	Piano Trio
1938	Piano Sonata
1940	Sonata for Violin and Piano
1942	Sonata for Clarinet and Piano
	Jeremiah, Symphony No. 1
1943	Seven Anniversaries, for Piano
	I Hate Music, A Cycle of Five Kid Songs for Soprano and Piano
1944	Fancy Free: Ballet, Suite [WW] and Three Dance Variations
	On the Town: Musical Comedy and Three Dance Episodes
	Dream With Me
1945	Afterthought, for Voice and Piano
	Hashkiveinu, for Cantorial Solo, SATB Choir and Organ
1946	Facsimile: Ballet and Choreographic Essay
1947	La Bonne Cuisine, Four Recipes for Voice and Piano
	Simchu Na, for Chorus and Orchestra/Piano
	Reena, for Chamber Orchestra
1948	Brass Music, Five Pieces for Four Brass Players and Piano
	Four Anniversaries, for Piano
1949	Two Love Songs, on Poems of Rilke, for Voice and Piano
	The Age of Anxiety, Symphony No. 2, for Piano and Orchestra
	Prelude, Fugue and Riffs, for Solo Clarinet and Jazz Ensemble
1950	Four Sabras
	Peter Pan, Songs and Choruses for the Play
	Yigdal, Round for Chorus and Piano
	Trouble in Tahiti, Opera in One Act
1951	Five Anniversaries, for Piano
	Silhouette (Galilee), Song for Voice and Piano
1953	Wonderful Town, Musical Comedy
1954	Serenade (after Plato's "Symposium"), for Solo Violin, String Orchestra, Harp and Percussion
	On the Waterfront: Film Score
1955	The Lark, French and Latin Choruses
	Get Hep! [WW]
	Salomé [WW]
	Symphonic Suite from On the Waterfront
1956	Candide: Comic Operetta and Overture
1957	Harvard Choruses (2), Male Chorus and Piano [WW]
	West Side Story, Musical
1958	The Firstborn, Incidental Music

1960	Symphonic Dances from West Side Story, for Orchestra
1961	Fanfares (2), for Orchestral Ensembles
1963	Kaddish, Symphony No. 3, for Orchestra, Mixed Chorus, Boys' Choir, Speaker and Soprano Solo
1965	Chichester Psalms, for Mixed Choir, Boy Soloist and Orchestra
1968	So Pretty, Song for Voice and Piano
1969	Shivaree, for Double Brass Ensemble and Percussion
1970	Warm-up, Round for Mixed Chorus
1971	Mass, A Theatre Piece for Singers, Players and Dancers
	Two Meditations from Mass, for Orchestra
1972	Two Meditations from Mass, for Violoncello and Piano
1973	"if you can't eat you got to," for Male Chorus
1974	Dybbuk, Ballet and Suites
1975	By Bernstein, A Musical Cabaret (based on deleted materials from previous theater works) [WW]
1976	1600 Pennsylvania Avenue, A Musical about the Problems of Housekeeping
1977	Three Meditations from Mass, for Violoncello and Orchestra
	Three Meditations from Mass, for Violoncello and Piano
	Songfest, A Cycle of American Poems for Six Singers and Orchestra
	Slava!, Overture for Orchestra/Band
	CBS Music, for Orchestra [WW]
1979	Up! Up! Up! and My New Friends, Songs for Voice and Piano
	Piccola Serenata, for Voice and Piano
1980	Divertimento, for Orchestra/Band
	A Musical Toast, for Orchestra/Band
1981	Halil, Nocturne for Solo Flute and Small Orchestra
	Moby Diptych, for Piano
	Touches, for Piano
	Olympic Hymn, for Mixed Choir and Orchestra [WW]
1983	A Quiet Place, Opera in Three Acts
1986	Jubilee Games, for Orchestra with Baritone Solo [WW]
	Sean Song, for Voice and Strings
	Opening Prayer, for Orchestra with Baritone Solo
	Yevarechecha, for Voice and Orchestra
1987	Trial Song, from The Race to Urga
1988	Missa Brevis, for A Cappella Chorus with Incidental Percussion
	My Twelve-Tone Melody, Song for Voice and Piano
	Thirteen Anniversaries, for Piano
	Arias and Barcarolles, for Piano Four-Hands, Mezzo and Baritone Solos
1989	Concerto for Orchestra (Jubilee Games)
	Vayomer Elohim
1990	Dance suite

MUSIC AND TEXT CREDITS

Introduction to *The Dance in the Place Congo* by Henry F. Gilbert, courtesy of the Boston Symphony Orchestra, Inc. *pp. 53–55*

"Wintergreen for President" by George Gershwin, copyright 1932 (renewed) by New World Music Corporation. All rights reserved. Used by permission. *p. 56*

Alborada del gracioso by Maurice Ravel, used by permission of Associated Music Publishers, Inc., agent for Editions Max Eschig. *p. 57 (top)*

Chants Populaires Hébraïques by Darius Milhaud, courtesy of Heugel et Cie, Publishers and Copyright Owners Worldwide. *p. 57 (bottom)*

Concerto for Piano and Orchestra by Aaron Copland, copyright 1929 by Cos Cob Press, Inc. Renewed 1958 by Aaron Copland. Reprinted by permission of Aaron Copland, copyright owner, and Boosey & Hawkes, Inc., sole publishers and licensees. *pp. 58–62; pp. 76–82*

Rhapsody in Blue by George Gershwin, copyright 1924 (renewed) by New World Music Corporation. All rights reserved. Used by permission. *pp. 67–71*

El Salon Mexico by Aaron Copland, copyright 1929 by Aaron Copland. Renewed 1966. Reprinted by permission of Aaron Copland, copyright owner, and Boosey & Hawkes, Inc., sole publishers and licensees. *p. 69 (note)*

Piano Sonata No. 1 by Roger Sessions, copyright 1931 (renewed) by B. Schott's Soehne, Mainz. Used by permission of European-American Music Distributors Corporation, sole U.S. agent for B. Schott's Soehne. *pp. 71–72; 93*

Three Chorale Preludes for Organ by Roger Sessions, courtesy of Edward B. Marks Music Corporation. *pp. 73–74*

Symphony in E Minor by Roger Sessions, courtesy of Edward B. Marks Music Corporation. *p. 75*

"Charleston" by Cecil Mack and Jimmy Johnson, copyright 1923 (renewed) by Warner Bros. Music Inc. All rights reserved. Used by permission. *p. 78*

Piano Variations by Aaron Copland, copyright 1932 by Aaron Copland. Renewed 1959. Reprinted by permission of Aaron Copland, copyright owner, and Boosey & Hawkes, Inc., sole publishers and licensees. *pp. 82; 86–88; 92*

Quartet No. 3, Op. 22 by Paul Hindemith, copyright 1923 by B. Schott's Soehne, Mainz. Renewed 1951 by Schott & Co. Ltd., London. Used by permission of European-American Music Distributors Corporation, sole U.S. agent for Schott & Co. Ltd. *p. 83*

Le Sacre du Printemps by Igor Stravinsky, copyright 1921 by Edition Russe de Musique. Copyright assigned 1947 to Boosey & Hawkes, Inc. Reprinted by permission. *p. 83*

A Song for Occupations by Roy Harris, copyright 1935 by G. Schirmer, Inc. Renewed 1962. Used by permission. *pp. 89–91*

Piano Sonata No. 2 by Charles Ives, copyright 1947 by Associated Music Publishers, Inc. All rights reserved. Used by permission. *pp. 94–98*

PHOTO CREDITS

[Every attempt has been made to trace the source of all the illustrations. Any omission is inadvertent and will be corrected upon notification.]

AMBERSON ENTERPRISES, INC. p. 303
AUTHOR'S COLLECTION pp. 11, 12, 15, 24, 119, 129, 145, 150, 161, 167, 175, 179, 218, 248, 252, 263, 269, 270 (left), 274, 310, 337, 339, 348, 349, 354, 365
HOWARD S. BABBIT, JR., p. 314
RICHARD BRAATEN p. 165
DOUGLAS M. BRUCE pp. 28, 334
CHRISTINA BURTON pp. 154, 173, 177, 231
CBS RECORDS pp. 101, 102, 149 (top left), 151, 157, 163, 211, 222, 261, 341, 344
BRUCE DAVIDSON/MAGNUM pp. 183, 289
"DIE WELT," HAMBURG p. 329
GIROLAMO DI MAJO pp. 2, 240
LAZAR DONNER/BETTMANN ARCHIVES pp. 113, 115
MIKE EVENS p. 326
WALTER R. FLEISCHER p. 27
RICHARD FUCHS p. 142
BILL GOTTLIEB p. 103
THE GRANGER COLLECTION p. 143
HENRY GROSSMAN p. 139
KEN HEYMAN pp. 144, 234
SIEGFRIED LAUTERWASSER pp. 106, 236, 297
JAMES LIGHTNER p. 356
LONDON WEEKEND TELEVISION p. 346
MCA RECORDS p. 131
GJON MILI p. 105
NEDERLANDSCH FOTOBUREAU p. 109
WALTER NICHOLLS p. 246
RUTH ORKIN pp. 130, 133, 215, 226, 228, 270 (right), 277, 281, 283, 316, 318, 320
IRVING PENN/CONDÉ NAST p. 257
BOB PHILLIPS p. 238
PHOTOHOUSE, TEL AVIV p. 123
ROGER PICARD pp. 265, 271
PINTO p. 140
POLYDOR p. 242
RADIO FRANCE/ROGER PICARD p. 31
RCA pp. 110, 127
RICK STAFFORD pp. 36, 305
ROCKFORD COLLEGE pp. 251
TEATRO ALLA SCALA pp. 331, 332
THEATER AND MUSIC COLLECTION OF THE MUSEUM OF THE CITY OF NEW YORK p. 149 (top right, bottom left, bottom right)
TIME-LIFE p. 272
VIVIANNE p. 111
WHITESTONE PHOTO pp. 152, 213, 351
EDWARD ZWERIN p. 212

"Life without music is unthinkable,
Music without life is academic.
That is why my contact with music is a total embrace."
—LEONARD BERNSTEIN, *Findings*

Award winners . . . bestsellers . . . familiar favorites . . . twentieth-century classics. Leonard Bernstein's unforgettable music-making can be heard on over 100 audio and video recordings in Deutsche Grammophon's renowned catalogue.

Among Our Highlights:

Bernstein: *West Side Story*—Te Kanawa/Carreras/Troyanos/Bernstein
Bernstein: *Candide*—Anderson/Hadley/Ludwig/Bernstein Grammy-winner!
Bernstein in Berlin—Bernstein's historic performance of Beethoven's Ninth Symphony in East Berlin on Christmas Day 1989, celebrating the fall of the Wall.
Bernstein: Final Concert—Beethoven's Seventh Symphony and Britten's "4 Sea Interludes" from *Peter Grimes*; Bernstein/Boston Symphony at Tanglewood on August 19, 1990.
Mahler: Symphonies—Bernstein/New York Philharmonic/Concertgebouw Orchestra/London Symphony/Vienna Philharmonic

For a free discography of Leonard Bernstein's Deutsche Grammophon recordings, write to: Bernstein Recordings, Deutsche Grammophon, PolyGram Classics and Jazz, 825 Eighth Avenue, New York, NY 10019, or fax your request to: 212-333-8402.

For other inquiries please write to: The Leonard Bernstein Society, Department D, 25 Central Park West, Suite 14, New York, NY 10023.

Leonard Bernstein, composer, conductor, pianist, teacher, and writer, was born August 25, 1918. Among his accomplishments, he served from 1957 to 1969 as conductor and music director of the New York Philharmonic, inaugurated two seminal television series on the performing arts, "Young People's Concerts" and "Omnibus," and lectured and mentored extensively on musical subjects. Books by Mr. Bernstein include *Leonard Bernstein's Young People's Concerts*, *Findings*, *The Joy of Music*, and *The Unanswered Question*. Leonard Bernstein died on October 14, 1990.